[英国]丹尼尔·K.加德纳 著　朱邦芊 译

牛津通识读本·儒家思想
Confucianism
A Very Short Introduction

译林出版社

图书在版编目（CIP）数据

儒家思想 /（英）丹尼尔·K.加德纳
(Daniel K. Gardner) 著；朱邦芊译. -- 南京：译林
出版社，2025.1. -- （牛津通识读本）. -- ISBN 978
-7-5753-0302-6

I. B222.05

中国国家版本馆CIP数据核字第2024T7K391号

Confucianism: A Very Short Introduction by Daniel K. Gardner
Copyright © Oxford University Press 2014
Confucianism: A Very Short Introduction was originally published in English in 2014.
This licensed edition is published by arrangement with Oxford University Press.
Yilin Press, Ltd is solely responsible for this bilingual edition from the original work which has been slightly adapted for the market, and Oxford University Press shall have no liability for any errors, omissions, inaccuracies, or ambiguities in such bilingual edition or for any losses caused by reliance thereon.
Chinese and English edition copyright © 2025 by Yilin Press, Ltd
All rights reserved.

著作权合同登记号　图字：10-2016-181 号

儒家思想　［英国］丹尼尔·K.加德纳　／著　朱邦芊　／译

责任编辑　许　丹
装帧设计　景秋萍
校　　对　王　敏
责任印制　董　虎

原文出版　Oxford University Press, 2014
出版发行　译林出版社
地　　址　南京市湖南路1号A楼
邮　　箱　yilin@yilin.com
网　　址　www.yilin.com
市场热线　025-86633278
排　　版　南京展望文化发展有限公司
印　　刷　江苏凤凰通达印刷有限公司
开　　本　890毫米×1260毫米 1/32
印　　张　8.75
插　　页　4
版　　次　2025年1月第1版
印　　次　2025年1月第1次印刷
书　　号　ISBN 978-7-5753-0302-6
定　　价　39.00元

版权所有·侵权必究

译林版图书若有印装错误可向出版社调换　质量热线：025-83658316

序　言

干春松

英文版的儒学通识类书籍，我印象最深的当推杜维明先生的《儒教》一书，此书最初是作为"世界宗教入门"丛书中的一本而刊行，后来台湾地区的麦田出版社和上海古籍出版社，有繁体和简体中文版出版。

将儒家列入一套宗教类的书籍，可能会引发一些争议。在以一神教为模板的"religion"定义的"刻板"印象下，关于儒家是否为一种宗教始终存在着"削足适履"般的争论。但作为强调儒家人文主义精神的思想家，杜维明对于儒家的宗教性的肯定，以及由此推论出的儒家注重内在精神修养和培育社群生活态度的思想品格及价值追求，给人以思想的震动。

作为现代新儒家的重要代表，杜维明在著作中体现出对儒家的"同情"和"敬意"，这种写作风格或许会让以"客观性"为衡量标准的学者们诟病。于是，我们可以选择英国学者丹尼尔·K.加德纳的《儒家思想》一书。

很显然，儒家的宗教性始终是海外学者对儒家的"特性"的独特关切。本书一开始就讨论到中西宗教差异这道"宇宙观的鸿沟",认为与西方的一神教所不同的是,中国人的世界中,并不是缺乏祖先和自然的神祇,而是不承认创始神或负责创造和维持自然秩序的"存在"或"实体"。所以,作者在讨论儒家的家庭伦理特性时认为,儒家与祖宗和地方神灵之间是"熟悉""亲近"的,并不像基督教信仰者与上帝之间那样是陌生的。同样,在对天人关系的理解中,儒家相信自然界与人类之间自然保持着平衡与和谐,圣人的作用就是通过礼乐来保持这种自然与人之间的和谐。

既然存在这样的出发点,我们就可以理解儒家的道德追诉和治理思想的基础。比如,就个人修身而言,每一个个体都可以对他人或社群产生影响,有人将之称为"道德乐观主义"。儒家义理坚信通过修身,将自己塑造成君子,并成为其他人的榜样,这构成儒家修身、齐家、治国、平天下的内圣外王之道。在这样的过程中,儒家的仁爱、礼乐、诚信的价值观念及其意义才能得到充分的呈现。

作者并不生活在儒家文化背景的社会环境中,但他十分敏锐地绕过对于"仁"的内涵的种种"规定性"的讨论,而是强调了儒家仁爱的"感同身受"的理解进路。他说:"一个人共情的感受和做法消失的那一刻,他的仁也随之而去。"(第23页)的确,仁爱的艰难性在于如何能在复杂的自然和人事环境中始终保持对于别人的爱憎、苦乐的敏感,从而真正对他们展现出爱心,而非表面的敷衍。这样的讨论可能要到二程兄弟才十分明确,但这恰好也能展现作者对儒学理解的深度和广度。所以,作者在讨论儒家的"家庭"观念及其"孝"的德性的时候,十分看重这些礼仪背后的情感因素，正是这些因素将人类对于长辈的亲情和对于动物的关爱区分开来。

儒家对于道德修养的目标是让自己成为君子，让自己成为这个社会的理想的治理者。与法家的严酷和道家的遁世不同的是，儒家的治理是通过展现统治者的道德感染力来展开的，这客观上导致了儒家思想在春秋战国时期的"不切实际"，但这也给后世的儒家带来了困难。在理念上儒家主张贤者居位的道德理想主义，这与大一统格局下的嫡长子继承制之间，存在着血缘法则和道德选择之间的紧张。孔子、孟子和荀子虽然是先秦时期最重要的政治观念提供者，但他们并无机会将他们的理念落地。

作者将孟子和荀子看作儒家的两个"变体"，这种说法可能会引发歧义，更好的说法可能是孟子和荀子朝不同的方向发展了孔子的思想。很显然，孟子的良知和性善论，是要为儒家伦理奠定发生学上的正当性，而荀子则更为强调礼与规范的重要性。在某种意义上，孟子式的儒者更接近于要成为世俗君主的老师，而荀子式的儒者则更倾向于成为君主的辅佐者。在战国末期这样一个混乱的时代，孟子式的理想主义遭受空前的质疑，而荀子则更为趋时地试图让儒家思想更符合时代的需要。在汉代的转折中，儒家更为现实地成为现实秩序的辩护者，并小心翼翼地试图通过恢复自然秩序的神圣性，来维护儒家理想对现实政治的批判性，这样的观点在董仲舒的天人观中得到了整合。

基于对经学传统的重要性的忽略，作者更为看重儒家"观念化"的精神传统的重要性。对于经学的忽略可能会导致作者在处理"四书"和"五经"的关系时产生一些认识上的扁平化，从而导致对宋代儒学的复杂性的理解略显不足。作者认为从"五经"转向"四书"是儒家的一种"哲学转向",更为注重经典中与修身相关的内容,这也是从哲学视野来看待宋代儒学的最为流行的看法。

本书充分意识到理气关系对于宋代理学的道德修养论的重要性,认为气的多变性促使人们认识到格物修身的重要性,从而既在天理的先在和后天的心性修炼之间建立起一种平衡,也让他们与先秦儒学之间建立起如下的共同点。

- 人是可以实现道德完善的;
- 学习是改善道德的关键;
- 古代的圣人提供了品德端正和在社会中表现得当的"道";
- 道德君子具有转化他人的影响力;
- 社会和谐是民众满足了各自角色所承担的道德责任的结果。(第88页)

作者对儒家的"制度化"表现出足够的关注,此为本书十分明显的优点。首先,他重视科举制度对儒家的道德理想和实践在整个中国社会传播的意义,这种官员选拔制度并非单纯地建构了社会流动的机制,更为重要的是将儒家经典作为考试的内容,促成了道德观念的普及和国家共同价值的建立。

与流行的儒学通识作品不同的是,本书特别设有儒学与女性的内容,既看到了传统中国社会中女性的从属地位,也肯定了女性对于教育子女、涵养个体的道德观念,以及促进家庭和谐的作用。作者引用曾国藩女儿曾纪芬的文字,从中看到了对传统女性的意义的最好阐述。他指出：

> 在家庭这个中国社会的基本单位内部，妇女作为母亲、教师和家务管理人，被赋予了合法的权威地位。（第113页）

在西方影响巨大的列文森的《儒教中国及其现代命运》一书曾经判定，儒家已经是"化石"，只具备怀念功能，而难以在未来的中国发展中产生作用。针对中西流行的此类说法，现代新儒学不断在为儒家的现代意义进行辩护。现代新儒家尤其强调了儒家与民主、科学之间的兼容性，以回应五四新文化运动以来，试图让儒家为近代中国的落后承担责任的做法。但本书作者的敏锐之处，在于他对21世纪以来儒学在中国大陆民间社会兴起的关注。虽然从今天的状况看，于丹及其《〈论语〉心得》已经成为过眼烟云，但由她通过电视媒体所引发的人们对于这本古老的儒家著作的兴趣，依然是本世纪以来十分重要的文化现象。

儒学的复兴，夹杂着经济崛起之后的民族主义的心理需求，也有普通民众寻求精神力量的原因，还有为维护国家统一寻求文化基础的因素，不一而足。如此多层面的混杂，可能难以为一个国外的学者充分体会，但他们已经不再将儒学视为博物馆的陈列物，而是看到了儒学对于中国社会建构和文化自觉的意义，这足以让人敬佩本书作者的视野之高远。

目 录

致　谢　**1**

年　表　**3**

第一章　孔子(前 551—前 479) 及其遗产：简介　**1**

第二章　儒家思想中的个人与修身　**15**

第三章　儒家思想中的治理　**33**

第四章　早期儒家思想的多种变体　**49**

第五章　儒家传统在公元 1000 年之后的转变：
理学的教义　**73**

第六章　儒家思想的实践　**91**

后记：20 世纪和 21 世纪的儒家思想　**114**

索　引　**119**

英文原文　**129**

致　谢

衷心感谢布朗大学的辛西娅·布罗考。她仔细聆听我的想法，阅读各章草稿，并在我疲惫拖沓之时敦促我继续努力。作为一个作者，拥有像她这样的同事和朋友真是三生有幸。

我在牛津大学出版社的编辑辛西娅·里德和她的助手夏洛特·斯坦哈特从项目之初便始终如一地给予我支持。出版社的匿名审稿人就草稿提出了极其周到详尽的审读意见。本书因为他们慷慨的专业建议而获益匪浅。克里斯蒂娜·约翰逊在编辑过程的最后阶段提供了协助。我对她的敏锐目光和准确判断深表感激。

年　表

商朝，约前1600—约前1045

周朝，约前1045—约前256

  西周，约前1046—前771

    文王（前11世纪）

    武王（前11世纪）

    周公（前11世纪）

  东周，前771—前256

    春秋时期，前722—前481

      孔子（前551—前479）

    战国时期，前403—前221

      孟子（前4世纪）

      荀子（前3世纪）

秦朝，前221—前206

汉朝，前206—220

  西汉，前206—9

汉武帝（前141—前87年在位）统治时期，儒家被确立为国学

王莽新朝,9—23

东汉,25—220

六朝,220—589

隋朝,581—618

全国实施科举

唐朝,618—907

五代,907—960

宋朝,960—1279

北宋,960—1127

主要的理学思想家：

周敦颐（1017—1073）

张载（1020—1077）

程颢（1032—1085）

程颐（1033—1107）

南宋,1127—1279

理学集大成者：

朱熹（1130—1200）

元朝,1279—1368

明朝,1368—1644

王阳明（1472—1522）派理学

清朝,1644—1912

科举制度废除（1905）

第一章

孔子（前551—前479）及其遗产：简介

孔子生活在公元前6世纪。但如果可以选择的话，他宁愿自己早生五百年，生活在周朝（前1045?—前221）初兴之时。在他的想象中，那是个黄金时代，统治者以德治国，民众遵循自古以来的礼法，到处都是一派和谐安宁。如今面目全非。中国不再由孔武德劭的周王一统天下。到公元前700年，国家已分裂成各自独立的小国，由各个封建领主统治，彼此间纷争不断，这些领主的权威不是通过道德行为和对民众福祉的真正关心，而是通过法律、惩罚和武力来维系的。

孔子一生对周初悠然神往。如果当时政通人和，同胞之间以礼相待——所有这些都通过得体的礼仪予以表达——他相信那一切会在自己的有生之年再次盛行。为此，他周游于各封国之间，希望找到一位与他观点相同的纳谏明君，授之以权，实施他的社会政治愿景。但他的周游无功而返，他从未得到过重用。

当时的统治者显然认为他的思想不切实际。毕竟在公元前6世纪，各国之间的战事依然连绵不绝；说什么以道德典范治国

2 图1 雕刻在石碑上的一幅唐朝(618—907)孔子像

即可战胜进驻边境的数万敌军,这种观点大概毫无说服力。另一种可能是,孔子的个性不大容易笼络封建统治者。正如他在《论语》中的教诲所示,他偶尔可能会赞美、同情、宽容错误,还有些幽默感,但往往都是一副批评、强硬、嘲讽和严苛的态度。

尽管如此,孔子却从未完全放弃希望,始终期待某地有某一位统治者会欣赏他的政治学说的真正价值。他的弟子子贡曾经问道:"如果你有一块美玉,你会把它装进柜子里藏起来呢?还是找个识货的卖掉?"孔子回应道:"卖掉它!卖掉它!我等着识货的人呢。"①(《论语·子罕第九之十三》)孔子始终没有遇到合适的机会,失望之余,他把毕生事业从政治转向教导弟子,希望弟子们信奉他的政治理想,在他本人失败的宦途上取得成功。根据传统的说法,孔子正式收入门下的弟子共有72人。

孔子名垂青史,不仅是因为他诲人不倦而受人敬重,也是对那些致力于传播其教诲的弟子和后世追随者的致敬。他们对孔子的格言和对话的记录构成了《论语》的基础,那是我们获知孔子思想的主要来源。《论语》的文本相当简短,号称有20卷——不妨将其理解为篇章——总共约有500个段落或"节",是由他的弟子们记录下来并经过历代人编辑的孔子教义集锦。早在公元前2世纪,孔子去世三个世纪之后,《论语》的文本就已经呈现为目前的形式了。

研究孔子思想,都要从这部相对简短的文本开始。但孔子与中国传统中的其他早期文本关系密切,特别是《易经》《诗经》

---

① 子贡曰:"有美玉于斯,韫椟而藏诸?求善贾而沽诸?"子曰:"沽之哉!沽之哉!我待贾者也。"(对于本书出现的典籍引用,统一在正文中采用白话文直译,并保留作者原有注释,另于脚注中附上经典原文,原文为译者所加。——编注)

3

《尚书》《礼记》,以及《春秋》。孔门弟子们从公元前2世纪便开始宣称,他参与了这五部文本的撰写、编辑或编写(五部文本大致都是在公元前1000—前200年间编写的)。尽管这种说法经不起深究,但从那时起,这些文本,即所谓的"五经",就一直被尊为儒家传统的经典。儒家将它们奉为传递圣人治世原则、描述正确礼仪、表达天人合一的信念,以及从春秋时期(前722—前481)的历史中汲取教训的著作,与孔子的教义完全一致。

儒家在中国的兴起

孔子召集了一群忠实的门徒,并不意味着他的教义立即赢得了普遍认可。在周朝所谓的春秋时期和战国时期(前403—前221)那动荡不已的数百年,很多思想家带着各不相同的主张,致力于解决各自的当务之急。道家、法家、阴阳家、纵横家、兵家、农家、墨家(墨子的追随者)和名家的教义均在探讨:怎样才算是有道明君?如何才能治国有方?国与民的理想关系是什么?中国怎样才能实现曾经的统一、稳定和繁荣?个人对家庭、族群和国家有何责任?人在天地之间的位置如何?

当然,并不是每一位思想家都对所有这些事项给予同等的重视。但这些就是春秋时期和战国时期所盛行的所谓"诸子百家"日夜思考之事。激烈的学术论争是这几个世纪的标志,代表不同学派的思想家争相劝说国君和知识界相信他们自己的教义才是真知灼见。虽然在这几个世纪里,儒家有几位杰出代表特别活跃,其中最著名的是孟子(前4世纪)和荀子(前3世纪),但仍须谨记,这一时期,儒家学说并未得到比其他思想家的教义更多的青睐。

这种情况在公元前2世纪发生了变化，汉朝（前202—222）的统治者越来越支持儒家的学说。然而在汉朝初兴之时，这些学说的前景并非一片光明。汉朝的开国皇帝刘邦对儒家充满鄙夷。司马迁写于公元前1世纪的《史记》中提到，此人早期还未统治江山时，曾对儒家学说充满敌意："许多人头戴儒生的帽子来见他，沛公就立刻把他们的帽子摘下来，在里边撒尿。和人谈话的时候，动不动就破口大骂。"①

然而在建立汉朝之后，刘邦（此时已是高祖皇帝，前202—前195年在位）最终发现，软化态度才是便宜之策。他的首席顾问陆贾在觐见他时，反复敦促他参照重要典籍《诗经》和《尚书》中儒家学说的治国之道。一日，皇帝显然厌烦了陆贾过于频繁的劝谏，他粗鲁地答道："你老子的天下是靠骑在马上南征北战打出来的，哪里用得着《诗经》《尚书》！"②陆贾不屈不挠，显然将个人安危置于度外，回答说：

> 您在马上可以取得天下，难道也可以在马上治理天下吗？……秦王朝〔汉朝所取代的短命朝代，以其严酷著称〕也是一味使用严酷刑法而不知变更，最后导致自己的灭亡。假使秦朝统一天下之后〔公元前221年〕实行仁义之道，效法先圣，那么，陛下您又怎么能取得天下呢？③

---

① 诸客冠儒冠来者，沛公辄解其冠，溲溺其中。与人言，常大骂。见《史记·郦生陆贾列传》。
② 乃公居马上而得之，安事诗书！（出处同上）
③ 居马上得之，宁可以马上治之乎？……秦任刑法不变，卒灭赵氏。乡使秦已并天下，行仁义，法先圣，陛下安得而有之？（出处同上）

汉高祖来了兴趣，请陆贾著书（《新语》）阐明这些思想。司马迁写道："每写完一篇就上奏给皇帝，高帝没有不称赞的，左右群臣也是一齐山呼'万岁'。"①

不过直到半个世纪之后，汉武帝（前141—前87年在位）长期统治期间，儒家学者才总算能够明确倡导该学派的学说，并在朝堂上给予儒家以特权地位，这种地位（尽管时有起伏）一直保持到20世纪初期。由于大臣们纷纷敦促尊崇儒家，废黜当时另外两派，即道家和法家的学说，武帝于公元前141年下令解职所有非儒家的官员，特别是倾向于法家之人。几年后，公元前136年，他制定了"五经博士"的制度，五经博士是指精通五部著作的专家，即儒家学者开始视为典籍的《易经》《诗经》《尚书》《礼记》和《春秋》。这些饱学之士靠五经的教诲和原则来辅佐皇帝。公元前124年，同一群饱学之士成为新近成立的太学的教员。在那里表现很好的学生，即因精通五经中的一部或多部典籍而通过考试之人，可以获得政府官方机构的任命。

这些步骤的重要意义不可估量，第六章还会详细谈到这一点。从这时起，儒家思想就成为中华帝国不可或缺的精神支柱。统治者依靠儒家学说的指导，并经由它来获得正统地位，还通过以儒学为主要内容的考试来招募官僚。此外，由于儒家思想在治国意识形态上的主导地位，中华帝国的教育也专注于对儒家著作的掌握。为官能够获得显赫声望和经济回报，但凡负担得起学费的人，都会努力掌握那些典籍，从而通过考试、获得官职。男孩从六七岁起就被寄予厚望，潜心学习记诵宣扬儒家价值的

---

① 每奏一篇，高帝未尝不称善，左右呼万岁。（出处同上）

启蒙读本，随后研读儒家经典。结果是，几乎每一个中国读书人都被儒家学说所教育和社会化，在中华帝国1912年终结前的一千年里尤其如此。因此，几乎所有受过教育的中国人，不仅是官员，还有诗人、散文家、小说家、艺术家、书法家、史家、学者、教师，乃至少数知识女性，都在某种程度上受到儒家经典所体现的信念和理想的陶染。

儒家思想在东亚的影响

儒家思想的影响并未止步于中国境内。本书作为一部通识读本，主要关注儒家思想在中国的影响，但我们应该认识到，在后来的若干个世纪，朝鲜和日本都发现，儒家的学说和理想经过改造后，可以满足他们的社会、政治和精神需求。

早在公元372年，朝鲜的高句丽王国就设立了一所儒家书院，贵族子弟可以在那里接受儒家经典的教导。几个世纪后（682年），新罗王国模仿高句丽的先例，也建立了一所国立儒家书院来培训官员；788年，新罗王国基于儒家经典，建立了一套初级考试制度。在高丽（918—1392）历代国王的统治下，该考试制度不断完善；招募官员的考试定期举办，此时对于官员的要求不仅包括经典本身，还要掌握中国人对这些典籍的注释。

儒家思想的影响越来越大，在朝鲜王朝（1362—1910）期间达到了巅峰。在儒家改革者的敦促下，建国者重建了沿袭自高丽的价值体系和社会习俗，自己担起了创建模范儒家社会的任务。他们设置了一套基于儒学的全国教育系统，只有那些在该考试制度中获得成功的人才会被任命为官，这成为朝鲜儒教国家的基础。

朝鲜也在中国典籍传至日本的过程中发挥了重要的作用。早在五、六世纪，朝鲜学者便开始把包括孔子的《论语》在内的中国典籍带往日本。公元604年，圣德太子颁布了日本的第一部"宪法"，即所谓的《十七条宪法》。儒家的影响显然无处不在。该宪法的第一条开头便直接引用《论语》中的"和为贵"（《论语·学而第一之十二》），第四条告诫大臣和官员遵行适当的礼，提醒他们如果抛弃礼仪，民众就会目无法纪。在日本历史的大部分时间里，儒家学说的影响都不及佛教和神道教的教义。但在德川时代（1603—1868），儒家前所未有地繁荣起来。部分日本学者接触了11世纪到16世纪在中国发展起来的各个儒家流派（参见第五章"理学的教义"），纷纷开设书院和学校教导他人。他们还向德川的幕府将军们传授儒家思想，敦促后者接受儒家教诲。他们认为，这些教诲当是日本政府和整个社会的道德基础。

尽管儒家思想被德川的幕府将军们尊为国学，它却从未像在朝鲜和公元10世纪之后的中国那样，成为独此一家的正统。究其原因，可能是日本从未有过科举制度，因而佛教、神道教以及其他思潮的繁荣发展拥有更大的思想自由和空间。在德川时代，儒家学说享有极高的人气并大获成功，大大改造了日本的道德观和社会关系。

越南也感受到了儒家思想的影响。公元前111年，汉帝国占领了越南的北方地区，在那里统治了逾一千年，越南一直到公元939年才最终获得独立。其间数世纪，中国文化以汉字、儒家典籍和礼仪，以及中国式行政管理等形式渗透到越南人的生活中。作为中央王国的一部分，该地区也引入了以儒学为基础的中国科举制度（参见第六章"儒家思想的实践"）。即便在10世纪赢得独立后，越南诸王朝仍继续依靠儒家考试来招募朝廷官吏，直到1910年代。进入20世纪后，科举制度的突出地位确保了儒家经典是国家教育课程的核心，以及受过教育的人和政治精英会捍卫与儒家教义相关的价值观和做法。

孔子的理想

孔子想象的未来世界将会再现社会和谐与圣人之治。这种愿景在很大程度上依赖于过去。孔子坚信在中国已知的历史中，曾经充分实现过一个黄金时代，为了拼凑起可以作为万世楷模的愿景，他认为有必要求助于那段历史，恢复他相信盛行于周初的政治制度、社会关系，以及个人修养的理想。这里与柏拉图作一比较很有启发意义，柏拉图生活的时代恰逢孔子去世几十年后。和孔子一样，柏拉图也渴望改进当时的政治和社会生活。但与孔子不同的是，他并不认为过往可以作为当今的规范模式。柏拉图在《理想国》中构建他的理想社会时，对于重建过去的兴趣远远少于诉诸哲学思考以及与他人的知性对话。

当然，这并不是说孔子没有进行哲学思考和与他人谈话，但他毕竟把大量精力投入过去以及对过去的学习中。这种学习采取研究标准文本的形式，特别是《诗经》和《尚书》。他向弟子们解释道："《诗经》可以引发思考，可以促进观察，可以扩大交际，可以抒发不满；在家可以用它来孝敬父亲，出外可以用它来侍奉国君。"[①]（《论语·阳货第十七之九》）孔子经常引用《诗

[①] 《诗》可以兴，可以观，可以群，可以怨；迩之事父，远之事君。

经》中的诗篇和《尚书》中的故事与传说，这表明他深深折服于这些篇章，以及它们所记载的价值观、礼仪、传说和制度。

但书本并非孔子获知过去的唯一来源，口述历史也是他了解富有教益的古代传说的来源。关于传说中的圣君尧、舜、禹，关于建立周朝并就此开启了社会与政治的非凡和谐时代的文王、武王和周公，以及关于伯夷、齐桓公、管仲以及柳下惠这些或闻名遐迩，或臭名昭著的统治者和官员的神话故事，或许是对他从经典文本中所学的补充，也让他对过去的全貌有了更多了解，孔子在《论语》中对这些故事都有所提及。

有趣的是，孔子的另一个知识来源是他同代人的行为。他观察他们，挑选出那些符合周初文化规范的礼仪和做法加以赞美，而对他认为促使周朝衰落的行为加以批评。从《论语》中可以看到，他谴责巧言、令色、足恭、谄上、有勇而无义，以及一味追求名利——他认为这些行为盛行于时人之间，而这恰是自周朝以来道德沦丧的表现。为了扭转这种堕落，人们必须再次学习如何真诚地尊重他人，敏于行而讷于言，信守然诺，坦率而温和地批评偏离正道的亲友和君主，贫而无怨难，富而无骄易，并坚持三年之丧，而丧期之俗早已为人弃之不用了，令孔子十分遗憾。总而言之，他们必须重新学习造就了周初和谐社会的那一套礼仪。

孔子把这一时期描述成黄金时代，这或许是一种理想化的看法，但无关紧要。与一个"黄金时代"衔接为他的理想增加了权威性和正统性，这种衔接也验证了他所提倡的礼仪和做法。在断裂和混乱的时期，这种对于历史权威和正统的渴望或许有助于解释孔子为何急于自称他不过是个传播者和好古之人①(《论语·述而第七之一》)。实际上,尽管孔子坚称自己只是个传播者,从他对周初时期的研究和重构来看,他无疑打造了一个创新而持久的社会政治愿景。然而,孔子自称依赖过往,说自己只不过是昔日既有现实的传播人,也就为未来的中国建立了一个文化模板。在中国的前现代传统中,与过去全然断绝关系的大革新并未受到多少重视。比方说,在中国,如果某个像杰克逊·波拉克②那样的人有意识地、自豪地否定艺术前辈,他不会像在西方那样被誉为创造性的天才。伟大的作家、思想家和艺术家之所为被认为伟大,正是因为他们精通传统——过去的那些最优秀的思想和技能。他们通过把自己与前辈伟人联系起来,充分汲取后者的风格与技巧,方能逐渐成为伟人。当然,仅靠模仿是远远不够的;模仿绝不应该是盲从。人们在掌握过去的同时,必须加进一些创新的东西,一些完全自成一家的东西。

因此,当人们走进一家美术馆观赏一幅幅比肩而挂的中国近代山水画时,它们乍看之下十分相似。但细察就会发现,这位艺术家形成了一种全新的笔触,那位艺术家发展了水墨的新用法,而另一位则拥有了一种描画草木的新风格。有了经过训练的更加敏感的眼光,才能看出山水画的各种高超技巧和表达上的微妙区别。但就算看出这些区别,也必须承认这些画作是从同一个山水传统演变而来的,艺术家们只是在历代大师的成就基础上自觉发展出了自己的风格。

---

① 述而不作,信而好古。
② 杰克逊·波拉克(1912—1956),有影响力的美国画家,抽象表现主义运动的主要力量。1947年,他开始使用"滴画法",取消画架,把巨大的画布平铺在地上,在画布上滴溅颜料作画。

理想背后的假设

为了打造他对完美和谐社会与圣人之治的愿景,孔子和所有的重要思想家一样,也有他自己的一套假设——那是他与生俱来的世界观,也对他的愿景的形成起到了重要作用。这种世界观的核心是,孔子认为宇宙由两个领域组成:人间和天地间(自然界)。他假定人间的秩序必须主动创设并由人(通过礼仪做法)来施为,与之相反,天地间有其内在的韵律与和谐,各部分之间自然维持了一种完美的平衡。世间万物都存在着一种有机的相互关联。实际上,《论语》认为,礼的一个重要功能便是确保人的活动与天地间的活动互为应和,彼此支持。

因此孔子的宇宙观里并没有上帝——既没有一神论的创世主,也没有任何负责创造或维持宇宙运行的存在或实体。宇宙看似自行运转,自时间之始便一直如此。这并不是说,孔子及其同时代人认为不存在一个由自然神祇和祖先构成的精神世界;各路神灵可以帮助人类掌控河流田地、村落城市,以及家庭宗族。但世间并没有负责创造今昔万物的至高全能的天神地祇。实际上,中国本土传统中完全没有可以被称作创世神的文字或考古证据。此事与盛行的西方一神论信仰之间的差异如此显著,以至于某些学者认为中国文明与西方文明之间有一道"宇宙观的鸿沟"。

尽管《论语》中没有上帝或一神论的创世神,但该文本的确提到了**天**,这个概念先前在《尚书》和《诗经》中也曾出现过。大多数学者认为,在那两个文本中,它是指一种天神或是周人的神化祖先。这个字过去一直被译作 heaven。孔子在与弟子的对话中提到的这个**天**,是即便当时的君主都不认同,也能够理解他、认同他的特质①(《论语·宪问第十四之三五》);在匡地之人短期监禁他时能够保护他②(《论语·子罕第九之五》);在桓魋企图刺杀他时,能再次保护他③(《论语·述而第七之二三》);而在他的爱徒颜回死时,抛弃了他④(《论语·先进第十一之九》)。如此看来,在《论语》出现"天"字的大多数语境中,它虽然不是我们西方的全能创世主上帝,却也是个拥有意识并专注人间事务的存在。《论语·为政第二之四》表明,这个"天"还可以在道德上指导人,孔子说,他在50岁时终于理解了"天命"。

孔子因而假设自行运作的宇宙的各部分之间毫不费力便达到了平衡(以及道德)的和谐。需要主动调节的乃是人间。在他的时代,政治与道德已经堕入可悲的境地。周初规范的社会政治秩序——孔子及其追随者称之为"道"——让位于混沌与无序。道家也谈论"道",但儒道两家为这个术语赋予的含义不同。道家的"道"远比社会政治秩序宏大得多;的确,在他们看来,它把社会政治秩序,甚至天地全都包含在内了。道家经典《道德经》的第一章便称其为"万物之母"。但尽管好的秩序不再,让它再次盛行却是孔子最深切的希望和热切的信念。他认为"道"可以恢复,但复兴的大业需要善良正直之人的努力。

结语:阅读孔子的《论语》

首次阅读《论语》会相当困难,因为它表面上没有明显的

---

① 子曰:"不怨天,不尤人,下学而上达。知我者其天乎!"
② 天之未丧斯文也,匡人其如予何?
③ 子曰:"天生德于予,桓魋其如予何!"
④ 颜渊死。子曰:"噫!天丧予!天丧予!"

逻辑。《论语》毕竟不是孔子在治学时付诸文字的经久不衰的文本，而是数代人所编辑的孔子语录集。因此，读者会看到孔子上一句刚刚说到德治，下一句就是孩童应该如何对待父母，其后又是一段关于学与思同等重要的言论。但是，无论它们看起来有多不相干，我认为全部大约500个段落都在直接或间接地探讨两个问题：一是什么造就了君子；二是怎样才是善政。在孔子看来，此两者密不可分。只有当君子为政府服务时，政府才会是他所理解的"好的"政府。同时，只有凭借德行与道义为政，才能引导它所治理的民众实现美好和谐的人际关系。如果读者能牢记这两个非常重要的相关问题——如何造就君子以及怎样才是善政——文本背后的连贯性和孔子的教诲就会清楚无碍。

第二章

儒家思想中的个人与修身

人们有句常说的话,都说"天下国家"。天下的根本是国,国的根本是家庭,家庭的根本是每个人自身。①(《孟子·离娄上之五》)

孔子及其追随者呼吁个人争做道德楷模。这些人会通过榜样的力量,推动他人做出得体恰当的行为。通过遵行礼仪和承担维持所谓五伦,即五种人际关系——父子、君臣、夫妇、兄弟、朋友——所必需的相互责任,他们为周围的人们提供了一个榜样,并因此给家庭、社会和帝国带来了和谐。

个人在建立良好的社会政治秩序中所起到的重要作用,解释了历代儒家学说为何如此深切地关注修身的过程。每一个人都被要求参与道德完善的过程,因为每一个人都有能力对他人产生有益的道德力量。儒家的经典之一《大学》直截了当地说:

---

① 人有恒言,皆曰,"天下国家"。天下之本在国,国之本在家,家之本在身。

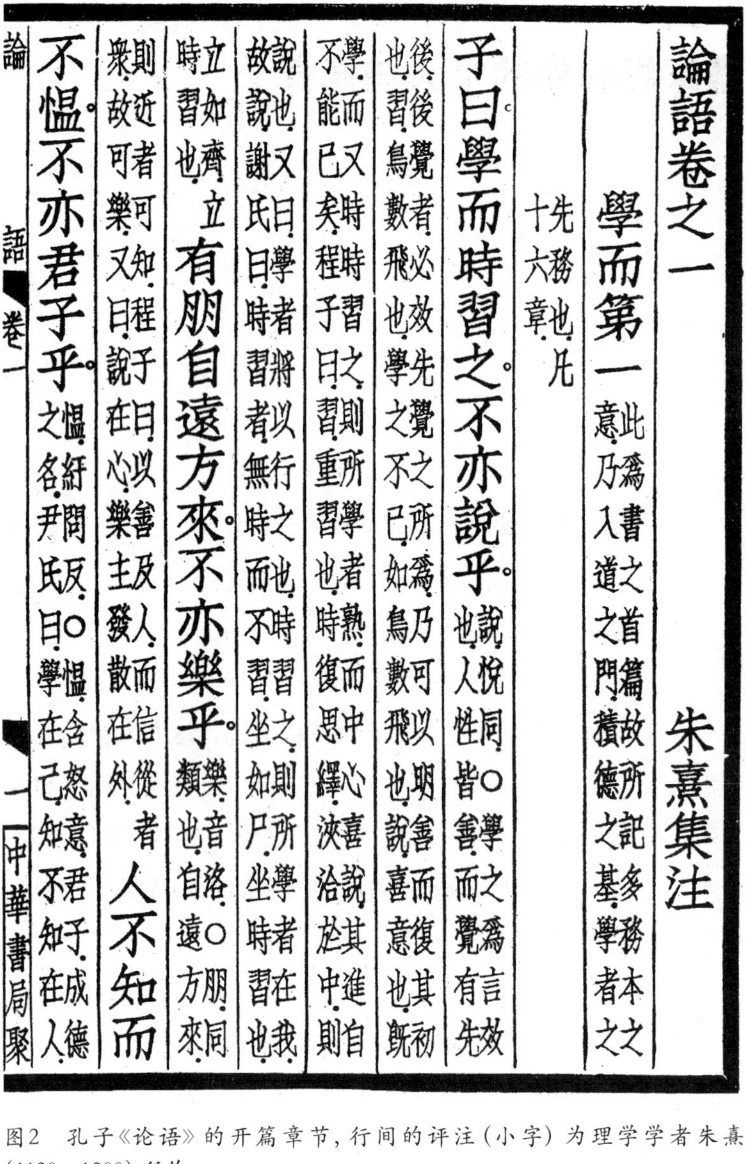
論語卷之一　　朱熹集注

學而第一　此爲書之首篇故所記多務本之意乃入道之門積德之基學者之先務也凡十六章

子曰學而時習之不亦說乎。說悅同○學之爲言效也人性皆善而覺有先後後覺者必效先覺之所爲乃可以明善而復其初也習鳥數飛也學之不已如鳥數飛也說喜意也既學而又時時習之則所學者熟而中心喜說其進自不能已矣程子曰習重習也時復思繹浹洽於中則說也又曰學者將以行之也時習之則所學者在我故說謝氏曰時習者無時而不習坐如尸坐時習也立如齊立時習也

有朋自遠方來不亦樂乎。樂音洛○朋同類也自遠方來則近者可知程子曰以善及人而信從者衆故可樂又曰說在心樂主發散在外

人不知而不慍不亦君子乎。慍紆問反○慍含怒意君子成德之名尹氏曰學在己知不知在人

論語　卷一　中華書局聚

图2　孔子《论语》的开篇章节，行间的评注（小字）为理学学者朱熹
17 （1130—1200）所作

"上自国家君王,下至平民百姓,人人都要以修养品性为根本。"①因此,儒家学说责成每一位追随者把修身作为他们追求真正之道的起点,无论其社会、政治和经济地位如何。这是孔子的忠诚门徒努力在中国社会再现文明、和谐与雅礼的基础,是"本"之所在。

个人修身的目标是成为**君子**。在孔子的时代,**君子**这个术语已经有很长的历史了。这个词由两个字组成,字面上的意思是"统治者的儿子",传统上曾用于指代周朝的贵族阶级。要想当上**君子**,就要出身社会政治精英集团;它是个世袭的社会身份,事关血统。孔子借用这个术语,赋予它全新的含义。按照他的用法,这个词转而指代道德上的——而非社会政治地位的——贵族。对于孔子而言,**君子**是在道德上高人一等的人,按照传统的礼制庄敬待人,并追求谦恭、真挚、诚信、正义和慈悲等美德。

孔子在整部《论语》中把道德优越的**君子**与**小人**对立起来。小人是不遵守礼仪规范、不遵循道德方式之人。他在**道德上**非常卑劣。孔子有一次直言不讳地对此二者进行了区分。孔子说:"君子懂得大义,小人只懂得小利。"②(《论语·里仁第四之十六》)随着孔子在《论语》中对**君子**的重新定义,一个重大的转变发生了。此前,一个人再努力也不能变成**君子**——是否拥有**君子**的社会身份在一出生就已经决定了——而现在,至少在理论上说,人人均可通过成功的修身而获得这个身份。孔子在这里向他同时代的人发出了一个全新的挑战:通过努力,你们所

---

① 自天子以至于庶人,壹是皆以修身为本。
② 子曰:"君子喻于义,小人喻于利。"

有的人都可以**变成**贵族。

学习的作用

为了变成**君子**，修身过程的基础便是学习。这或许可以解释《论语》为何一开篇就大声疾呼："子曰：'学而时习之，不亦说乎？'"(《论语·学而第一之一》)在遍布《论语》全篇的议论中，孔子自我评价说，如果有什么能让他不同于他人的话，那就是他热爱学习。孔子说："哪怕十户人家的小村子，都一定有像丘这样忠诚守信的，只是没有丘这么好学。"[①](《论语·公冶长第五之二八》)正是这种对学习的热爱，让他出类拔萃，并成为他人的道德榜样。

与他认为人人皆可成为**君子**的观点一致，孔子认为，学习的机会应该向所有的人开放。不应有任何社会或经济障碍："有教无类。"(《论语·卫灵公第十五之三九》)关于他本人的教学，他说："自己主动送十条干肉来，我没有不教诲的。"[②]正是孔子的坚定信念，才使得真正渴望学习之人，无论其社会地位如何，都有望在道德上改善自身，甚至获得"君子"的身份。

学者们立即指出，尽管孔子主张对全民开放学习，事实上在他的时代，只有少数人有望得到他提出的那种教育——此话不假。当时大多数中国人都是勉强维持生计的农民，对于他们来说，教育的代价过于奢侈。少数家庭能够负担得起让一个儿子不染指家庭的农活；如果可以的话，接下来就要被迫购买学习用品了——笔、墨、纸，以及当时只能由人力以相当大的成本辛苦

---

① 子曰："十室之邑，必有忠信如丘者焉，不如丘之好学也。"
② 自行束脩以上，吾未尝无诲焉。见《论语·述而第七之七》。

抄写的课本；最后，因为教育并非由国家出资支持，哪怕只是读书识字都往往要找老师辅导，而后者则需要每个学生的"礼物"或报酬维生。

孔子愿意教导任何到场之人，但要符合一个重要的条件：学生必须真心实意地有**志**于学。在回忆自己的道德轨迹时，孔子告诉弟子们，他从15岁便开始追寻道德上的完美了："吾十有五而志于学。"① 孔子招收学生时，也必须从后者身上感受到同样的激情和投入："那些不感到兴奋的，我不去教导；那些不急于表达的，我不去启发。举一个例子而他不能联想到别的情况，就不要再啰嗦了。"②（《论语·述而第七之八》）孔子想必是借鉴了自己的经验。他知道，学习可能非常艰难，道路也会非常漫长。成功需要渴望与毅力，还需要真正的参与和智识上的主动。

对于孔子来说，学问就是了解过去，了解古人及其仪轨、音乐、社会和政治制度，以及他们的规范关系。这种过去是历史经验的宝库，在其中可以找到如何维持——以及破坏——良好秩序的"经验资料"。由于孔子本人就受到了尤其是《尚书》和《诗经》的启发并深受其影响，他把这些经典作为他的教义的基础，敦促弟子们极其仔细地研读它们（例如，学而第一之十五，为政第二之二，为政第二之二一，宪问第十四之四十，季氏第十六之十三，阳货第十七之九，阳货第十七之十）。

孔子告诫说，学习绝不能仅仅是积累知识的问题。孔子说："赐（弟子子贡）啊，你以为我是博学多闻的人吗？"子贡

---

① 见《论语·为政第二之四》。
② 不愤不启；不悱不发。举一隅，不以三隅反，则不复也。

回答说:"对啊,不是吗?"孔子说:"不是的,我是靠一个原则贯穿始终的。"①(《论语·卫灵公第十五之三》)学习礼仪、音乐、制度、得体的关系,以及历史,很可能只能了解一系列细节和事实,除此之外一无所获。需要一个全面的框架,方能把所学的一切联系成一个整体。如果不能以整体性的观点把它们联系起来,即"一以贯之",所习得的各种细节便没有多少意义可言。

因此,好学生有望以他的所学为基础,从点滴的知识碎片推导,得出更全面的理解。以孔子的一个爱徒颜回为例。孔子之所以厚爱颜回,部分原因恰恰是他杰出的推理能力。孔子问子贡说:"你和颜回哪个更强?"他回答说:"我吗?我哪里敢比颜回?颜回听到一件事,就能理解十件事;赐听说一件,只能理解两件事。"孔子说:"你比不上他。我们俩都比不上啊。"②(《论语·公冶长第五之九》)此外,好学生还应该知道如何运用推论得来的知识。孔子说:"三百首《诗》背熟了,把政务交给他,却办不了;派他出使四方,也不能相机行事。背诗虽多,又有什么用呢?"③(《论语·子路第十三之五》)这里的要旨是,仅仅把书本知识记在头脑中是刻板而无用的,绝非能实现自我转变和改善社会的真学问。

因此,孔子所说的"学习"指的是道德学习,即研究那些让人成为**君子**的价值观并身体力行。他哀叹在他本人的时代,学

---

① 子曰:"赐也,女以予为多学而识之者与?"对曰:"然,非与?"曰:"非也,予一以贯之。"

② 子谓子贡曰:"女与回也孰愈?"对曰:"赐也何敢望回!回也闻一以知十,赐也闻一以知二。"子曰:"弗如也。吾与女,弗如也。"

③ 子曰:"诵《诗》三百,授之以政,不达。使于四方,不能专对;虽多,亦奚以为?"

习已经沦为获得世俗成功或赞扬的一种手段："古人学习是为提高自身学养，今人学习是为让别人钦佩。"①（《论语·宪问第十四之二四》）他的目标是让人回到正确的轨道上来，让学习再次成为道德上的自我提升。

孔子坚持认为，儒家追求道德完善或成圣的责任必须扎根于持之以恒地致力于学习，这在很大程度上源于他本人的生活经历。在《论语》著名的"自传式"段落中，他说：

> 我十五岁全神贯注于求学；三十岁能够自立；四十岁没什么迷惑；五十岁得知天命；六十岁耳根顺了；七十岁随心所欲，没有不合情合理的。②（《论语·为政第二之四》）

尽管是自传式的陈述，这番言语却显然旨在成为儒家学派全体学生的顺序模板。这段话建议，通往道德完善之路必须始于坚定不移地学习。通过学习，学生也可以成为圣人——其一举一动都本能地符合"道"。

道德君子：礼仪之中的仁

《论语》并没有为道德君子提供一个简洁明晰的定义，却连篇累牍地讨论了道德君子的各种特质。最重要的是，道德君子是仁者。在儒家的理想中，仁是最高的美德，这种美德涵盖了包括诚信、正义、慈悲、礼仪、智慧，以及孝顺在内的一切。没有一

---

① 古之学者为己，今之学者为人。
② 吾十有五而志于学；三十而立；四十而不惑；五十而知天命；六十而耳顺；七十而从心所欲，不逾矩。

种翻译能够精确描述这个词的全部意义。它被译成了五花八门的benevolence（仁爱）、humanity（仁慈）、humanness（人性），如此等等；我在本书中把它翻译成true goodness（真善），希望这种译法能够传达"仁"在孔子教诲中包罗万象、至高无上的地位。

仁不是与世隔绝，与其他人断绝往来培养不出这种品质。仁只能存在于与他人的关系以及对待他人的方式中。正是在具体的行为中，作为美德的仁才得以实现。例如，孝子向其父鞠躬，就"施行"了他的孝心。因此，仁与礼仪密切相关，因为孔子认为，仁主要通过践礼才被赋予了有意义的表达。出于这个原因，我们发现孔子在《论语》中的大部分教导都在讨论恰当的礼仪。孔子认为，在道德上高人一筹，就是对礼仪有敏锐的认知。

关于仁

虽说仁的概念在孔子的学说中至关重要，他却从未就他所谓的至德做出大致的解释或定义。这让弟子们倍感挫败，在《论语》中，他们自始至终都在用如下的问题烦扰他："仁是什么？""某某人是仁者吗？""某某人的行为是仁行吗？"孔子的回答各不相同，似乎取决于提问之人以及所论及之人。仁可以是"爱人"（《论语·颜渊第十二之二二》），是"克己复礼"（《论语·颜渊第十二之一》），是"恭、宽、信、敏、惠"（《论语·阳货第十七之六》），是"有勇"（《论语·宪问第十四之四》），是"不忧"（《论语·子罕第九之二九》），或是"刚毅"（《论语·子路第十三之二七》）。孔子向弟子们所做的解释不过是仁的概况或部分面向。他也知道他们很沮丧，渴望他能更加开诚布公，就说道："朋友们，我知道你们认为我有什么瞒着没教。但我对你们没什么可隐瞒的。"①(《论语·述而第七之二三》)看来,仁似乎无法被完全表达,充分定义,它有一种不可言喻的性质。

像他的追随者们一样,我们倒是可以从《论语》中梳理出对这个基本道德品质的更加深刻的理解。该文本中的一些段落尤其发人深省。子贡问:"有没有一个字可以终生去做的呢?"孔子说:"应该是恕吧:自己不乐意的,就不要强加于人。"②(《论语·卫灵公第十五之二四》)仁就是感同身受的境界。在与他人打交道时,我们应该以自己乐于接受的方式来对待他们。为了判断他人的感受,我们需要易地而处,体会一下自己的感受。这就是孔子的同理心。将自己的这些同理感受成功地延伸至他人,使得我们与其他人的关系能够真正达到感同身受之时,就实现了仁:"我们老师的道,就是忠于自己,宽恕他人,没别的。"③(《论语·里仁第四之十五》)

在任何一个特定时刻或特定场合,感同身受或许不难。孔子认为,其困难在于我们与各式各样的人交往时,整天都保持着共情的感受与做法,这些人包括关切的学生、悲伤的友人、哭闹的孩子、病弱的邻居、咄咄逼人的乞丐、心烦意乱的同事、筋疲力尽的配偶,不一而足。如果一整天可以称作挑战的话,那么整周或整月就更是难上加难。这或许解释了孔子何以拒绝称任何人为仁者,他自己也不例外④(《论语·述而第七之三四》)。一个人共情的感受和做法消失的那一刻,他的仁也随之而去。颜回

---

① 二三子,以我为隐乎?吾无隐乎尔。
② 子贡问曰:"有一言而可以终身行之者乎?"子曰:"其恕乎!己所不欲,勿施于人。"
③ 夫子之道,忠恕而已矣。
④ 子曰:"若圣与仁,则吾岂敢。抑为之不厌,诲人不倦,则可谓云尔已矣。"

比大多数人都能保持仁,但就连他的成功也是有限的。孔子说:"颜回能做到心中三个月不违背仁。其余弟子能一天做到一次,或者一个月做到一次就不错了。"①(《论语·雍也第六之七》)如此说来,有必要认识到,仁不是可以一劳永逸地达成的一种内心状态;它是一种涉及身心的持续**行为**,需要始终保持警惕。正因为此,孔子的另一个著名的弟子曾子才会说:"读书人必须博大坚毅,因为他们重任在肩,征途漫长。将仁爱作为自己的负担,不也沉甸甸吗?到死方休,不也漫长吗?"②(《论语·泰伯第八之七》)。在儒家的传统中,作为君子和仁者,需要终身的承诺,至死方休。

中文"仁"字的词源本身也能给我们一些启发。"仁"字由两部分组成,一部分是"人",另一部分是"二",表明一个人只有与他人交往方可成就"仁",即真正的善。在儒家传统中,仁并不是一种可以孤立培养并表达的品质。儒家思想中没有为"上帝的竞技者"③这种闪米特传统留有立足之处,那位竞技者坐在叙利亚沙漠里40英尺高的石柱上,当着上帝的面为自己扬善除恶。在孔子看来,仁是人际关系,是只有与其他人交往才会实现的一种美德。

关于礼

孔子在《论语》中坚称,君子的共情关切必然与传承下来并经过数世纪改善的一系列"礼"(传统上译为"仪轨"或"礼仪规

---

① 子曰:回也,其心三月不违仁。其余,则日月至焉而已矣。"

② 士不可以不弘毅,任重而道远。仁以为己任,不亦重乎?死而后已,不亦远乎?

③ 指柱上苦行者圣西缅(Saint Simeon the Stylite,约390?—459),叙利亚苦行圣人。他以在阿勒颇附近的一个柱顶上的狭小平台生活了37年而闻名。

范",但也有译作"仪式""礼节""得体行为的准则""礼仪规范"以及"习俗"的)有关,既受到后者的规训,也要通过它来表达。但正如"仁"一样,他没有尝试为弟子们定义"礼",也没有对其意义和作用给出大致的解释。然而,我们在后世的《礼记》一书中找到了一些有用的段落。例如:

> 礼是用来决定亲疏、判断嫌疑、分别异同、明辨是非的。践礼时不胡乱取悦、讨好他人,也不说多余的话。践礼时不逾越节度,不侵犯侮辱,不轻佻亲狎。修养自身、实践所言,叫作善行。行为有修养,说话合乎道理,这是礼的本质。①

给人赋予了"人性"或"文明",让人有别于兽类的,正是践礼:

> 鹦鹉虽能说话,终究不过是一种飞鸟;猩猩虽能说话,终究不过是一种禽兽。而今要是作为人却没有礼,虽然能说话,不也还是禽兽之心吗?但如果人和禽兽一样不知礼,父子俩就可能拥有同一个配偶。因此圣人兴起,制定礼法来教导人,使人从此而有礼,知道把自己与禽兽区别开来。②

---

① 夫礼者所以定亲疏,决嫌疑,别同异,明是非也。礼,不妄说人,不辞费。礼,不逾节,不侵侮,不好狎。修身践言,谓之善行。行修言道,礼之质也。见《礼记·曲礼上第一》第5章。

② 鹦鹉能言,不离飞鸟。猩猩能言,不离禽兽。今人而无礼,虽能言,不亦禽兽之心乎?夫唯禽兽无礼,故父子聚麀。是故圣人作,为礼以教人。使人以有礼,知自别于禽兽。见《礼记·曲礼上第一》第6章。

"礼"为民众之间的多种交往提供指导,正是在它的指导下,才有了社会的和谐。践行恰当礼仪的父亲就应该表现得像个真正的父亲;践行恰当礼仪的儿子也应该表现得像个真正的儿子。"礼"因而有助于实现规范性的五伦。孔子认为,周初的良好秩序就建筑在这五伦之上,这些关系因而成为任何良好的社会政治秩序的基础。正如《礼记》所说:"君臣之道,父子之道,夫妇之道,兄弟之道,交友之道。这五种就是天下人共行的大道。"①

人自幼便开始在家礼中学习如何致敬祖先,如何哀悼亡者,以及如何庆祝人生的重大转变,比如冠礼——代表成年的仪式——以及婚礼。他逐渐熟悉了祭祀祖父要用多少以及具体使用哪些礼器,穿衣和悼词的规矩,以及哀悼期间的饮食事项。他甚至还知道不能佩戴紫色或紫红色的饰品,或是在便衣上使用红色或朱红色,以及吊唁时不戴黑色的帽子。但在孔子看来,践礼并不限于我们能够想到的宗教和仪式场合;于他而言,人生的方方面面都受到一系列礼仪的支配,就连最平凡的日常事项也不例外。我们如何进食,如何说话,如何彼此问候,如何穿衣,以及公开和私下里如何为人处事,都由礼仪的预期和传统所决定。因此,关于进食,《礼记》告诫说:

不要把米饭团成饭团;不要狼吞虎咽地进食;不要大口地喝汤;吃东西时不要发出声音;不要用牙嚼骨头;不要把拿起的鱼肉又放回食器;不要把骨头扔给狗吃;不要一个劲地专挑某种食物吃;不要迫不及待地扬去饭中的热气。

---

① 君臣也、父子也、夫妇也、昆弟也、朋友之交也。五者,天下之达道也。见《礼记·中庸第三十一》第19章。

不要用筷子吃黍饭。不要不咀嚼羹汤里的菜就急忙喝下；不要往盛给自己的羹汤里再添加调味品；不要一直剔牙；不要喝调味的蘸酱。①

在很多西方人看来，这些禁令或许看似无关紧要——不过是礼貌和规矩而已，谈不上道德的培养。但孔子无疑将其视作"礼"，正确践行它们可使人培养并表现出"仁"："所以，礼的教化作用很微妙：它在邪恶还没形成时就加以预防，让人每天在不知不觉中趋向善良、远离罪恶。"②

当然，礼只有在真心诚意施行时，才有这种"教化"之力。孔子唯恐学生们把践礼看作没有意义的表演和姿势而已。为了让"礼"具有真正的意义，演礼就必须注入得体的情感："如礼行事却不恭敬，料理丧事但不悲哀，我如何看得下去呢？"③（《论语·八佾第三之二六》）向祖先奉献酒和食物必须伴以尊崇和挚爱的情感；在长者面前鞠躬必须伴以敬意；礼貌的言谈、衣着和用餐礼仪必须伴以对他人的得体举止与客套。因此，践礼是人用于表达自己最具人性的品质的方式。正是通过这种方式，他内心的感受与外在的举止才能合二为一。

在《论语》的教诲中，践礼看来既是一种彰显人性的手段，又是培养让我们之所以为人的那些品质的方法。通过献祭，我们加深了对祖先的尊崇之情；通过鞠躬，我们加深了对长辈的敬

---

① 毋抟饭，毋放饭，毋流歠，毋咤食，毋啮骨，毋反鱼肉，毋投与狗骨。毋固获，毋扬饭。饭黍毋以箸。毋嚺羹，毋絮羹，毋刺齿，毋歠醢。见《礼记·曲礼上第一》第29章。
② 故礼之教化也微，其止邪也于未形，使人日徙善远罪而不自知也。见《礼记·经解第二十六》第5章。
③ 为礼不敬，临丧不哀，吾何以观之哉！

意；通过高雅的言谈、衣着和用餐礼仪，我们加深了对他人的得体举止与客套之情。在孔子看来，亲身实践礼仪会向施礼者反复灌输与这些礼有关的情绪与感受。孔子在整部《论语》中呼吁沉浸在这些礼仪中，如此可以让人从外部习惯于良好、规范的社会行为，而这种已成习惯的行为又可以引导和重塑他的道德意识。一次，在被问及构成"仁"的要素时，孔子干脆答道："非礼勿视，非礼勿听，非礼勿言，非礼勿动。"（《论语·颜渊第十二之一》）

于孔子而言，礼与乐密切相关。古人早就意识到了音乐能够激发德行。正如《礼记》所说："音乐是圣人所喜爱的，它可以使民心向善。因为它感人至深，还可以改变民情民俗，所以先王特别强调乐教。"①因此，孔子认为，弟子们应该学习音乐——或者更准确地说，学习他认为有道德提升作用的某些类型的音乐——这是昔日礼仪环境的重要组成部分。他特别推荐韶乐（即圣王舜的宫廷音乐），说它甚至对他本人都有巨大的影响（《论语·八佾第三之二五》《论语·述而第七之十四》《论语·卫灵公第十五之十一》）②。音乐的重要性——及其在儒家学说中与礼的密切关系——在这句言简意赅地劝诫弟子们的话中得到了恰如其分的总结："以《诗》动人，以礼仪立人，以音乐成人。"③（《论语·泰伯第八之八》）

---

① 乐也者，圣人之所乐也，而可以善民心，其感人深，其移风易俗，故先王著其教焉。见《礼记·乐记第十九之四·乐施》第4章。

② 相关原文分别为：子谓《韶》："尽美矣！又尽善也！"谓《武》："尽美矣！未尽善也！"；子在齐闻《韶》，三月不知肉味，曰："不图为乐之至于斯也！"；颜渊问为邦，子曰："行夏之时，乘殷之辂，服周之冕，乐则《韶》《舞》。放郑声，远佞人，郑声淫，佞人殆。"

③ 兴于《诗》，立于礼，成于乐。

作为道德熔炉的家庭

家庭为我们提供衣食住行，但在儒家学说中，它最重要的作用是让我们踏上通往美德的道路。家庭是社会的缩影，也是学习人际关系及其规范的地方。在理想情况下，我们正是在这里被灌输了适当的价值观和做法，才使得和谐的儒家社会得以建立：服从和尊重权威，敬老爱幼，等等。

《论语》的第二个段落谈到了家庭在塑造有德行的个人以及促进和平稳定的社会和政治秩序中的重要作用。有子[①]表达了孔子的观点：

图3　李公麟（约1041—1106）《孝子跪奉双亲图》摹本（14世纪？）

[①] 有子（前518—前458），即有若，字子有，鲁国人，孔门七十二贤之一。

> 一个人能够孝顺父母，敬重兄长，却喜好违犯上司，那是少有的。不喜欢违犯上司，却醉心于捣乱，这样的人从来不会有。君子抓根本。根本扎稳了，一切为人处世之道自然生发出来。孝敬父母，尊重兄长，这就是仁的根本吧！[①]
>
> （《论语·学而第一之二》）

如此看来，个人的道德修养始于家庭。这里是人开始学习行孝友悌，尊敬长辈的地方；是人学习礼仪规矩名称的地方。在这里学到的功课可以随时应用在外部世界。好儿子自然会服从统治者；好弟弟自然会尊敬长兄；好女儿和妻子也自然会顺从男人。家庭承受着巨大的压力，必须提供正确的道德环境，因为一个任性的儿子——不顺从村里的长者或统治者——不仅会让他本人，也会让他的整个家庭名誉扫地，特别是他的父母。他的失败就是他们的失败；作为父母，他们没有培养起儿子的道德感和规范意识，如今却让社会承担了严重后果。

在家庭里学到的各种美德中，孝顺是最基础的。孝顺的本质就是服从父母的权威：尊重他们的意愿，关心他们的福祉。《礼记》总结了与这个基本美德有关的责任：

> 孝子的养老，首先在于使父母内心快乐，不违背他们的意愿；其次才是言行循礼，使他们听得高兴，看得快乐，使他们起居安适；在饮食方面尽心侍候周到——孝子终生皆须如此。所谓"终生"孝敬父母，不是说终父母的一生，而是

[①] 其为人也孝弟，而好犯上者，鲜矣；不好犯上，而好作乱者，未之有也！君子务本，本立而道生；孝弟也者，其为仁之本与？

终孝子自己的一生。所以，父母生前所爱的，自己也要爱；他们生前所敬的，自己也要敬。就是对他们喜欢的犬马也都是如此对待，更何况对他们爱敬的人呢！①

在儒家思想中，尽孝并不会随着父母的过世而终止。真正的孝道需要子女终生表现得像父母希望的那样，其处事为人应有利于家庭的美名：

> 父母虽然去世了，儿子将做好事，想到这会给父母带来美名，就一定果敢地去做；如果是将做坏事，想到这会使父母跟着丢人，那就一定敛手不敢去做。②

因此，孝敬并不只是在家庭关系网内部发挥，而是作为良好有德的行为，在更广大的社会关系网里实现的。

有关笼统的"礼"的教义，也同样适用于更为具体的孝顺：形式背后的感情至关重要。这个要旨在儒家学说中一遍又一遍地重复，比如弟子子游问孝，孔子明确回应："如今行孝道的，只知道能够给父母提供膳食。可是就算狗啊马啊，我们也都能把它们养起来。没有孝敬心，怎么区别这两种养呢？"③（《论语·为政第二之七》）正如他对所有的"礼"的态度一样，孔子

---

① 孝子之养老也，乐其心不违其志，乐其耳目，安其寝处，以其饮食忠养之，孝子之身终，终身也者，非终父母之身，终其身也；是故父母之所爱亦爱之，父母之所敬亦敬之，至于犬马尽然，而况于人乎！见《礼记·内则第十二》第11章。

② 父母虽没，将为善，思贻父母令名，必果；将为不善，思贻父母羞辱，必不果。见《礼记·内则第十二》第2章。

③ 今之"孝"者，是谓能养。至于犬马，皆能有养。不敬，何以别乎？

坚持认为,外在的孝顺行为是内在的真诚感受的忠实表达。

　　在儒家的理想中,家庭对维持中国的社会政治秩序至关重要,因为正是在这里,在家庭中,子女开始慢慢适应在中国社会占主导地位的义务承担和价值观。孩子在家庭里得知,世界本来就是有等级的;当存在明显的地位差异和明确的角色分工时,等级制度才会有效地发挥作用;每一种社会身份都有与之相连的固定、规范的责任(例如,作为好儿子或女儿有一整套行为规范);在等级分明的网络中,好人就是履行与其社会地位相关的责任之人;以及,等级制度中的每一个人认真履行了他被界定的角色所应承担的责任,整体的和谐也就实现了。

第三章

儒家思想中的治理

季康子[鲁国非法的实际统治者]问孔子如何理政,孔子回答说:"政就是正。先生自己带头改正自己,谁还敢继续不当的行为呢?"[1](《论语·颜渊第十二之十七》)

作为楷模的统治者

修身以道德的自我实现为目标。但是,正如这句话所暗示的那样,个人的自我实现本身绝非目的。孔子认为,自我实现会促成他人的自我实现,这样的连锁反应会引发全社会的道德转化。当然,这正是为什么道德先锋的存在对于儒家学说如此关键,也是孔子为什么致力于解释良善、道德,以及成为君子之意义。与治理手段相比,道德精英树立的榜样更能有力地促进社会和谐。至少在理想情况下,这种道德精英阶层的顶端当是堪称典范的统治者,他以绝对的正确性为全体民众做出榜样。

---

[1] 季康子问"政"于孔子。孔子对曰:"'政'者,正也。子帅以正,孰敢不正?"

儒家的统治者拥有"德"。这种"德"可以对他人发挥一种精神伦理的力量。民众被这种"德"所吸引，因而也就聚集在他的身旁。孔子将其与自然世界进行了比较："治理国政用道德，就好比北极星：它安住本位，群星围着它转。"①（《论语·为政第二之一》）民众对优秀的儒家统治者的归顺，显然不是屈服于某种强制权力，而是对辐射整个王国的一种固定、可靠的道德权威的服从。这种道德权威是能够指导他人行动，让他们走向正确方向的一股力量。以道德劝说来指导和管理民众的主题贯穿于《论语》以及儒家的其他经典著作；实际上，这正是儒家政治哲学的一个与众不同的特点。

上文引述的季康子在不少其他地方重提政府治理的主题。季康子问孔子如何理政，他说："要是杀掉坏人，引进好人，怎么样？"②孔子几乎没有掩饰自己对篡位者季康子的厌烦乃至鄙视，回答说："您搞政治，哪里用得着杀人？您一心做好人，老百姓就好了。君子好比风；百姓好比草。风一吹过来，草就伏贴了。"③（《论语·颜渊第十二之十九》）季康子就是不得要领。在孔子看来，依赖于惩罚和武力的苛政不起作用，且恰好说明"治国无方"。好的政府只需道德领导就够了。道德会孕育道德。在与季康子交谈结尾处使用的风与草的比喻，无疑是中国传统中最著名的说法之一。民众容易接受统治者的道德劝说的影响；而他对他们的影响完全呈现为一派"自然"，就像风自然会吹倒草一样。这里要注意的是，正如有道的统治者会让民众朝

---

① 为政以德，譬如北辰，居其所，而众星共之。
② 季康子问政于孔子曰："如杀无道，以就有道，何如？"
③ 对曰："子为政，焉用杀？子欲善，而民善矣。君子之德，风；小人之德，草；草上之风，必偃。"

着善的方向前进一样，缺乏道德权威的统治者则会让民众走向伤风败俗。因此，在儒家的传统中，无德的统治者会对整个道德社会的秩序构成严重的威胁。

孔子坚信德行的教化力量，并坚信它能够吸引其他人过上一种道德的生活，以至于他有一次表达了想要在东方九夷部落安家的愿望，有人问道："九夷蛮荒无礼，怎么办？"他坦然答道："君子在那里住，怎么还会蛮荒无礼？"①（《论语子罕第九之十四》）。有了正确的道德领导，连"九夷"也会举止得体。

孔子对季康子说，好的统治者本人一定渴望良善。他希望臣民培养怎样的道德，自己必须以身作则。相反，当一个国家目无法纪的行为猖獗，统治者就必须扪心自问，思考自己有无过失。季康子遇到了盗窃的麻烦。他问孔子该怎么办。孔子回答说："假如您自己不贪，您就是悬赏让人去偷，也没有人偷窃的。"②（《论语·颜渊第十二之十八》）孔子坚称，如果鲁国盛行偷窃，那就是季康子的责任。民众毕竟是从统治者那里学习道德的。如果统治者高尚而不贪婪，那么民众也会高尚而不贪婪。如此一来，就没有什么能诱使他们偷窃。因此，只要统治者本人没有私欲，就可以在他的国家和民众中实现儒家倡导的和谐。

如果好的政府取决于道德先锋的存在，那么统治者就有责任识别那些由于品格诚信而有资格做官的人。选择合适的人至关重要。鲁哀公问孔子说："怎么做才可以服众？"孔子回答说："推举正直的人来管理邪佞的人，老百姓就服；重用邪佞

---

① 或曰："陋，如之何？"子曰："君子居之，何陋之有？"
② 季康子患盗，问于孔子。孔子对曰："苟子之不欲，虽赏之不窃。"

的人来支使正直的人，老百姓就不服。"①（《论语·为政第二之十九》）这个段落谈到了一个熟悉的主题：榜样的力量，风自然而然地吹弯草叶的力量。执政者的正直会促进他们管理的人品行端正。但这个段落也提到了另一个相关的要点。如果统治者在选择官员时不偏不倚，如果他避开那些不合格的腐败之人而只提拔良善之人，便显然是在为民众谋福利。反过来，看到他把他们的福祉放在心上，人们也会继续给他以信任和支持。

孔子继而说，这样的信任正是国家和统治者正统性的基础：

> 子贡问如何理政。孔子说："粮食充足，军备充足，民众信任。"子贡问："万不得已要去掉三者其中的一个，先去掉哪一个？"孔子说："去掉军备。"子贡问："万不得已再去掉一个，先去掉哪一个？"孔子说："去掉粮食。自古以来，人总是要死的；但如果得不到民众信任，政府就没法立足了。"②（《论语·颜渊第十二之七》）

言外之意，民众如果对其统治者有信心，相信他把他们的福祉放在第一位，就愿意忍受一切艰难困苦。统治者只要真诚地关心民众的福祉，就一定会得到他们回报的忠诚与支持，哪怕他们自己的生命危如累卵。

高尚贤德的统治者是完美的君子，行为举止始终得体。他

---

① 哀公问曰："何为则民服？"孔子对曰："举直错诸枉，则民服；举枉错诸直，则民不服。"

② 子贡问政。子曰："足食，足兵，民信之矣。"子贡曰："必不得已而去，于斯三者何先？"曰："去兵。"子贡曰："必不得已而去，于斯二者何先？"曰："去食。自古皆有死，民无信不立。"

是完美的榜样，毫不费力地按照正确的行为准则行事。他正是通过自己有号召力的道德榜样来教化和引导民众，并让他们步入正轨。孔子认为，在这种理想的统治之下，法律、命令和惩罚这些常规的执政工具就无关紧要了。这并不是说它们完全没有必要，但在孔子看来，对这些工具的依赖越少，对统治者个人、他的道德之光及礼仪范例的依赖越多越好。自上而下的法律和惩罚或许的确能够在表面上维持民众的社会秩序，但想用它们向民众灌输是非观并引导他们改善道德则收效甚微。而且它们对于提升真正的社群精神，即民众共同致力于创造和谐社会也无甚助益。在孔子的所有言论中，这一段最好地总结了孔子关于善政之基础的观点：

> 用政令训导人，用刑法统制人，老百姓就力求免遭刑罚，却没有廉耻心。用道德教导人，用礼仪规范人，老百姓除了有廉耻心之外，还会匡正自己。①（《论语·为政第二之三》）

个人的道德改善，以及社会的和谐，都不是法律和惩罚等外部威胁和强迫的结果。相反，它们源于民众，后者受到了统治者重建社群和国家的榜样的启发，通过践礼以及自幼在家庭生活中形成的那种流畅而规范的关系，方能实现。

孔子在这里指出，就塑造民众的行为和理想而言，文化与传统是比法典和刑罚更加有效和强大的工具。通过榜样和道德劝说，好的统治者会倡导一整套共同的价值观和做法，这可以有

---

① 道之以政，齐之以刑，民免而无耻；道之以德，齐之以礼，有耻且格。

效地规范民众的行为,并使每一个人受到社群及其规范的约束。孔子认为,违反这些规范会导致严重的后果,有时其影响会长期存在。一个人吃黄鱼用手抓而不用筷子,或者在大庭广众之下咒骂年迈的父亲,或是在哀悼父母期间身穿华服,都有可能被他人视作蒙昧无礼。说到底,他不了解作为真正的中国人意味着什么,就要冒被同村之人排斥的风险。尽管没有正式的法律对此类"不轨行为"给予罚款或其他处罚,但惩处的威胁仍不可小觑。这正是孔子何以相信在共同文化治理之下的社会,民众不会随意跨越习俗行为的界限,而会培养出一种强烈的羞耻感。

  以礼治国的统治者承担了文化旗手的角色,因而巩固了他的合法性;同时,他还作为导师,为民众示范他们应当接受的信念和做法。孔子相信以礼治国的功效,这在他与弟子们的对话中得到了反复证明。孔子说:"能够以礼让来治理国家,那还有什么困难呢?如果不能以礼让治国,又怎么能施行礼呢?"[①](《论语·里仁第四之十三》)然而,**只有**当统治者施行时辅之以适当得体的情感,即谦卑或尊重的精神之时,礼仪才会有效。正是这种情感让统治者的演礼具有权威性,并赋予那种演礼以指导民众和"格"(《论语·为政第二之三》)民的力量。

  然而,如果根据这些,就说孔子认为法律和惩罚在治理中没有一席之地,却是错误的。他呼吁以德和礼来统治,却也把刑法看作政府机构的常规组成部分。例如,他谈到君子时,说"君子关注法度",与之形成对照的小人则"关心恩惠"。[②](《论语·里仁第四之十一》)而在和子路交谈时,他说:"如果礼乐不兴盛,

---

① 子曰:"能以礼让为国乎,何有? 不能以礼让为国,如礼何?"
② 君子怀刑,小人怀惠。

刑罚就不会恰当；刑罚不恰当，百姓就手足无措。"①(《论语·子路第十三之三》)的确，孔子非常看重的《尚书》和《诗经》都提到了贤德的周初统治者公正地使用法律和惩罚(如《尚书·康诰》)。他可能意识到，为了维持社会秩序，偶尔诉诸法律和惩罚是不可避免的。尽管如此，他显然希望越少使用这些手段越好。当孔子论及"断案子，我和别人差不多。总要竭力使大家没有官司可打了才满意"②(《论语·颜渊第十二之十三》)时，他所阐述的，是儒家学说的一个核心原则：最好的政府是在最小程度上依赖法律的政府。

《论语》中呈现出来的理想统治者的面貌，是一个人的德作为一种有强大号召力的道德力量向外发散，让民众走向"仁"和践礼，从而实现社会和谐。这股力量是非强制性的，其影响也看似自然，就像草随风动。因此，理想的统治者甚至无须主动统治。孔子说："无为而治的，大概就是舜吧！他做了什么呢？他只是庄重端正地面向南，坐在王位上罢了。"③(《论语·卫灵公第十五之五》)注释者们认为，这段话的意思是称颂圣王舜的美德如此伟大，如此丰沛，以至于他不必采取任何行动，就毫不费力地感化了民众；这是对《论语·为政第二之一》的呼应，后者将统治者比作北极星，"它安住本位，群星围着它转"。道家也使用"无为"一词来表明"行为"和"做"应该是自发的，没有目的性，也绝不会以任何方式违背万物的自然过程。注释者们在这里赋予这个词以道德意义，从而将孔子对这个词的用法与道家区分

---

① 礼乐不兴，则刑罚不中；刑罚不中，则民无所措手足。
② 听讼，吾犹人也；必也使无讼乎！
③ 子曰："无为而治者，其舜也与！夫何为哉？恭己正南面而已矣。"

开来，他们解释说舜之所以能够"无为"，完全是因为他的"德"极其强大。换言之，"无为"是他的道德状况的直接结果。但我们也要记住，舜之所以能在政府具体的日常事务中"无为"，是因为他是一个道德高尚的统治者，对民众充满同情，选择了像皋陶①这样正直高尚的人来实施政府的日常管理（《论语·颜渊第十二之二二》）。

好的统治者必然善于判断人品，在选择官员时只挑选那些与他共同致力于儒家原则和民众福祉的人。从这里我们就能够大致了解到，始于公元前2世纪，延续了逾两千年的著名的中国科举制度为何如此重要了。

政府与民众的福祉

因此，在儒家的理想中，民众的福祉在很大程度上取决于统治者的品行。在治理王国的过程中实现其仁德的责任由他和他任命的官员共同承担。像统治者本人一样，理想的官员也应该是仁者；是一位经历过修身的过程，埋头于学习且努力成为道德君子的人。实际上，我们已经看到，《论语》在某种程度上就是孔子教导学生如何有道德的一个尝试，希望他们能成就他本人未竟之事——谋得一官半职。他认为，只有正派的人才会成为好官，而只有好官才会使善政变为现实。

好官并非掌握某种特殊技能或履行特定功能之人。实际上，孔子言简意赅的说法"君子不器"②（《论语·为政第二之

---

① 皋陶，偃姓，舜帝和夏朝初期的一位贤臣。传说中生于尧帝统治的时候，曾经被舜任命为掌管刑法的"理官"，以正直闻名天下。他还被奉为中国司法的鼻祖。

② 指君子不能只有一种用途。

十二》),说的就是这种理想。何晏①(活跃于3世纪)对这句话的传统注释是:"每种器皿都有限定的用途。但说到君子,凡事他都可以做到。"②之所以"凡事都可以做到",是因为他是德的化身。作为德的化身,他充满同情和仁慈,且一以贯之推己及人。有了自己精心训练的共情技巧,他便做好了准备,能够应对国家和社会面临的各种事务。这并不是说他在某些领域一定不在行,如灌溉控制、税收或行政技术等,而是这些专业技能并不是他成为好官的充分条件。让他成为一个好官的,是他做好了准备,愿意改善民众的命运,及时关注民众的需求。

儒家学说认为君子有义务为政府效力,帮助统治者在全国上下实施"道"。毕竟,所谓"仁"就是服务和改善他人的生活。但按照孔子的说法,君子有时候也可以拒绝效力。孔子提到过一个名叫蘧伯玉的魏国大臣在公元前559年辞官,感叹道:"君子啊蘧伯玉!国家有道,就出来当官;国家无道,就能把原则珍藏起来。"③(《论语·卫灵公第十五之七》)此外,孔子还说过类似但更为抽象的话:"天下太平就出来做事,天下大乱就隐藏起来。"④(《论语·泰伯第八之十三》)

这类说法看似与《论语》通篇的主旨,即君子有责任改变桀骜不恭的社会,让它重新恢复道德,并不一致。孔子怎么会允许君子在社会最需要他现身的时刻"隐藏"起来呢?再考虑

---

① 何晏(196—249),字平叔,东汉末年大将军何进之孙,曹操的婿养子,三国时期玄学家,魏晋玄学贵无派创始人,与王弼并称"王何",玄学代表人物之一。其著述完整存于世者甚少,以散文和赋为主,散文多是哲学、政治论文。
② 器者各周其用,至于君子,无所不施。见何晏、邢昺:《论语注疏·卷二》。
③ 君子哉蘧伯玉!邦有道,则仕;邦无道,则可卷而怀之。
④ 天下有道则见,无道则隐。

图4 木刻版画,一个官员履行儒家宣扬的义务,关怀其子民的福祉。画中的说明文字为"开仓赈济"。摘自傅惜华编《中国古典文学版画选集》(1981年)

到孔子虽然生活在"道"显然势衰的时代,但正如我们在前文中引述的他与子贡的对话(参见第一章)中所见,他仍在焦急地等待"识货的人"①(《论语·子罕第九之十三》)。他从来都没有怀疑过自己如果有机会,一定能把愚昧无知的统治者和社会引入正轨的能力。孔子说:"如果有人用我主持国家政事,一年之内可以见到成效,三年就会成就显著。"②(《论语·子路第十三之十》)这么说来,君子**通常**就应该为统治者效力。但在上文这样的段落中,孔子语带谨慎,暗示一个国家及其统治者有时候可能会堕落得不可救药,以至于他们根本不会受到君子的道德转化的影响。这样的国家里没有君子生存的空间,也不会准许践行他的原则。实际上,任何坚持这样做的人只会招来统治者的怒火和严厉的惩罚。在面对敌视道德改革的统治者时,君子最好还是"卷而怀之"。

由于在儒家的理想中,善政在很大程度上取决于统治者以及他任命为他效力之人的德行,孔子的教义并没有像美国宪法那样就政府组织的规划方式或行政权力的划分,也没有就政府应当采纳哪些具体措施或政策提供太多指导。孔子认为,有道的统治者出于怜悯和仁慈,一定会行正确之事,也会采取适当的步骤,满足其臣民的需要。

话虽如此,读者还是可以从《论语》的某些段落中推断出一些笼统的政策建议。例如,孔子说:"治理一个千辆兵车的国家,就应该谨慎地处理国家大事,表现出自己值得信任;节约财政开

---

① 善贾。
② 子曰:"苟有用我者,期月而已可也,三年有成。"

支爱惜民力；适时征发力役，不违农时。"①（《论语·学而第一之五》）孔子认为，统治者有责任改善民众的物质生活。开销过高的政府必定税赋也过重；政府必须谨慎对待财政问题，留意民众沉重的税务负担。政府还须记住不要在农忙季节动用劳力从事公共事业项目。干预民众的农业活动只会降低农业的生产力，这是他们的基本生计。

在与弟子冉求的对话中，孔子指出民众物质生活的富足为何是政府的关键问题：

> 孔子到卫国去，冉有为他驾车。孔子说："真是人口众多啊！"冉有问："人口已经很多了，还要再做什么呢？"孔子说："让他们富裕。"又问："富裕起来后又要做些什么？"孔子说："教化他们。"②（《论语·子路第十三之九》）

这里隐含的主张是，只有当民众的物质需求得到满足后，他们才容易受到道德教育的影响。以这种观点来看，民众是否能够接受统治者个人魅力的影响，取决于社会经济条件，而统治者对此负有责任。

孔子赞美传说中的圣王禹致力于造福民众的农业项目。孔子谈到禹时说："自己的宫室简陋不堪，却竭尽全力兴修水利。对大禹，我挑不出一点毛病。"③（《论语·泰伯第八之二一》）禹试图驯服持续的洪水，改善田地的灌溉，他的政府所做的正是政

---

① 子曰："道千乘之国，敬事而信，节用而爱人，使民以时。"
② 子适卫，冉有仆。子曰："庶矣哉！"冉有曰："既庶矣，又何加焉？"曰："富之。"曰："既富矣，又何加焉？"曰："教之。"
③ 卑宫室，而尽力乎沟洫。禹，吾无间然矣！

府当做之事：尽其所能地促进民众的农业繁荣（参见《论语·宪问第十四之五》）。长期以来，农业繁荣一直是中国统治者关注的问题。的确如此，在代表中国最早历史记载的商朝（前约1600—前约1045）甲骨文中，王朝的统治者为了求雨和确保丰收，几乎从未停止过舞蹈、祷告和祭祀。

天　命

以德治国的理想绝非始于孔子。《尚书》中保存的很多周初文献中都贯穿这一主题。

这些文献讲述道，商朝本是由英明而仁慈的统治者以合乎道德的方式开启的。但随着时间的推移，统治者的品行发生了变化，王位被一向极端下流淫荡的邪恶之人占据。商朝的最后一位统治者纣王尤其堕落，文献中对他的描述不遗余力地表达了对他的蔑视。周朝的奠基人武王在召集兵力攻打商朝的军队时说：

> 现在商王纣不尊敬上天，降祸灾给下民。他嗜酒贪色。他敢于施行暴虐。他用灭族的严刑惩罚人。他凭世袭的方法任用人。他把宫室呀、台榭呀、陂池呀、奢侈的衣服呀当作自己的追求，用这些东西来残害你们万姓人民。他烧杀忠良，解剖孕妇。皇天动了怒，命令我的先父文王严肃进行上天的惩罚，可惜大功没有完成。①

---

① 今商王受，弗敬上天，降灾下民，沈湎冒色，敢行暴虐。罪人以族，官人以世。惟宫室、台榭、陂池、侈服，以残害于尔万姓。焚炙忠良，刳剔孕妇。皇天震怒，命我文考，肃将天威，大勋未集。见《尚书·周书·泰誓上》。

纣王不是一个"好"人,因而也不是一个"好"的统治者。《尚书》继而说道,在他的治下,民不聊生。因此"悲哀地呼告上天,诅咒纣王灭亡,企图脱离困境"①。上天出于怜悯和对百姓的同情,收回了曾经给予商朝初期统治者的任命,将其重新授予了周朝。

《尚书》的这个段落是中国历史上第一次出现"天命"的概念。当年被授予周公(他是当时辅佐年幼的成王的正直摄政者)的天命,从周朝到20世纪初期一直是中国政治意识形态的基础。但奇怪的是,尽管孔子在他的教义中坚持认为,只有美德才会成就好的统治者,但他在《论语》中却没有使用表示"上天授予"之意的"天命"一词。这或许是因为这个词当时尚未特别广泛地流行;反过来,也可能是因为这个词已经广为流传,他认为弟子们知道,他与他们进行的大部分讨论都不过是对这个词的某种注释。无论如何,他的教义赞同并宣扬了天命所体现的理想,这一点是毫无疑问的。

表面看来,天命理论非常简单。一个心系苍生、关注百姓福祉的上天(参见第一章),把统治权授予了像上天一样致力于为民众谋福利的有德而仁慈之人。根据《尚书》文献所载,商朝的早期统治者正是如此。这些人——及其继任者——为了维持这种授权,绝不可放弃美德。一旦他们失德,一旦统治者腐败变质,他们就会丧失统治权,上天也会收回授权。

这里必须注意的是,上天不会自行采取行动,而只会响应民众的希望和意愿。民众通过"悲哀地呼告上天",表达**他们**对统治者和国内普遍存在的情况的烦恼和不满。诚然,上天是政治

---

① 以哀吁天,徂厥亡出执。见《尚书·周书·召诰》。

态势中的一支重要的力量——也是一种强大的制裁,但它是代表民众的利益而运作的媒介。《尚书》的一句名言精准地抓住了这一重点:"上天的看法和人民的看法一样;上天的听闻和人民的听闻一样。"①在为民众办事时,上天并非恣意或专横的力量。它并不会仅凭自己的喜好,肆意任性地赐予和收回委任。

因此,天命显然绝非"宿命"。统治者通过高尚和仁慈的统治赢得天命,也会因为抛弃高尚和仁慈的统治而失去它。这并非上天心血来潮。《诗经》里有一首诗警告周朝杰出的奠基人周文王的继任者说,天命的去留取决于他们自身:

> 天命归周不容易,
> 天命别断你手上。
> 光大文王好名声,
> 殷商灭亡天命定。
> 上天意志难揣测,
> 没有气味没声响。
> 只有效法周文王,
> 万邦诸侯都敬仰。②

这里传达的信息非常明确:做有德之人,天命就归于你;抛弃美德,就会失去天命。说到底,决定天命去留的是统治者与民众的关系,以及他对待民众的态度,而不是上天。因此,"天命"与欧

---

① 天视自我民视,天听自我民听。见《尚书·周书·泰誓中》。
② 命之不易,无遏尔躬。宣昭义问,有虞殷自天。上天之载,无声无臭。仪刑文王,万邦作孚。见《诗经·大雅·文王之什·文王》。

洲的"君权神授"说截然不同,后者宣称,统治者的统治权是上帝直接授予他们的,而他们的行为只须对上帝负责。他们不受民众意志的约束,享有绝对的权威。

周公正是在公元前11世纪中叶周师伐纣之际,第一次阐述了"天命"的原则。如果天命理论只是精彩的政治宣传——为周师伐纣的合法性服务——的话,那么它同样可以赋予他人伐周的合法权利。这正是《诗经》中的诗篇和《尚书》中的文献恳请周朝的领袖们致力于培养美德,以维护其正统性的原因。天命来去不定,得失都在一念之间。

所以,天命的观念如此根深蒂固,以至于当外来的"野蛮的"满族人在1644年进入北京城,并宣布建立清朝(1644—1912)时,其领袖颁布的第一个要求汉族接受满族统治的法令,就引用了天命的精神和语言:

> 天下者非一人之天下,有德者居之;军民非一人之军民,有德者主之。我今居此。①

---

① 见《明季南略·卷之八·大清国摄政王令旨》。

第四章

早期儒家思想的多种变体

　　我们在思考儒家传统的成功,考察它何以能够持续两千年,甚至延伸到21世纪时,必须铭记这样一个简单的事实:儒家思想一直在变化。这不足为奇,因为一切重要信仰体系能够持续,都是由于它们不断变化且具备多样性。毕竟,很少有人会说托马斯·阿奎那[①]的基督教就是圣保罗[②]的基督教,或者洛约拉的伊格内修斯[③]的基督教就是约翰·加尔文[④]的基督教。诚然,这些人的神学观点都出自《希伯来圣经》[⑤]和《新约》所述的一般概念,因此

[①] 托马斯·阿奎那(1225—1274),欧洲中世纪经院派哲学家和神学家。天主教会认为他是史上最伟大的神学家,也称他为神学界之王、天使博士(天使圣师)或全能博士。
[②] 圣保罗(约3—约67),早期教会最具有影响力的传教士之一,基督徒的第一代领导者之一,因为他首创向非犹太人转播基督的福音,所以被奉为外邦人的使徒。《新约》诸书约有一半是由他所写。他在整个罗马帝国的早期基督教社群之中传播耶稣基督的福音。
[③] 洛约拉的伊格内修斯(1491—1556),又译作"罗耀拉的依纳爵",西班牙人,耶稣会创始人,罗马公教圣人之一。他在罗马公教会内进行改革,以对抗由马丁·路德等人所领导的宗教改革。
[④] 约翰·加尔文(1509—1564),法国、瑞士著名的律师、牧师、宗教改革神学家,新教的重要派别——改革宗(或称加尔文派)的创始人。
[⑤] 又称"希伯来经卷",是圣经研究学者用来指代犹太教正统经籍《塔纳赫》的专业术语,它既是犹太人的正典文献,也是《旧约》的教义来源。

某些核心信念是一致的。但与此同时，这些思想家生活在不同的年代和地点，自然会在根本教义的基础上反思当前的一系列社会和宗教优先事项，从而产生了重点各不相同，有时甚至迥异的各种"基督教"。基督教这种始终对不同的人群以及不断变化的时间和地点保持关切的能力，正是它得以存续至今并生命力旺盛的原因。

　　基督教——以及犹太教和伊斯兰教——的规律同样适用于儒家思想。但是大部分西方世界直到20世纪初期依旧把儒家思想看作某种永恒不变的顽石，这种停滞不前的传统自其创始人的时代至今没有过什么变化，是中国19世纪和20世纪"落后"的罪魁祸首。无论这种观点是出于对儒家传统的无知，还是源于西方对自己在同一时期所取得的物质进步的自鸣得意，从20世纪到21世纪这段时期，它逐渐让位于一种更加丰富的理解，认识到儒家思想在东亚共同历史特别是中国历史中的勃勃生机。

　　孔子概述的理想适宜于各种不同的解读。尽管这些解读立足于一系列共有的基本观点，它们却像基督教一样，可以演进为相当独特的"儒学"。中国的学者们称之为经典儒学、孟子儒学、荀子儒学、汉儒、宋儒、理学、功利主义儒学、王阳明儒学，如此等等。读者不必害怕：我无意在本书中列举儒家所有不同的学派或阐述它们之间的重大差异。我只是想说明，孔子的理想在不同的解读者那里可以得到不同的阐述。我将重点关注他最著名的早期门徒——孟子（约前4世纪）和荀子（约前3世纪），他们对孔子理想的"角逐式"解读贯穿着帝制中国的全部历史。（本书第五章将讨论"理学"，这种儒家思想的重新诠释有很大的影响——是帝国后期对孔子学说的标准解读。）

　　我们无从知晓孟子和荀子准确的生卒年份，但孟子生于公元前4世纪中期，而荀子生于公元前4世纪晚期，但主要活跃于公元前3世纪，应该是没有问题的。孟子来自中国东北部的小国邹国。他从邹国出发，去寻找支持他的观点的统治者，正如与他同名的文本中所述，他找到了一些听众。但他未能如愿找到知音，所以就像在他之前的孔子一样，改行教书了。分作七篇的《孟子》据说是其弟子编纂的，是孟子与当时的统治者、他的弟子，以及哲学对话者之间的谈话记录。

荀子是赵国人，赵国位于华北中部。他后半生的大部分时间都在稷下学宫做学者，稷下学宫位于中国东北部的齐国的宫廷里，知识分子们在那里展开激烈的辩论。他的同名著作《荀子》分为32个章节，与《论语》和《孟子》都不一样：它不是谈话记录，也不是箴言体，而是一系列自成一体的文章，被认为是荀子本人所作。因此，我们在《荀子》中看到的是有理有据的论证，文章结构的整体性远胜《论语》和《孟子》。

孟子和荀子两人都完全支持孔子的核心信念：一、人可以成为圣人；二、道德的良善来自修身；三、学习是修身过程的一部分；四、先锋精英阶层在提升民众的道德方面起着至关重要的作用；五、良好的治理取决于统治者的德行，他要创造适宜的条件，方能使民众变得良善，社会更加和谐。

然而，这两位伟大的思想家也有一些根本分歧，尤其是关于人的道德完善的根源是什么这个问题。孟子认为根源在于内在的人性，主张人的天性生来向善，就像水自然会向山下流淌一样[①]（《孟子·告子上》第二章）。人为了实现道德完善，必

[①] 人性之善也，犹水之就下也。人无有不善，水无有不下。

须学会如何发展这种与生俱来的善,并与可能导致他误入歧途的外部力量相抗衡。荀子强烈反对,他毫不含糊地宣称:"人性恶。"(《荀子·性恶篇第二十三》)人需要求诸外部,到环境和文化中去寻找可以改变顽固人性的道德资源。既然对于人类的天性——以及随之而来的人的道德源于何处的问题——的基本假设截然不同,他们就实现道德完善的具体路径存在分歧也就不足为奇了,在修身和学习等重要领域尤其如此。

孟 子

1. 关于人性与修身

在陈述人性之善正如高山流水时,孟子并没有主张所有的**人都是**良善的,而是说就他们的天赋秉性而言,人都**倾向于善**。不是每一个人都会实现这种善,就像水并不**总是**顺势而下(孟子说,想一想被堰塞或被迫逆流而上的水①)。善是人性中内在的一种潜力,必须加以发展或培养。按照孟子的解释,人性的善就像幼苗,必须得到生长的机会:

> 每个人都有怜悯体恤别人的心情。……之所以说每个人都有怜悯体恤别人的心情是因为:如果今天无论是谁突然看见一个小孩要掉进井里面去了,必然会产生惊惧同情的心理。这不是因为他想要巴结这孩子的父母;不是因为想要在乡邻朋友中博取声誉;也不是因为厌恶坏名声。由此看来,没有同情心,简直不是人;没有羞耻心,简直不是

---

① 激而行之,可使在山。

人;没有谦让心,简直不是人;没有是非心,简直不是人。同情心是仁的发端;羞耻心是义的发端;谦让心是礼的发端;是非心是智的发端。人有这四种发端,就像有四肢一样。……我们自己都有这四种发端;如果我们知道要扩大充实它们,它们就会像火刚刚开始燃烧,泉水刚刚开始流淌那样。能够扩充它们的人,就能保全四海之内的一切;不能扩充它们的人,就连赡养父母都成问题。①(《孟子·公孙丑上》第六章)

孟子认为,每一个人生来都有仁、义、礼、智这四端。如果没有这四端,就"不是人";它们和四肢一样,都是人的正常自然构造的一部分。为了说服我们相信他的观点的正确性,他请我们这些读者想象一下,自己遇到一个即将跌落井中的无助的孩子时会怎么做。他认为,我们每一个人都会**本能地**生出恻隐之心,这就说明我们每一个人都有怜悯之端。

但敏锐的读者或许注意到了,孟子在这一段中没有继续说我们生出恻隐之心后,**都**会赶忙去救那个孩子。这绝不是孟子的疏忽。这是孟子的哲学立场中至关重要的一点,他认为我们天赋的"四端"不一定能够发展成为仁、义、礼、智,二者之间存在着差距。也有人会在遇上孩子几乎必死无疑时,驻足思

---

① 人皆有不忍人之心。……所以谓人皆有不忍人之心者,今人乍见孺子将入于井,皆有怵惕恻隐之心;非所以内交于孺子之父母也,非所以要誉于乡党朋友也,非恶其声而然也。由是观之,无恻隐之心,非人也。无羞恶之心,非人也。无辞让之心,非人也。无是非之心,非人也。恻隐之心,仁之端也;羞恶之心,义之端也;辞让之心,礼之端也;是非之心,智之端也。人之有是四端也,犹其有四体也。……凡有四端于我者,知皆扩而充之矣,若火之始然,泉之始达。苟能充之,足以保四海;苟不充之,不足以事父母。

忖:"我会因为救孩子而获益吗?""在救助过程中,我会受伤吗?""我要对孩子的死负责吗?"孟子认为,这些人与他人的人性并无二致;他们也拥有仁、义、礼、智四端。但与那些冲过去救孩子,毫不计较利弊,也不顾及个人安危的人不同,他们的道德幼苗没有被培养长大。修身的重要作用,就在于此。

为了说明人对自己的道德幼苗不事培育的后果,孟子讲了一个牛山的故事。在这个故事里,孟子还相当隐晦地指出,恶的根源是循环往复的日常生活。人日常的生存需求,加上与他人争夺有限的资源,使得他极有可能丧失与生俱来的善:

牛山的树木曾经十分茂盛。但是由于它地处都城的郊外,一棵一棵地遭到刀斧的砍伐,还能够保持茂盛吗?当然,山上的树木有雨露滋润,日日夜夜都在生长,并非没有抽条萌芽。但随即又有人赶着牛羊去放牧。这就是它变成光秃秃的荒山的原因。人们看见它光秃秃的,便以为牛山从来也不曾有过高大的树木。这难道是山的本性吗?

人的本性也是一样:他会真的没有仁义之心吗?他舍弃自己本初的良心,正如刀斧砍伐树木一样:天天砍伐,还可以保持茂盛吗?当然,日夜生息再加上每日破晓的清明之气,他的好恶与旁人仍有一丝相近之处。但他白天的所作所为,又使它[本初的良心]完全窒息而消亡了。如果反复窒息,夜晚的息养之气便不足以维系良心的存在。而一旦夜晚的息养之气不足以维系它的存在,此人也就与禽兽无异了。人们见到禽兽,会觉得它从未曾有过向善的天性。但这难道真的是人的天赋秉性吗?所以,假如得到滋养,没有什么不会生长；假如失去滋养，没有什么不会衰亡。孔子说："把握住就能维持，放弃就会失去。……"这就是指人心而言的吧？①（《孟子·告子上之八》）

这个段落强调的观点是，所有的人，无论看起来有多堕落，都生而具有完全相同的良善的人性。就算连环杀手也有同样的秉性，虽然乍看之下，我们很难发现这一点。正如樵夫持续伐木，加之牛羊吃掉嫩芽和花蕾，让牛山的自然植被不复繁茂，人性之外的力量也可能砍断他道德的幼苗，让他看似毫无人性。这正是"操"（把握）本初之心何以如此迫切的原因；因为这里，这种心念，正是美德的四端之所在。

因此，能否把握这种心念，恰是道德君子的超拔出众之处。孟子说，这种心念能让人思考和省察；而人只有通过思考和省察才能坚持正确的道路——免于外部世界的危险和诱惑，从而给他与生俱来的仁、义、礼、智四端的幼苗发育成熟的机会——获得充分的发展。正是这种成长使人在道德上日臻完善。

2. 关于统治者

孟子认为，帮助臣民努力坚持正确的道路是统治者的明确责任。因此，文中有一个特别雄辩的段落，责成统治者确保其民

---

① 牛山之木尝美矣。以其郊于大国也，斧斤伐之，可以为美乎？是其日夜之所息，雨露之所润，非无萌蘖之生焉，牛羊又从而牧之，是以若彼濯濯也。人见其濯濯也，以为未尝有材焉，此岂山之性也哉？虽有乎人者，岂无仁义之心哉？其所以放其良心者，亦犹斧斤之于木也。旦旦而伐之，可以为美乎？其日夜之所息，平旦之气，其好恶与人相近也者几希，则其旦昼之所为，有梏亡之矣。梏之反复，则其夜气不足以存。夜气不足以存，则其违禽兽不远矣。人见其禽兽也，而以为未尝有才焉者，是岂人之情也哉？故苟得其养，无物不长；苟失其养，无物不消。孔子曰："操则存，舍则亡。出入无时，莫知其乡。"惟心之谓与！

众获得物质上的富足:

> 至于百姓,如果没有固定的生计,也就没有固定的道德观念。一旦没有固定的道德观念,那就会胡作非为,什么事都做得出来。引导他们犯罪,然后再去处罚,这等于是陷害他们。哪里有仁慈的人在位执政却去陷害百姓的呢?所以,贤明的国君监督百姓的生计,一定要让他们上足以赡养父母,下足以抚养妻子儿女;好年景丰衣足食,坏年景也不致饿死。然后督促他们走善良的道路;这样一来,百姓也就很容易听从他了。①(《孟子·梁惠王上之七》)

孔子也认为,只有当民众的基本物质需求得到满足后,他们才更容易受到道德教化。但孟子就此问题的论述篇幅要长得多,提出了好的统治者为促进民众的福祉应该采用哪些明确而具体的措施:

> 不违背农时,那粮食就吃不完;密孔的渔网不入池塘,那鱼鳖就吃不完;砍伐林木有定时,那木材便用不尽。粮食和鱼鳖吃不完,木材用不尽,这样便使老百姓能够养活家小,葬送死者而无遗憾了。老百姓养生送终没有缺憾:这正是王道的开始。在五亩大的家园种上桑树,上了五十岁的人就可以穿着丝绸了;鸡鸭猪狗不失时节地繁殖饲养,上

---

① 若民,则无恒产,因无恒心。苟无恒心,放辟邪侈无不为已。及陷于罪,然后从而刑之,是罔民也。焉有仁人在位罔民而可为也?是故明君制民之产,必使仰足以事父母,俯足以畜妻子,乐岁终身饱,凶年免于死亡;然后驱而之善,故民之从之也轻。

了七十岁的人就可以吃到肉了。百亩的田地不误农时得到耕种，数口之家就不会闹饥荒了。注重乡校的教育，强调孝敬长辈的道理，须发花白的老人们就不再会肩挑头顶，出现在道路上了。年满七十岁的人能穿上丝绸、吃上肉，年轻力壮的人不缺衣少食，做到了这些而不称王于天下的是绝不会有的。现在，猪狗吃的是人吃的食物而不知道设法制止，路上出现饿死的人而不知道赈济饥民，人死了反而说"与我无关，是年成不好的缘故"，这和把人杀了反而说"与我无干，是武器杀的"又有什么不同呢？大王要是能够不归罪于荒年，这样，普天下的百姓便会涌向他这儿来了。①（《孟子·梁惠王上之三》；参见同篇之五和七）

这些显然都是"王道"的政策和做法。

孟子批评他那个时代的统治者，声称他们对于自身利益和财富的关注胜过了对民众福祉的关心。他在著作中的第一个段落里就表达了对梁惠王的不满：

孟子拜见梁惠王。梁惠王说："先生，你不远千里而来，一定是有什么对我的国家有利的高见吧？"孟子回答说："大王！何必说'利'呢？只要说仁义就行了。如果大

---

① 不违农时，谷不可胜食也；数罟不入洿池，鱼鳖不可胜食；斧斤以时入山林，材木不可胜用也。谷与鱼鳖不可胜食，材木不可胜用也，是使民养生丧死无憾也。养生丧死无憾，王道之始也。五亩之宅，树之以桑，五十者可以衣帛矣。鸡豚狗彘之畜，无失其时，七十者可以食肉矣。百亩之田，勿夺其时，数口之家可以无饥矣；谨庠序之教，申之以孝悌之义，颁白者不负戴于道路矣。七十者衣帛食肉，黎民不饥不寒，然而不王者，未之有也！狗彘食人食而不知检，涂有饿莩而不知发，人死，则曰："非我也，岁也。"是何异于刺人而杀之，曰："非我也，兵也。"王无罪岁，斯天下之民至焉。

王说'怎样使我的国家有利',大夫说'怎样使我的家族有利',士人和百姓说'怎样使我自己有利',结果是上上下下互相争夺利益,国家就危险了啊!……所以,大王只说'仁义'就行了,何必说'利'呢?"①(《孟子·梁惠王上之一》)

谈论利益的统治者也会促使其民众谈论并追求利益,这不但会导致他们堕落,疏忽对其道德幼苗的培养,而且讽刺的是,这么做不会给统治者和国家带来任何好处。正如孔子早先说过的那样,统治者的工作是做一个道德榜样:"君主仁爱,就没有人不仁爱;君主公正,就没有人不选择公正。"②(《孟子·离娄下之五》)简而言之,孟子认为,好的政府就是要提供食物和住所,并为民众树立道德榜样,从而创建一个物质和道德环境,以便与生俱来的仁、义、礼、智的幼苗得以自然生长,不受任何阻碍。

孟子甚至断言,只有实施这种善政、把民众放在首位③(《孟子·尽心下之十四》)的统治者,才是真正的统治者。传说中夏朝的最后一位国王桀,以及商朝最后一位国王纣,都是残酷的暴君。因此当齐宣王问道:

"商汤流放夏桀,武王讨伐商纣,有这些事吗?"孟子回答道:"文献上有这样的记载。"宣王问:"臣子杀他的君主,可以吗?"孟子说:"败坏仁的人叫'贼',败坏义的人叫

---

① 孟子见梁惠王。王曰:"叟!不远千里而来,亦将有以利吾国乎?"孟子对曰:"王!何必曰利?亦有仁义而已矣。王曰:'何以利吾国?'大夫曰:'何以利吾家?'士庶人曰:'何以利吾身?'上下交征利而国危矣。……王亦曰仁义而已矣,何必曰利?"
② 君仁莫不仁,君义莫不义。
③ 民为贵。

'残'；贼、残这样的人叫独夫。我只听说杀了独夫纣罢了，没听说臣杀君啊。"①（《孟子·梁惠王下之八》）

在论述只有当君主本人的行为举止符合一位"真正的"君主的标准时，他才可以被称作君主，孟子赞同孔子所呼吁的"正名"，即名与实必须完全一致的理念。（《论语·子路第十三之三》）按照孟子的看法，杀死纣王不是弑君，而是杀死了一个偏离统治者的正道，从而放弃成为一个真正统治者的废物。孟子此处的观点将在中国的整个帝国史上得到有力的回响，凡表现得不像一个真正的君主以仁义来关怀民众的统治者，都有可能遭到废黜。

尽管统治者可以被废，文中却没有呼吁人民革命，因为只有大臣们才有权废黜邪恶的统治者②（参见《孟子·万章下之九》）。然而按照这个段落的说法，统治者关怀民众福祉的责任，即提供一个好的环境，以便民众的美德幼苗可以生长发育，得到了一个强大的制裁机制作为后盾，即强行除去这个统治者。若干个世纪以来，这一段落时而被视为支持民众起义的权利，当然，正如我所说，这种看法未必完全准确。

荀 子

1. 关于人性与修身

关于人性的问题，这两位哲学家的分歧非常明显。如果说

---

① "汤放桀，武王伐纣，有诸？"孟子对曰："于传有之。"曰："臣弑其君，可乎？"曰："贼仁者谓之'贼'，贼义者谓之'残'。残贼之人谓之'一夫'。闻诛一夫纣矣，未闻弑君也。"

② 君有大过则谏，反复之而不听，则易位。

在孟子看来，人性中包含有仁的幼苗的话，那么在荀子看来，人性正是人道德败坏和刚愎自用的根源。荀子直接质疑自己的前辈，宣称："孟子说：'人的本性是善良的'，而我说这是不对的。"[1]（《荀子·性恶篇第二十三》）在一篇从头到尾讨论"人性恶"的章节的开头，荀子解释道：

> 人的本性是恶的；善良是人为的。人从一生下来就有贪图私利之心，如果他沉迷于这种嗜好，人与人之间就要发生争夺，也就不再讲求谦让了。人一生下来就有忌妒仇恨的心理，如果他沉溺于此，就会导致他诉诸暴力犯罪，这样忠诚信实就丧失了。人生来就有爱好声色的本能，喜欢听好听的，看好看的。如果沉湎于这些，就会发生淫乱的事情，礼仪制度和道德规范也将丧失殆尽。因此，放纵人的本性，顺着人的情欲，他就一定会卷入争吵抢夺，违反等级名分，扰乱礼仪制度，最终变成一个罪犯。[2]（《荀子·性恶篇第二十三》）

荀子认为，人要变得良善，就必须远离他的本性。因此——像他之前的孟子一样——他非常重视培养的过程。但荀子的目标并非培养人与生俱来的天性，而是约束和改变人的天生冲动。

鉴于他关于人性及其需要"改造"的观点，荀子对学习和礼义在培养过程中的作用比孟子要重视得多。学习和尊礼是教化

---

[1] 孟子曰："人之性善。"曰：是不然。
[2] 人之性恶，其善者伪也。今人之性，生而有好利焉，顺是，故争夺生而辞让亡焉。生而有疾恶焉，顺是，故残贼生而忠信亡焉。生而有耳目之欲，有好色焉，顺是，故淫乱生而礼义文理亡焉。然则从人之性，顺人之情，必出于争夺，合于犯分乱理而归于暴。

人、重塑其桀骜不驯的天性的必备工具。孟子认为人性生来向善，因而他不认为这些工具有多么必要。这并不是说孟子完全舍弃了这些，而是与荀子相比，它们在他的思想中没有同样的突出地位，在他看来，小心培育内在的新生幼苗更加重要。

学习在荀子宣扬的这一派儒家思想中的重要作用，在《荀子》这部著作的第一个段落中就有所揭示：

> 学习不应该停止不前。靛青是从蓼蓝中提取而来的，但比蓼蓝更青；冰是由水凝固而成的，但比水更寒冷。笔直如墨线的木材可以弯成一个圈，曲度就像圆规画的一样，即使再经过烘干，也不能恢复原样。正是弯曲的过程使它变成这样的。所以木材压在矫直板上才能取直，金属在磨刀石上磨过才能锋利；君子如果博学多闻，又能每天检查反省自己，那就会见识高明而不会犯错误了。①（《荀子·劝学篇第一》）

这里指出，学习拥有强大的力量去接受人性中原始、顽劣和自私的东西，继而将其改造——实际上是**强迫**——成为对道德敏感的机体组织。

正如我们所见，相比之下，孟子不像荀子那样，认为学习是强迫性的重塑工具，理由无非是在他看来，人的道德"幼苗"需要小心的培育，而不是咄咄逼人的弯折、模塑或折磨，方能成长

---

① 学不可以已。青，取之于蓝而青于蓝；冰，水为之而寒于水。木直中绳，輮以为轮，其曲中规。虽有槁暴，不复挺者，輮使之然也。故木受绳则直，金就砺则利，君子博学而日参省乎己，则知明而行无过矣。

为"仁"。因此，虽说孟子也会像孔子那样（例如，《论语·雍也第六之二七》①，《论语·子罕第九之二》②）鼓励人"博学"③（《孟子·离娄下之十五》），也敦促真正的王像值得称道的夏、商、周三朝的统治者那样建立学校，阐明正确的社会关系④（《孟子·滕文公上之三》），但他并不像荀子那样认为严格的研究或教育意义上的学习有多大的迫切性，因此，他对学习的全面关注也远逊于荀子。

如果说在荀子看来，学习是一种有效的转化工具的话，那么它就必须是**正确**的学习。出于这个原因，他制定了一个示范课程以供人终生遵循：

> 学习应该从哪里开始，又在哪里终结呢？我说，就学习的科目而言，应从诵读经典开始，到读礼义为结束；就学习的目标而言，应从做一个有教养的人开始，到成为圣人为止。真正努力，日日积累，才能达到最高境界。学到老死后才停止。所以，从学习的科目来说是有终结的，但若从学习的目标来说，是片刻也不能停顿的。做到了这样，人才能成为人；半途放弃学习，就成禽兽了。⑤（《荀子·劝学篇第一》）

---

① 子曰："君子博学于文，约之以礼，亦可以弗畔矣夫！"
② 达巷党人曰："大哉孔子！博学而无所成名。"子闻之，谓门弟子曰："吾何执？执御乎？执射乎？吾执御矣！"
③ 博学而详说之，将以反说约也。
④ 夏曰校，殷曰序，周曰庠，学则三代共之，皆所以明人伦也。
⑤ 学恶乎始？恶乎终？曰：其数则始乎诵经，终乎读礼；其义则始乎为士，终乎为圣人。真积力久则入，学至乎没而后止也。故学数有终，若其义则不可须臾舍也。为之，人也；舍之，禽兽也。

荀子还提供了更详细的课程说明,描述了所涵盖的主题和"课本"——甚至还对学习的顺序提出建议:

> 《尚书》记载的是古代的政事,《诗经》收集了有和谐乐律的诗歌,礼是法制的前提、事物的规范。所以学习到礼就算达到尽头了,因为它们据说代表了道德及其力量的顶点。礼的恭敬规矩,乐的中正和谐,《诗经》《尚书》的广博,《春秋》的微言大义,这些典籍囊括了天地间的一切事物。①(《荀子·劝学篇第一》)

在漫长的儒家传统中,这一段落是最早尝试为学"道"的学生建立的一个连贯的课程表。

显然,"礼"是荀子学习课程的核心内容。荀子认为,正是通过"礼"的指导,人的邪恶倾向才可能受到约束,长此以往,他的行为才会变得惯于向善:

> 挺直的木头不用矫直板就自然挺直,它的本性就是挺直。弯曲的木材一定要放在矫直板上熏蒸定型才会挺直,这是因为它本性弯曲。同样,因为人的本性恶劣,必定要依靠圣王的治理,礼义的教化,然后才能实现社会安定,合乎善良的标准。②(《荀子·性恶篇第二十三》)

---

① 故《书》者,政事之纪也;《诗》者,中声之所止也;礼者,法之大分,类之纲纪也。故学至乎礼而止矣。夫是之谓道德之极。礼之敬文也,乐之中和也,《诗》《书》之博也,《春秋》之微也,在天地之间者毕矣。

② 直木不待檃栝而直者,其性直也;枸木必将待檃栝烝矫然后直者,以其性不直也。今人之性恶,必将待圣王之治,礼义之化,然后皆出于治,合于善也。

荀子以贯穿于其著作的精彩叠句结束了这个段落——有目的、有意识地努力改造或改变我们顽劣的天性："所以，人性本恶的道理已经很清楚了，那些善良的行为是人为的结果。"①

如我们所料，孟子认为礼并没有这种"直"（矫正）或约束的效果，因为他既然主张人性中存在与生俱来的善，它就并不需要约束。按照孟子的理解，正确的礼——就像仁、义、智一样——只是人的善良本性的自然实现；用他的话来说，它是仁和义的"文"（装饰）(《孟子·离娄上之二七》②；参见《孟子·尽心上之二一》③)，而不是产生这些美德的手段。

可是荀子就认为礼是修身的必要组成部分。正如他在上文引用的段落中所解释的那样，礼的确有"直"（矫正）的作用，但也在情感和心理上给人以滋养。正确的礼允许人表达自己的情感而不必冒扰乱社会秩序的风险。通过节制或"教化"自己顽劣的内在情感和欲望，礼使得人可以使其情感世界与他周围的广阔世界相协调："礼，是要做到取长补短，减少有余的，弥补不足的，既表现出爱慕崇敬的仪式，又养成按礼行事的美德。"④(《荀子·礼论篇第十九》)如此一来，即便礼约束了人最无法无天的情绪冲动，仍可以使他获得情感上的满足。荀子说："一切的礼，开始时简略，以后以优雅的形式逐渐完备，最后会令人喜悦。"⑤(《荀子·礼论篇第十九》)所以，施行完备的礼有一种强大的美，这种美学上的诉求使人激昂，并获得情感上的愉悦。

---

① 用此观之，人之性恶明矣，其善者伪也。
② 礼之实，节文斯二者是也。
③ 君子所性，仁义礼智根于心。
④ 礼者，断长续短，损有余，益不足，达爱敬之文，而滋成行义之美者也。
⑤ 凡礼，始乎梲，成乎文，终乎悦校。

最后，礼还有划分社会各个阶层的重要功能——孔子本人显然也很认可这种功能。荀子说：

> 倘使名分地位平齐，就没有足够的物资分配；权力分配平均，就会缺乏统一；人人平等，就谁也不能役使谁。……如果人们的权势地位相等，而好恶又相同，那么由于物资不能满足需要，就一定会发生争夺。争夺一定会导致混乱，而混乱一定会引发枯竭。古代的圣王痛恨这种混乱，所以制定了礼义来建立名分地位。①（《荀子·王制篇第九》）

礼强化了社会的等级制度。它使等级制度拥有凝聚力和稳定性，鼓励所有的人——无论"贫富""贵贱"——发挥其应有的作用。②

2. 思想与道德的可完善性

荀子对人性的悲观看法不该掩饰一个基本要点：他像孟子一样热切地坚信人是可以实现道德完善的。他写道：

> 路上的人也可以成为禹[圣王]那样的人。……路上的任何人都具备了解仁义法度的基本素质，也有将其付诸实施的能力。因此，他显然也可以成为禹那样的人。③（《荀子·性恶篇第二十三》）

---

① 分均则不偏，埶齐则不壹，众齐则不使。……埶位齐，而欲恶同，物不能澹则必争；争则必乱，乱则穷矣。先王恶其乱也，故制礼义以分之。

② 贵贱有等，长幼有差，贫富轻重皆有称者也。

③ 涂之人可以为禹。……然而涂之人也，皆有可以知仁义法正之质，皆有可以能仁义法正之具，然则其可以为禹明矣。

简而言之，正是因为人生来具有认知和识别是非的能力，他能够从生活的周遭环境中逐渐了解道德。如果在孟子看来，人与禽兽最明显的区别在于人的本性的话，那么在荀子看来，人与其他物种的最大区别则在于人可以通过自己的主观能动性了解事物并付诸实践。

然而人或许有能力理解道德，但他又为何要这样做呢？生来邪恶，带着"天然的"自私欲望，热爱私利，还有忌妒和仇恨的感情的人，为什么会有向善的冲动呢？换句话说，首先，性恶的他为何要选择服从学习和礼制这些矫正工具呢？荀子的解释引人入胜：

> 每个渴望为善的人之所以这么做，恰是因为人性本恶。浅薄的人希望变得丰厚；丑恶的人希望变得美丽；狭隘的人希望变得宽大；贫穷的人希望变得富足；卑贱的人希望变得高贵。如果本身没有，就必定要向外寻求。但如果人已经富足，就不再羡慕钱财；如果地位高贵，就不再羡慕权势。如果本身已经拥有，当然不必再向外寻求。从这里我们可以看出，人之所以想要为善，正是人本性恶的缘故。[①]（《荀子·性恶篇第二十三》）

显然是因为我们生而有之的自私的欲望与贪婪和忌妒的情感，才让我们积极寻求拥有我们现在还不具备的善。也就是说，人

[①] 凡人之欲为善者，为性恶也。夫薄愿厚，恶愿美，狭愿广，贫愿富，贱愿贵，苟无之中者，必求于外；故富而不愿财，贵而不愿势，苟有之中者，必不及于外。用此观之，人之欲为善者，为性恶也。

并非为了善的缘故而追求善，至少起初并非如此，而是为了满足他对于不属于自己的东西的渴望。说来讽刺，对道德的追求竟然源于自私和贪婪。

但是，单靠人的自私天性本身，无法解释他寻求善的冲动。善的冲动还源于人从思想上认识到，如果他放任自己顽劣的天性，就会导致"悖乱而互相残害"①（《荀子·性恶篇第二十三》）。想到悖乱和互相残害并不符合他的自身利益，最终也无法满足他的欲望，他便希望能约束他的天性，寻求礼和经典教义的指导。

3. 关于统治者

按照荀子的说法，统治者的责任是在天生厌恶秩序的民众中间建立秩序。统治者知道，要想实现社会的有序与和谐，就必须对人与生俱来的激情和欲望加以约束。通过日常的礼仪指导，他谨慎地提出遏制这些激情和欲望，从而教化民众培养出得体的社会行为模式。

然而，荀子认为，对于某些臣民来说，相对温和的礼仪的力量是不够的，这些人的冲动如此顽劣，需要采用其他更坚决的控制手段。出于这个原因，他认为统治者还应该运用法律和惩罚作为维持秩序的手段。荀子的理想是这样的一个社会，其间的秩序与和谐在很大程度上是通过践礼的变革性影响来产生并维持的；然而当礼不起作用时，统治者必须依靠法律和惩罚这些更具强制性的工具。

这种理想的社会只有在"真正的王"统治之下才会实现。

---

① 天下悖乱而相亡不待顷矣。

只有良善而正直的统治者才能够真正摸清民众的情况，决定如何最有效地抑制他们的自私。他是个热心而公平的法官，准确无误地知晓何时应当以礼引导，何时应当通过法律和惩罚来强制实施。因为他充满关爱和仁慈地对待民众，民众也心甘情愿地支持他。

荀子对于在他本人所在的时代，"真正的王"能否实际执政的考量相当现实。孟子的人生大半都花在劝说当时的统治者努力成为真正的王，荀子则不同，他承认往最好处想，大概也只能期待一个能够在自己的国家推行秩序的统治者，无论是通过法律和惩罚，还是通过武力。他断定，贤明统治者的时代早就过去了；如今，如果民众无法通过礼实现道德完善与和谐的话，那就需要一个至少能确保稳定治理和有序社会等级制度的霸主。

孟子与荀子对人与上天的看法

公元前4世纪的孟子认为，上天是一个道德实体。短短一个世纪后，荀子把上天描述为一个按照其自身的内部节奏运行、没有任何道德驱动力的自然实体；在他看来，上天近似于"自然"或"自然法则"。鉴于这些基本观点的不同，两位哲学家对于上天在人的生命中发挥的作用自然有着全然不同的理解。

孟子主张，人与上天之间存在着一种密切的道德联系：

> 有天然的爵位等级，有人间的爵位等级。仁、义、忠、信，乐于行善而不厌倦，这是天然的爵位等级。[①]（《孟

[①] 有天爵者，有人爵者。仁义忠信，乐善不倦，此天爵也。

子·告子上之十六》）

人的道德是上天赋予的。因为人正是从上天那里得到了他美德的幼苗。如果他想成为一个充满良善之心和人性的人，他就有义务让这些幼苗生长发育。通过培育这些幼苗，他也就遵从——并满足——了上天为他制定的道德计划。因此，从某种意义来说，上天从生物学角度决定了人的行为规范。

《孟子》中有一个段落提出了相当独特的宇宙观和宇宙统一论，这位哲学家说道：

> 人如果能竭尽心力，就会知道本性，知道了本性，就会知道上天了。保存自己的本心，修养自己的本性，就可以侍奉上天了。①（《孟子·尽心上之一》）

这里，孟子意在向弟子们强调，人与上天之间存在着一种密不可分的道德联系。如果上天是人的道德、人的心灵中内嵌的道德潜力的发起者，那么随着这种道德的实现，人便会洞悉上天的意图。这就是了解上天的渠道。完成上天在我们降生时便赋予我们的任务，履行它在我们身上播下的道德责任，就能侍奉上天。"侍奉"一词也提醒我们，说到底，我们都必须服从上天强制性的道德立法权。

荀子对上天的理解与孟子简直就是天壤之别。在他看来，上天是自然主义的，没有任何意图可言，因而与人类也没有道德

---

① 尽其心者，知其性也。知其性，则知天矣。存其心，养其性，所以事天也。

联系。实际上，荀子严厉批评当时广泛存在的信念，说什么上天可以与人交流，可以通过预兆和征兆等形式表达赞同和反对：

> 流星坠落、树木发出异响，举国上下都害怕，四处询问：这是为什么呢？我回答说：这没有什么啊。这不过是天地变异、阴阳互化，时常发生的现象啊。你可以觉得它们奇怪，但不该害怕它们。①（《荀子·天论篇第十七》）

这里的天是自然的秩序。其表现形式正是宇宙间自发的"阴阳互化"。这不是某个对我们感兴趣或任性而为的上天与人类活动的"交流"或响应。有些人认为，上天是一个实体，能对他们的乞求做出回应，荀子在其著作中坚持不懈地驳斥他们："祭神求雨就下雨了，为什么呢？我回答说：没有特别的原因。假如你不去祭神求雨，也会下雨。"②他还提醒他们："上天并不因为人们厌恶寒冷就取消冬季。"③（《荀子·天论篇第十七》）他的锲而不舍显示了他认为当时的"迷信"做法和信仰非常普遍。而他希望传达的讯息非常明确：上天对人根本毫不关心！

正是因为不存在什么与人类有道德联系或者关怀人类的上天，人必须到圣人及其制定的礼仪那里寻求道德指引。上天既没有赋予道德，也不会提供道德支持。的确，在荀子看来，过去之所以会产生值得尊敬和赞美的圣人尧、舜和禹，是因为只有他们能够领会到，人需要一套礼法和教义，才能认清道德的方向。

---

① 星队木鸣，国人皆恐。曰：是何也？曰：无何也！是天地之变，阴阳之化，物之罕至者也。怪之，可也；而畏之，非也。

② 雩而雨，何也？曰：无何也，犹不雩而雨也。

③ 天不为人之恶寒也辍冬。

当人一帆风顺，社会万事顺遂之时，一切皆在人为。人必须逐渐认识到，与许多人的想法相反，他的命运与上天的意志或宿命无关：

> 社会的安定或混乱，是由上天决定的吗？我回答说：太阳月亮、行星恒星，在禹的时代和桀的时代都一样运转。禹使天下安定；桀使天下混乱。可见社会的安定或混乱并不是由上天决定的。①（《荀子·天论篇第十七》）

人的命运只取决于他自己的努力。

尽管上天存在的目的并非支持人类，但荀子也承认，在其"阴阳互化"中，上天的确对人有着强大的影响。荀子告诫人们要警惕这些影响，并尽可能地利用好它们。

> 认为上天伟大而思慕它，
> 哪里及得上滋养它的产物而控制它？
> 顺从上天而颂扬它，
> 哪里及得上掌握天命而利用它？
> 盼望时令而等待它，
> 哪里及得上因时制宜而使它为我所用？
> 依靠万物自然增殖，
> 哪里及得上拓展它们的产能并转化？②（《荀子·天论

---

① 治乱，天邪？曰：日月星辰瑞历，是禹桀之所同也，禹以治，桀以乱；治乱非天也。
② 大天而思之，孰与物畜而制之！从天而颂之，孰与制天命而用之！望时而待之，孰与应时而使之！因物而多之，孰与骋能而化之！

篇第十七》）

荀子认为，上天是独立的他者，对人世间或人的福祉毫无兴趣。但通过这里描述的有意识的努力，人可以在上天不断互化的阴与阳中，在它恒常的变化中，发现很多对人类生活有益的影响。

总而言之，早期儒家的两个重要分支的创立者孟子和荀子一致同意：一、人可以实现道德上的尽善尽美；二、为了实现道德完善，人必须经历修身的过程。但在孟子看来，人的道德潜力的根源是内在的，存在于人的本性之中；而在荀子看来，它存在于外部，在文化中，尤其是古代圣贤们创立的一整套礼制中。因此对于孟子而言，修身在很大程度上是一种小心培养、保护不断成长的内在的善不受社会上有害和败坏影响的过程；而对于荀子而言，这个过程必然更加宽泛和主动，并直接依赖于社会，寻求能够"矫正"或重塑人天生扭曲的本性的工具。孟子认为，理想的统治者有责任为他的臣民建立道德高尚、物质富足的环境，在这样的环境中，人的道德潜力才能自然发展而不受任何阻碍；而荀子则认为，统治者更像是一种存在，他积极引导臣民的行为，并让他们认识一系列文化工具——礼、法律、惩罚，这些工具是遏制他们鲁莽冲动，使他们习惯于与其天性相悖的善的必要工具。

纵览中国历史，荀子对学习和礼的改造力量的信念对中国的教育与社会实践有着不可磨灭的影响。但孟子的影响却更大：一千年后，负责儒家思想传统大变革的思想家们会排斥荀子的人性观，支持孟子的更加乐观的看法：人生来便拥有至善的幼苗。

第五章

儒家传统在公元 1000 年之后的转变：理学的教义

孔子、孟子和荀子为其后一千多年的儒家传统设定了哲学方向。但 11 世纪出现了一个儒学思想家的小团体，他们开始重新思考古代前辈们的学说。他们的儒家"学派"被称作道学，通常又被称为理学，很快就在中国的知识界和政治生活中占据了主导地位。的确，到 13 世纪，这个学派已经成为国家的正统，它所主张的原则成为中国帝国政府表面上的指导原则，也是科举制度的基础——其正统地位一直持续到 20 世纪初。

理学重写了儒家传统。它捍卫经典儒家思想的价值观和道德标准，但在两个重要的方面改变了儒家思想：一、它把 11 世纪和 12 世纪产生的一个复杂的形而上体系（即对存在和认知之本质的解释）作为经典儒家思想的价值观和道德标准的坚实基础；二、在这个形而上体系的基础上，它建立了一个结构化的修身计划，也就是"成为圣人"的进阶模板。

理学为什么会出现在这个特定的时期？宋朝（960—1279）的儒家士大夫认为他们的世界危机四伏——无论政治上、智识上,还是道德上皆是如此。自从10世纪宋朝建立之初,华北平原的部分地区,即中华文明的腹地,就被一连串非汉族的部落占据。1127年,这些部落中的最后一个——女真人,攻陷了宋朝的都城开封,并建立了金朝(1115—1234),迫使宋廷南逃。北方的失陷极大地震动了中国的士大夫阶层。在他们看来,这远不仅仅是一场简单的军事或政治失败;它意味着"道"的急剧衰落。如果中国的皇帝及其大臣们的一贯表现能像儒家的圣贤统治者和大臣们那样品行端正的话,"道"就会占据优势,而北方也就不会在"蛮族"的进攻下不堪一击了。是什么使得这些人偏离了道德修养和德政的儒家道路呢?

很多人指责更早期的另一次"蛮族"入侵:佛教。这种外国的学说于公元1世纪从印度传入中国,在6世纪后日益盛行。儒家坦承,它的吸引力如此之大,"不管是大人还是小孩,官员、农夫还是商人,无论男女,都入了佛门"[①]。甚至很多本应遵行和发扬儒家之道的学者,也逐渐被佛教(特别是像禅宗这样的精英学派)对人性、心灵、认知方法、自我实现,以及人与宇宙的关系等哲学探索所吸引。儒家沮丧地看待这种流行,担心佛教对个人启蒙的专注会分散社会各阶层人士的注意力,而他们作为中国人——以及儒家弟子——的基本义务本是在道德上完善自我,以便服务社会和促进他人的福祉。

从10世纪和11世纪开始,很多认同儒家传统的学者们已经留意到"儒家之道"的重要地位面临挑战,对如何应付他们的"道"所面临的挑战给予了深刻的反思。他们带着近乎宗教的热

[①] 不问大人小儿,官员村人商贾,男子妇人,皆得入其门。引自《朱子语类·卷一二六之释氏》第118。

情阅读经典文本，在其中寻找那些可以雄辩地说明当时的急务，从而力挽狂澜于既倒的教义，也就是真理。很多人参与到10世纪和11世纪的这场研读经典、寻找其当代意义的大潮中。在这些思想家中，最主要的有周敦颐（1017—1073）、张载（1020—1077）、程颢（1032—1085），以及程颐（1033—1107）。

但宋朝的这场对儒家传统之意义的反思，其最有影响力的人物要属下一个世纪的朱熹（1130—1200），他是宋代理学的集大成者。朱熹基于宋代早期这些思想家的著作所作的集大成式研究，充分体现在他对儒家经典所作的一系列精彩的行间注释中。朱熹的天才之处就在于，他所提出的这种"全新"的儒家哲学依赖于在他那个时代已属古代文献的读物——的确，它们早已是陈旧过时的文本——而这种全新哲学也要从对这些文献的阅读中寻求解释。他受到宋代先驱们的思想的深刻影响（无疑也关注了佛教所引介并推广的某些问题），以他那个时代的形而上学的语言，从经典文本中构建了一个自我实现的系统过程，如果认真遵行这套过程，就会引导人成为圣人。与顿悟的佛教徒不同，按照真正的儒家方式，这个实现了道德完善的人会全心全意地服务于社会，并给民众带来和谐。通过他以及其他志同道合者的努力，便可复兴曾经伟大的"道"。

朱熹理学的形而上

古典的儒家思想家孟子和荀子尽管立场不同，却都认为人是可以实现道德完善的。朱熹也认为人在道德上可以日臻完美，但他发展了一种形而上学，用新的哲学术语来支持这种假设——或者更确切地说，他用的是旧的术语，却赋予了它们全新的意义。他支持孟子的人性善理念,认为所有的人都生来具有仁、义、礼、智这四种主要美德的开端,并为其提供了本体论支持。实际上,正是因为朱熹的学说,孟子关于人性的观点才最终战胜了荀子,成为正统。但朱熹进而回答了孟子遗留下来、在很大程度上并未解决的哲学问题:如果人生而良善,邪恶又来自何方,是如何产生的呢?此外,在确定了人的邪恶根源后,朱熹又规划了一份按部就班的详细计划,用来根除邪恶,滋养人与生俱来的善。

朱熹声称,整个宇宙都由"气"所组成,这个汉字有物质力量、质能、生命力、心理物理学要素等各种各样的翻译(但本书干脆就把它音译为"qi")。这种"气"无休无止地动态循环,在具体的构造中彼此结合,组成了宇宙中的具体事物。无论物体的形式或形状有多不同,它们都是由"气"所组成的。用他的前辈张载的话来说:

> 气以各种方式,朝着各个方向移动流散,其两种元素[阴与阳这两股原始力量]聚集在一起组成了具体的万事万物。这样产生的人和物象才会千差万别;通过阴阳两种元素永无休止的循环,建立起天地之间万物的大道理。①

因此,是"气"把宇宙中的万物结合在一起。在朱熹和他的理学同道们看来,假设存在一种弥漫于宇宙间的共有之"气"有着强烈的道德含义。因为如果万物都由"气"所组成,那么宇宙中的

---

① 游气纷扰,合而成质者,生人物之万殊;其阴阳两端循环不已者,立天地之大义。见《张载集·正蒙·太和篇第一》。

万物和人就是相互关联的。张载有一篇著名的文章以如下的字句作为开篇：

> 天是我的父亲，地是我的母亲；我如此藐小，却混有天地之道于一身，而处于天地之间。
> 这样看来，充塞于天地之间的，就是我的身体；而引领统帅天地万物的，就是我的本性。
> 世人都是我的兄弟姐妹，而万物皆与我为同类。①

在共有之"气"的关联下，人们像对待"兄弟姐妹"一样对待他人。这种准生物学的人际关系有助于解释人为什么会像孟子在数世纪前所说的，自发地对他人怀有同情。说到底，人类就是一个大家庭。

因此，这种"气"证明了宇宙之间的万事万物——无论生物还是非生物——的相互关联。但也正是这种"气"解释了众多事物之间的差别。万物出生时接收到不同份额的"气"，质量和数量皆不相同。理学家们解释说，总的来说，人类接收到的"气"最为清澈纯净，正是这种"气"的质量，让人类与宇宙间的其他生物和事物有了最为明显的区别。朱熹的前辈周敦颐写道：

> ［阴和阳］两种气交合感应，变化产生出万物。万物生生不息，也就变化无穷。只有人，得到了其中最纯粹、最有

---

① 乾称父，坤称母；予兹藐焉，乃混然中处。故天地之塞，吾共体；天地之帅，吾其性。民吾同胞，物吾与也。见《张载集·正蒙·乾称篇第十七》。

灵性的"气"。①

74 他继而解释说，正是因为拥有"最纯粹、最有灵性的'气'"，一切生物中只有人具备道德判断力，了解善与恶的差别。树木接收到的是树木的"气"，因而不具备类似的能力。

但"气"并非人与生俱来的善的**根源**。因为正如宇宙间的万物都是由"气"所组成的，万物也都有"理"，即原则（有时会译作"道德原则"）。朱熹解释说："天下未有无理之气，亦未有无气之理。"②如果说"气"赋予了事物以具体的心理物理学形式，那么用朱熹的话来说，该事物所固有的原则便是"它之所以如此的原因，以及它应该符合的规则"③。宇宙间的每一件物体、活动、关系、物质和事件都有原则。船有船的属性或规范性质，车有车的属性，树有树的属性，人有人的属性，父子关系有父子之间基于原则的关系属性。人这个物种之所以天性善良，也是因为人固有的原则。

因此，原则存在于万事万物之中。但朱熹坚持认为，原则最终只有一个。在他看来，船、车、人、树，以及父子关系的原则只是同一个普遍原则的具体表现。他经常重复"原则只有一个，其表现却多种多样"（理一分殊）这句话。因此，"原则"一词的最佳解释或许是类似于宇宙的基础模式或蓝图，蕴含在宇宙万物之中；原则的具体表现标注出每一个事物在这个统一的宇宙蓝图中所扮演的更具体的角色。朱熹的简明定义重新阐述如下：

---

① 二气交感，化生万物。万物生生，而变化无穷焉。惟人也，得其秀而最灵。见《周元公集·卷一·太极图说》。
② 见《朱子语类·卷一之理气上》。
③ 知夫所以然之故，与其所当然之则。见《朱子语类·卷十七之大学四或问上》。

每一个事物都有其原则的表现，但万物在宇宙中所遵循的规则或模式最终只有一个，正如万物之所以如此一般。原则虽然没有形状或生产能力，却为千变万化的"气"所组成的宇宙提供了连贯性和秩序。

朱熹赞同孟子的看法，认为每一个人的人性完全一致，因为每一个人在出生时都被赋予了同样的四种主要美德。但是，朱熹在完全接受孟子关于人性善的观点的同时，也赋予了它一个当代的形而上学基础，主张人类之所以拥有自己的本性，是**因为人性与人的原则，即"理"，完全一致："人性就是这种原则。"**①

但如果人性就是原则，因而永远不变，永远良善的话，又该如何解释"坏"人和"坏"的行为呢？朱熹及其理学同道没有将目光局限于孟子（后者从未真正就这个问题给出圆满的答案），而是基于他们对"气"的理解，对恶做出了详细的解释。他们得出的结论是，尽管人与宇宙间的其他万物均有关系，却接收到了最高等级的"气"，每一个人接收到的"气"的份额均不相同；该份额的质量和数量也因人而异——这与每一个人完全一致的人性形成了鲜明的对比。某些"气"相对更加澄澈，某些相对更加纯净，而某些则较为稀薄。

"气"的这种分配，造成了每一个人独特的外形和个人特征，也解释了人为什么会有个性差别。而且，正是"气"的这种基于澄澈稠密程度的分配，要么让一个人内在的善良品性璀璨耀眼，要么令其黯淡无光。朱熹对弟子们说："人性就是原则。人之所以有善恶之分，就是因为每个人所分配到的'气'有昏明厚薄的

---

① 性即理也。见《朱子语类·卷四之性理一》。

差别。"①

每一个人出生时被特别赋予了什么样的"气"是命中注定的。我碰巧接收到**这种**数量和质量的"气",而你碰巧接收到**那种**数量和质量的"气"。但是,我们被赋予的"气"是可以改变的,如果我们想要理解理学的计划,了解这一点至关重要。正是因为"气"是流动易变的,因为人可以通过自己的努力引导它的变化,人才会上进,甚至成为圣人。最澄澈纯净的"气",如果没有得到适当的照料,也会变得浑浊粗糙,而浑浊粗糙的天赋也可以被培育得更加纯净清明。每一个人的艰巨任务是照料他所得到的"气",保持或使它纯净清明,以便天性中的善可以毫无阻碍地自我发展。

这种日臻完善的可能性产生了理学家们眼中的人的道德困境:人自来都有能力实现道德完善,却常常无法做到道德完善。他拥有一种与生俱来的道德潜力,但这种潜力必须通过积极而有意识的努力才能加以实现。为此,他天赋的"气"必须得到培育滋养,因为决定他作为人能否实现道德潜力的,正是他所得到的那部分"气"的状况。朱熹同意孟子的观点,认为人可以达到完美;但通过对"理"(原则)和"气"这两个术语之意义的详细阐述,他和他的理学同道们为人应当**如何**改善自身提出了一种详尽的本体论解释。

修身与格物

这种道德困境解释了修身过程在理学哲学体系中的核心地位。修身是调节的过程,是个人改善本人之"气",并因此让

---

① 若人品之不同,固是气有昏明厚薄之异。见《朱子语类·卷四之性理一》。

他人性中的善得以实现的手段。朱熹思考儒家传统的经典文本时，在《大学》第一章里找到了他认为的理学修身计划的基础，以供"儒家之道"的追随者学习：

> 古代那些人……要想修养自身的品性，先要端正自己的心思；要想端正自己的心思，先要使自己的意念真诚；要想使自己的意念真诚，先要使自己获得知识；获得知识的途径在于认识、研究万事万物。①

因此，修身取决于调查研究万事万物的努力，也就是所谓的"格物"，这个词在若干个世纪里一直存在着争议。

朱熹在一个评论的章节里阐述了《大学》的这个段落，成为"致知在格物"的正统解读：

> 经书所说的"致知在格物"的意思是：如果我们想要获得最多的知识，就应当在接触外物时极力探索每一事物的道理。人的头脑是有智慧的，它拥有认识事物的能力，而天下的事物也无不包含着道理。只要人没有极力探索那个道理，他的认识就不可能完备。因此，《大学》一开始的教诲，就是教育学生，无论遇到天下的任何事物，都要根据他们已经认识的道理，进一步深入探索，力求达到认识的极点。如此长久用功，终有一天会突然领悟，融会贯通；如此一来，一切事物的特质，无论表面的还是隐含的，精微的还是粗浅

---

① 古之……欲修其身者，先正其心；欲正其心者，先诚其意；欲诚其意者，先致其知，致知在格物。见《礼记·大学第四十二》。

的,终将被认识,我们的认识在总体上、在运用上也都能洞察明白。这就是所谓"对事物穷尽探索"。这就是所谓"对事物认识透彻"。①

　　这里建议的过程是归纳性的。无论何时,遇上何物何事,或任何关系,人必须透过表面看透事物的本质。为了了解它隐含的真理,他必须探究其内含原则的具体表现,并加以思考。付出一定的时间和努力之后,他对万事万物的了解便可得到加深和拓宽,对周遭世界的领悟也能越来越清晰。因此,探究原则始于具体的事物,但最终会有助于理解让万事万物息息相关的普遍原则。

　　当然,这种研究的目标并不在于为理解而理解世界,它所提议的也并非科学探索。相反,如果一个人确实了解万事万物的本质,如果他真的认识到事物、事件和关系何以如此,他就完全能够妥善应对自己在世上遇到的那些事物、事件和关系。了解原则的各种表现就能洞悉宇宙的秩序,继而对人在那样的宇宙秩序中应该如何应对万事万物有一种道德意识。

　　按照朱熹的说法,每个人之所以能领悟原则,就是因为如荀子所说,我们生来具有能够理解的心智——这种智慧能够参透事物的基本原理。但他同时承认,并非每一个人都实现了完全澄明这种修身的目标。因为虽然心智能认识到原则,能够理解万事万物,但它也可能因为泛滥的人类情感或兽性欲望而偏离

---

① 所谓致知在格物者:言欲至吾之知,在即物而穷其理也,盖人心之灵莫不有知,而天下之物莫不有理。惟于理有未穷,故其知有不尽也。是以大学始教,必使学者即凡天下之物。莫不因其已知之理而益穷之,以求至乎其极。至于用力之久,而一旦豁然贯通焉。则众物之表里精粗,无不到,而吾心之全体大用,无不明矣。此谓物格。此谓知之至也。见《四书章句集注·大学章句》。

了这种领悟。因此，朱熹时常呼应孟子的话，告诫弟子们要"坚持明确的信念"①或"找回迷失的信念"②。正如他有一次所说："正是因为人放弃了自己的信念，他才堕入了邪恶。"③还有一次，他说："如果一个人能够保持自己的信念，使它格外澄明，他自然就能融入正道了。"④在朱熹看来，纯粹由最纯净的"气"所组成的信念就是"根本"。如果人循规蹈矩，合乎原则，就必须照料这种"气"并保持它的纯净。

帮助给信念指引正确方向的是"志"（意志），朱熹将其解释为信念的意图或倾向，或者按照字面意思，是"心之所向"⑤。人必须努力使这个意志保持坚定；因为如果意志坚定，必然会引导信念走向领悟原则的正确道路，远离阴险的欲望。"立志"显然是朱熹在与弟子讨论时最常见的口头禅之一。当然，孔子本人在《论语》（"为政第二之四"）中就有一段"自传式"评价⑥，将十五岁立志于学习作为他走上道德完善之路的第一步，而在那以前很久，就有人提出了意志的关键性。

朱熹的学习计划

正如朱熹所解释的那样，在任何地方、任何物事上都可以研究原则。通过观察自然世界及其各种现象、考察一个孝子、考虑历史事件和人物、思索个人经历和关系，都可以帮人找到原则。

---

① 持其志。见《朱子语类》文中多处。
② 求放心。见《朱子语类》文中多处。
③ 只缘自放其心，遂流于恶。见《朱子语类·卷十二之学六》。
④ 人能操存此心，卓然而不乱，亦自可与入道。见《朱子语类·卷十二之学六》。
⑤ 见《朱子语类·卷五二之孟子二》。
⑥ 子曰："吾十有五而志于学；三十而立；四十而不惑；五十而知天命；六十而耳顺；七十而从心所欲，不逾矩。"

毕竟，原则存在于万事万物之中。但朱熹担忧的是，这种广泛而没有边界的探索领域会让个人勉为其难，阻止他们对事物进行严肃的调查。他希望给学生们指明更有重点的方向，提出哪些具体的"物事"有可能会引导学生对原则得出清晰而直接的领悟。

在朱熹看来，这些"物事"就是古代圣贤的著作，即儒家的经典："世间万物都有原则，但其精髓存在于圣贤的著作中。因此，为了寻找原则，我们必须阅读这些著作。"[①]因为经典是古代至圣所撰，那些圣贤本人生前就曾逐渐改善自己的"气"，完全领悟了原则，那些经典中的原则是最清晰、表达最明确的。原则或许还有其他的调查方法，但研究圣人的著作显然是最有效的。

为了给"儒家之道"的追随者们进一步指明方向——希望可以尽可能方便他们学"道"——朱熹制订了一个连贯的、按部就班的经学计划。到11世纪末，儒家经典已经由最初的"五经"扩充到了"十三经"，他在那些经典中挑选了四部——在13世纪后，它们一般被称为"四书"——让学生们在研习其他著作之前先行阅读：《大学》、《论语》、《孟子》和《中庸》。这四部著作"易读、直观而简洁"，拥有其他经典文本所不具备的可读性。它们是儒家所有学问的基础：

> 读书应该从容易理解的段落开始。例如，《大学》《中庸》《论语》《孟子》这四书的道理就非常清晰。人们只是不去读它们。如果能理解这些文本，任何书都可以读了，任何

---

① 夫天下之物，莫不有理，而其精蕴则已具于圣贤之书，故心由是以求之。见《朱文公文集·卷五九之辛亥答曹元可》。

道理都可以探究了，任何事物也都可以应对了。①

掌握了这四部著作之后，学生们才开始阅读所谓的"五经"，自汉朝以来的一千五百年里，这些始终是儒家传统的重点著作：《易经》《诗经》《尚书》《礼记》，以及《春秋》。

朱熹在这里把儒家学习的重点从"五经"转向"四书"，强调了一个虽然显而易见但还是应该明确道出的观点：正如基督教的《圣经》提出了各种教义，引得读者解读出各种含义，儒家"十三经"正典也是一样，包括内容和重点不同的各种著作。"五经"和"四书"或许有着共同的基本道德、社会和政治理想，但在这两个系列中，这种理想的表达形式显示出很大的差别。

笼统地讲，"五经"用古代的事例和教训来解释儒家的道德观；指明从过往汲取的理想制度和治理方法；详细描述了人在生活的各种境遇中应该如何做人；并详细说明了维持一个安定有序的社会应秉持哪些礼仪做法。统治者从"五经"中学会了如何统治，大臣们学会了如何管理国家，父母学会了如何当家长，子女学会了如何表达孝心，长幼学会了如何互相表达尊重，朋友也学会了如何结成深厚友谊。

"四书"没那么强的历史性、描述性和具象性。这些著作主要关注的是人的天性、其道德的内在根源，以及他与广袤宇宙的关系。它们介绍和解释了得体行为和行动的一般原则，与"五经"不同，理解它们无须对古代中国的制度和社会实践研精钩深。

---

① 读书，且从易晓易解处去读。如大学中庸语孟四书，道理粲然。人只是不去看。若理会得此四书，何书不可读！何理不可究！何事不可处！见《朱子语类·卷十四之大学一》。

从"五经"转向"四书"不仅仅是课程层面的转移；它代表了儒家传统的一个重要的哲学改向，"向内"诉诸经典的教诲，这些经典更加注重人之道德的内在领域，以及至关重要的修身过程。从13世纪起，"四书"以及朱熹对这些经典的行间注释就成为儒家传统的"核心课程"，是通向自我实现和真正领悟的门径。

因此，在朱熹的学习计划中，有一套合适的阅读文本，还提出了阅读它们的正确顺序。但同样重要的是，还有一个正确的阅读**方式**。朱熹用多年时间为自己的学生发展了一套详尽的阐释学（或者用他自己的话来说，叫作"读书法"），这是阅读经典文本的一套系统的理论和方法。他告诫说，只是用眼睛扫过文本并不会产生真正的理解。要想让圣人的著作揭示真理，读者必须带着严肃的目标和端正的心态来阅读。他必须全神贯注，心无旁骛："读书，须是要身心都入在这一段里面，更不问外面有何事，方见得一段道理出。"[①]为此目的，朱熹提倡静坐或沉思的做法，因为这样可以让读者静下心来，完全开放心智，接受圣人的教诲。

读者应该一遍又一遍地吟诵经典，直到他对文本不再"陌生"。反复吟诵便能记住文本，但这个过程绝不是机械式的"死记硬背"；每一次的阅读与吟诵都会产生对文本更加深刻精妙的个人领悟。朱熹对文本并没有规定的阅读次数，他只是说"次数足够了就可以停止"[②]，但他承认，在某些情况下，阅读50到100遍也并不算太多。朱熹的阐释学目标很明确："道"的追随者通

---

① 见《朱子语类·卷十一之学五》。
② 数足则止矣。见《朱子语类·卷十之学四》。

过吟诵和记忆经典来内化或体现圣人的言语。真正把它们变成自己的思想,他本人也可成为圣人一样的人。

应当明确的是,对于朱熹而言,研习经典的重要性主要并不在于它是一种智力活动,而在于这是通向一种道德乃至精神目标的智识手段。通过经典著作,特别是"四书",有悟性的读者可以领会宇宙的根本原则,并因此像朱熹所写的那样,"竭尽全力地实践'道',这样便可进入圣贤的境地"①。因此,格物可能会转向"外部"世界的事物,特别是"四书",但这个过程的终极目标在于内在的道德培养。通过领会万事万物内含的原则,我们完全唤醒了作为人性的原则,并因此在我们日常的生活中,充分表达我们每一个人在出生时被赋予的仁、义、礼、智。探索原则直至"它的极点"就是在道德上完善自己。

理学之"新"

宗教或哲学的传统因为能够顺应时代、与时偕行而历久弥新。无法对变化的世界做出回应的传统就必然会消亡。儒家传统之长闻名遐迩,在很大程度上得益于它的灵活性,以及它能够有效地构建其要旨,来解决当代的紧迫问题。"道学",或称理学,就是儒家学派能够主动不断地重新诠释其基础教义的例证。11世纪和12世纪对儒家传统和备受推崇的经典文本的反思,产生了一种对该儒家要义的有意义的理解,那种理解与11世纪和12世纪的受众息息相关。随着"玄学"(曾经被称作"新道教")和佛教等其他学派在第一个千年的引进,这些受众已经习惯于

---

① 须是物格、知至,方能循循不已,而入于圣贤之域。见《朱子语类·卷十五之大学二》。

思考宇宙形而上的本质、人在其中的位置,以及人理解和接触宇宙真相的能力。

11世纪和12世纪"新"儒家所用的"新"方法,或与古典儒家有别的方法,简列如下:

- 使用形而上的语言;
- 将人置于原则与"气"的宇宙环境之中;
- 将"格物"即探究原则作为儒家修身过程的**唯一**基础;
- 缩小焦点,重点关注人的内心生活;
- 建立一套学习计划,给予"四书"高于"五经"的地位。

理学体系的形而上特征尤其让人们很难意识到,这个后期的儒家学派竟然与古典儒家思想共有一套最基本的信仰:

- 人是可以实现道德完善的;
- 学习是改善道德的关键;
- 古代的圣人提供了品德端正和在社会中表现得当的"道";
- 道德君子具有转化他人的影响力(《大学》第四章①);
- 社会和谐是民众满足了各自角色所承担的道德责任的结果。

如此说来,诚然,理学学派把原则和"气"这一套形而上学术语纳入其教义之中,但该学派最终重申——并向11世纪和12世纪的当代受众宣传了——道德-伦理的教诲,这是孔子、孟子

---

① "有斐君子,终不可喧兮"者,道盛德至善,民之不能忘也。

和荀子等早期儒家思想的核心内容。

朱熹之后的理学

在13世纪和14世纪,朱熹的集大成理学成为中国智识和政治中事实上的正统。然而,对其学说的质疑也的确存在。其中最著名的是15世纪的王阳明(1472—1529),他发展出一种颇有竞争力的理学思想的变体。王阳明起初是朱熹学说和修身计划的拥护者,后来则认为朱熹的道德完善方法过于书生气,其格物过程也过于艰巨。他提出"心理合一",而**不是**像朱熹所坚持的,心性合一。

其影响非常深远。学生们再也不必冗长拖沓地学习经典,也不必在"外部"世界寻求领悟原则了。按照王阳明的理解,出自《大学》的"致知"之意并非通过**外部**调查来扩充自己对原则的理解。相反,它是指扩大或应用人**与生俱来**的道心——人天生的分辨儒家所谓的是非的能力——来应对自己遭遇的万事万物和情境。在王阳明看来,学习分辨是非,在一切境遇中行为端正,并不取决于持续艰苦的学习,而只须注意自己的所作所为,应用每个人出生时便有的道德良知,即儒家的良心即可。

王阳明学派的一个明显的吸引力在于,道德的自我实现要比朱熹所说的容易得多,因为经典的研读和学习不再必不可少。朱熹学派在理论上坚持认为,任何人都可以达到道德完美,但实际上,它严格的经典学习计划使得这一领域仅仅局限于那些有足够的财富、手段和闲暇来全身心地投入学习之人。总而言之,王阳明的学说至少在理论上给那些目不识丁的人,或者王阳明本人所谓的"无知"的男女,提供了儒家修身的可能性。

一直到20世纪初期,朱熹学派一直是理学的主流,理学的学说和注疏成为教育课程的基础。但王阳明学派也获得了相当的人气,特别是在明朝(1368—1644)末期。随着他们各自的学说进入朝鲜和日本,朱熹和王阳明两个理学学派都在中国境外有了不少忠诚热情的拥护者。

第六章

儒家思想的实践

到目前为止,我们讨论到孔子"传播"了一种来自周初时期的理想化的社会政治理想;忠诚门徒们详细阐述这种理想,并在此过程中赋予其不同的重点和意义;又论述了在他过世一千多年后,思想家们重新定位了这种理想,解释了它在由"理"与"气"组成的宇宙环境中的重要性,这两个哲学术语对孔子本人大概毫无意义。我们关注的重点一直是思想领域,探讨孔子最初的理想在若干个世纪里如何被赋予了各种诠释和解读。

然而,这些教义并不局限于思想领域。它们出现在人们的践礼、家庭的日常生活、农民和精英的道德教育,以及国家的行政管理之中。将前现代的中国社会和政治笼统地定性为"儒家"或许是一种过度简化——这种说法有过强的排他性——但要说它们严重"儒家化",受到儒家信仰原则的影响和指导,却是完全贴切的。

儒家思想的"制度化"

早在汉朝,儒家思想就已经被作为中国国家意识形态的重要支柱了。正如我们在第一章中所见,公元前141年汉武帝登基之后,下旨免除了所有非儒家学者的职务;短短数年后的公元前124年,他又成立了以"五经"为核心课程的太学。太学的学生如果在年底的考试中证明自己精通"五经"中的一部或多部,就会成为候补官员,在官僚机构出现空缺时填补那些位置。

在此之前,儒家还只是众多思想学派之一。但在汉武帝采取这些措施之后,儒家便在中国官方意识形态中承担起中心角色。公元10世纪前后,随着科举更经常的使用,儒家成为**事实上**的主导学说,近乎国家的正统。因此,从公元前2世纪开始,中国日益成为"儒家"的国度——儒家精英治理国家,其政策和原则至少在理论上植根于儒家学说。(当然,就像西方基督教国家一样,中国国家的理想与其实际做法之间经常存在着相当大的脱节。)

在儒家看来,为官是社会上最高尚也最重要的职业。这种观点反映在职业等级排序上,该等级(虽从未获得正式的立法)对中国历史的进程产生了深远的影响。在这种排序中,(儒家)士大夫占据榜首;随后是靠劳作为民众提供食物的农民;再其后是提供日常使用的产品和工具的工匠;最后是商人。商人排在最底层,表明儒家认为商人是寄生虫,自己不事生产,而是买卖有生产力的"阶级"——农夫和工匠——的物品。随着儒家的价值观日益成为社会的主流,这种对商人的蔑视在中国的大部分帝国史上贯穿延续下来。(还要注意,军人在这种等级制度上没有立足之地,预示着这种文化赋予文职的特权高于武职,以及在后来的帝国时期,对军人及其职业普遍缺乏尊重。)

最不受社会尊重的商人或许可以积聚大量财富,生活豪华舒适，而农民却通常要为生存挣扎。实际上，商人的财富可以轻易超过哪怕最显要的官员。但这种财富却绝不会给商人带来为官者的社会地位和威望，也许正是出于这个原因，成功的商人往往会坚持让儿子努力学习参加科举，而不是子承父业。据信，官员是通过非凡的天资和品行而获得文官任命的——这种天资和品行如此出色，以至于引起了皇帝本人的注意。他们奉召做官，站在帝王身边，为他出谋划策，探讨如何给帝国带来和平与和谐。他们是社会的精英，按照流行的说法，是"天上的星宿"。

中国各朝各代的政府使用各种方法来招募文官。最常见的包括：一、举荐，地方当局将杰出人士的名单上呈首都，以供任命为文官；二、"门荫"，这是有一定地位的官员拥有的一项特权，他们可以提名自己的一个或多个儿子或家庭其他成员出任文职；三、国家发起的考试，成功者即使没有获任官员，也总会得到官员的身份。在这些方法中，科举考试后来成为招募的主要途径，到目前为止也是最负盛名的。

科举制度

隋朝（589—618）的统治者拓展了考试的用途，在整个帝国施行考试。其后的唐朝（618—907）继续并拓展了隋朝的做法，更经常地举办考试，通过考试过程产生了数量更多的官员，不过他们并非主流。到了晚唐，向考试成功者授予最高官职的做法，才使得考试制度得到了极大的发展势头。到9世纪，就连那些可以通过世袭特权得到文官任命的人也觉得，若想得到真正重要的职位，就有必要参加考试。自那以后直到20世纪初的整整一千年，考试制度一直是中国通向精英地位的必由之路。

从晚唐时期发展完备直到20世纪初期，考试制度基本上完全基于已成体系的儒家学说；其目的毕竟是招募官员，协助治理一个自我定义为儒家的国度。考试采用的具体形式，以及对考试的不同特征所赋予的具体权重（例如明经、写诗、策问、文体、书法等），或许会在若干个世纪中发生变化，但考试中测试的知识始终都是儒家的范畴。在13世纪之前，考生需要表现自己对"五经"尤其精通，那是考试课程的核心。1313年，随着朱熹学派的影响与日俱增，政府下令做出改变，宣布从这时起，以"四书"，特别是朱熹对"四书"的理解，作为考试的基础。

科举对中国社会的影响，无论怎样夸大都不为过。孩子们通常在母亲的辅导下，使用《三字经》等儒家入门读物在家里开始接受教育。如果他们继续受教育——由于家庭资源有限，只有极小比例的中国孩子有此机会——到七岁左右，他们会跟随家庭教师或村塾先生，开始学习《大学》《论语》《孟子》和《中庸》。学习过程枯燥，而且未必挑战或刺激智力。大多数时间都以"回课"的方式花在机械式的记忆上。在"回课"时，学生会走向老师的书桌，背对着老师，凭记忆大声背诵老师要求他准备的字句。如果他的背诵完美无瑕，就可以回到自己的书桌，开始学习课本里的下一行。但如果他忘了一个字，或是弄错了顺序，他就会挨一记竹板重击，继而听命回到自己的座位上，继续努力记忆。这个学习法保证他在15岁的时候能"通晓""四书"；他将能从头到尾一行不差地背诵其中的每一篇文章，没有任何错误。

15岁时，如果他被认为天资聪颖，并且家庭资源也足够充分的话，他就可能继续接受教育，此时的目标便专注于科举了。在考试中赢得最高等级（即进士出身）的机会非常渺茫。考生

图5　19世纪的中国课堂。站在老师桌前的学生们正在"回课",即大声背诵他们记忆的课文

首先要通过地方考试;成功后才有资格参加三年一度的省级考试;考中以后便获准前往帝都,参加同样是三年一度的会试。①

研究表明,参加地方考试的人,最终通过会试的比例不到百分之一。然而,即便机会如此渺茫,实际上中国所有的读书人都会走上考试的道路。他们当中最有雄心的会希望赢得进士的出身,在中国帝国社会的晚期,这几乎可以确保获得官职的任命、财富,以及崇高的社会地位。其他很多人深知自己几乎没有什么希望金榜题名(也就是获得进士身份),他们走上考试道路为

---

① 文中所说的地方考试,指的是各州府县举办的童试,赴考者称作"童生",考中后称"秀才"(即"生员"),第一名叫"案首"。随后参加的省级考试称为乡试,考中者称"举人",第一名称作"解元"。在首都礼部举行的考试称作"会试",考中之后称"贡士",第一名是"会元"。最后的殿试在紫禁城的保和殿举行,由皇帝亲自主持,考中者称"进士",殿试的第一名为"状元"。

的是该制度提供的其他福利。生员考生在地方级别的第一套重要考试中取得成功后,虽然仍没有资格当官,却也能获得某些特权:免除徭役和体罚。此外,生员地位的持有者(更高级别的举人更是如此)可以获得对中国传统的伟大文本一定程度的学问和知识,这样的资质可以帮助他们从事一系列职业——其中包括教书、经商和地产管理等,还有助于构建有用的社交网络。

在这些考试中取得成功的压力与它们的吸引力一样巨大。考生们要花费数年甚至数十年准备考试。很多人在乡试和会试中反复落选,却一次又一次地重返考场。实际上,在首都获得进士出身的成功者们,其平均年龄都有三十多岁了。坚忍不拔的考生献身考试生涯的艰难岁月,成了中国讽刺作家和小说作者

图6　1873年前后的广州科场。进入科场后,考生会在成排的标号考房里被分配一间"号舍"。这个科场有7 500间号舍

笔下的丰富素材。无论准备得有多充分，无论他们对儒家学说的了解多么深刻和纯正，考生们都很清楚，他们在统计学上的成功机会微乎其微。难怪很多人会寻找竞争优势——而那种优势并不总是光明磊落的。

考生可能会采取许多常见作弊技巧中的一种，其中包括：一、穿着抄写着"五经"文本或考试范文的内衣；二、把小抄裹挟在食物和铺盖里；三、雇人"冒名顶替"——此人须是个经验老到的作文高手——来假扮他们的身份，在分配给他们的号舍里就座；四、预先从考官那里买考题；五、贿赂考官；六、安排人在科场内外作答，一旦开始唱名，就把答案递进他们的号舍。国家不断采取各种措施，防止这些舞弊以及围绕该制度产生的很多其他手段。但考生们足智多谋，而且考虑到一定与成功相伴而来的回报，提升自身机会的诱惑实在太大了。在整个科举制度史上，腐败随处可见。这里有着深刻的讽刺意味：考试制度的明确宗旨是要在帝国寻找对儒家的道德–伦理学说理解最深刻之人，但考试中的作弊却泛滥成灾。

然而，正是这个制度促成了与儒家学说有关的道德理想和实践在整个中国社会的传播。正如前文所述，中国的大多数教育都是面向考试的学习，因此强化了考试中所要宣扬的价值观。无论是生活在北京、西安还是广州的学童，读的都是一样的儒家启蒙读本，一样的"四书五经"；并且在学习"四书五经"的过程中，阅读的都是被国家宣布为正统的注释。同样，无论是在浙江省、山东省，还是四川省参加考试的知识精英，精通的都是同样的经典著作，最终也都在这个过程中彰显儒家的美德和理想，至少人们希望如此。如果他们足够幸运，获得了官方的任命，人们

图7 以蝇头小楷写下数百篇考试范文的内衣。像这样抄满儒家经典或范文的"夹带衫"可以缝进考生长袍的夹层中,在考试期间用作"参考"

期待他们弘扬的也正是这些美德和理想。这就是说,考试制度是中国历史上的一股强大的整合力量。它确保,尽管中国的领土广袤,人口数量庞大而多样,却始终存在着一种广泛共有的文化,一种价值观、信仰和风俗习惯体系,在民众中间创造出一种统一的表象,使他们看似更容易被中央集权的政府治理。

有趣的是,尽管科举考试促进了儒家学派的价值观和利益,但从唐朝开始,考试制度却受到了儒家学者们的一连串批评。常见的对该制度的反对意见包括:

- 它奖励死记硬背,坚持僵化的文学制度,而不是独创性或分析思维。

- 它提倡学究式的古老知识，而不是对治国有实效的知识。
- 它不是评估考生品行的有效手段；举荐制度对于寻找品行端正之人更加有效，因此应该取代考试制度，或为其作补充。
- 它分散了学生对真正的学问，也就是为了道德修养而学习的注意力；相反，学习的目的变成了追求空洞的名望和世俗的成功。
- 它引发了激烈而粗野的竞争，而据孔子说，儒家的君子是不应该竞争的。

这些反对意见并未遭到即时驳斥，有时还会引发严肃的辩论。实际上，考试制度在若干个世纪里经历了频繁的变革。然而，作为一种制度，它在将近一千五百年里基本保持不变，成为塑造和维持中国的文化及社会规范的一股最为强大的力量。它是中国帝国秩序的根基所在。

儒家思想与平民

如果士大夫精英可以被称为儒家的话，那些没有受教育机会的普通百姓又该当如何？他们有多"儒家"呢？他们显然认同与孔子及其传统有关的很多信念和理想。毫无疑问，大多数人也承认他们有孝顺父母和祖父母的义务（即便他们不一定能做到）；而负担得起通过供奉来祭拜祖先的人也大多会如此行事。中国社会通过正式和非正式的种种手段，鼓励精英和平民采用国家准许的社会实践和信仰：村塾以基本的儒家学说和原则来教导孩子们，哪怕有些孩子不会为参加科举而继续接受严肃教育；地方官员和村落长者大声朗读提倡正当社会行为的公告和所谓乡约；皇帝在整个帝国传播儒家口吻和观点的道德教育；而普通家庭则遵守儒家学派编纂的家庭和祭祖礼仪，并将其一代一代地传递下去。

至于以主流文化的价值观和做法来与他人交际的平民百姓是否会把这些价值观和做法看作"儒家"，却很值得怀疑。他们更有可能只把这些看作中国文化中受人喜爱的习俗。但在孝敬父母、尊重长辈，以及祭拜祖先等方面，他们信奉的却是自公元前2世纪以来就与儒家学说密切相关的做法和理想。在描述中国的平民时，我建议宁可过于谨慎：他们大多不能被称作"儒家"，因为他们并没有致力于儒家学说的研究，也没有以任何实质性的方式认同自己是儒家学派的拥护者；但他们的生活却在很大程度上受到了儒家思想的教义和做法的影响。

的确，在历史上，区分"儒家的"和"中国的"一直都是研究中国的学者面临的难题。以孝顺为例。这是孔子学说的核心。在帝制中国，无人能一面合情合理地宣称自己是"儒家"弟子，一面却公然违背孝顺的价值观。但这种价值观在孔子颂扬它之前很久便已存在了。孔子对弟子们说"述而不作"(《论语·述而第七之一》)时，孝顺可能只是他心中所想该传统的许多教义与做法之中的一种。那么，是否应该把孝顺归为"中国的"？因为它起源于中国文化史的深处，早于孔子及其学派的出现。还是应该把它归为"儒家的"？因为孔子在从过往中进行选择时，为一个风雨飘摇的理想赋予了新的现实意义与生命，并确保它通过与国家的儒家正统的有机联系，在中国人中间持续扩散。我认为两者皆是。

无论如何，我在本书里提到孔子从中国早期传统中挪用为"儒家思想"的那些理想时，我相信读者会明白，我并不是说它们起源于孔子，也不是说它们的实施仅限于他真正的信徒。他的学说所获得的正统地位保证了它们在中国社会中广泛而普遍的传播。

儒家思想与统治者

中国的独裁传统可以追溯到儒家思想在公元前2世纪被制度化以前很久，不迟于公元前1400年，甲骨上的铭文就证明了商王们的权威和势力。但儒家的教义高度赞扬独裁的优点，无疑给中国传统的独裁治理制度增加了更多的合法性。

孔子当然认为独裁可行，因为统治者作为**一家之主**，像父亲对待子女一样，以仁慈温和的权威引导臣民，爱护和关心他们的福祉。他的独裁统治的正当性源于他完美的品行和道德魅力，自然会引来其臣民"子女"的忠诚和服从——平民百姓没有受过自行治理的教育，也没有应有的美德。他通过自己的善良和示范性的践礼，教导民众行为得体，尊重等级秩序，从而在整个国家建立起和谐。而且，就像一个父亲应该代表家人做出决定一样，统治者也应该代表民众做出决策。在孔子看来，理想的政府是**民享**的政府，却不是**民有**或**民治**的政府。

如果统治者的确仁慈，这个制度的运作就会很好。但实际上，孔子理想化的这种统治者很难有代表性。问题在于：按照儒家的制度，如果没有真正高尚的儒家统治者，政治秩序还会有效地运行吗？孔子当然认为并希望儒家培养的官员可以制约统治者的权力——并提供后者所需要的指导。但实际情况仍然是官僚体制里配备的都是"他的"人。他们是通过他的恩惠,通过在他的政府举办的科举考试以及他亲自监督的附加殿试中取得成功而上任的。皇帝负责他们的任免,甚至一句话就可以将他们流放或杀死。这并不是说士大夫对皇帝的决定不置一词,而是他们这样做会冒巨大的个人风险。我想,挑战皇帝的权威绝非等闲之举,亦非寻常之事。

中国帝国史上的基本问题是:当儒家的意识形态在事实上无法引导和约束皇帝的意志时,就别无他法了。对于皇帝的权力或行为没有宪章或立法限制,在皇帝的行为远离儒家理想时,也没有机构或部门拥有合法的权威对其加以制约。因此,统治者可以滥用自己的权力,或者无视自己的责任而不受到任何惩罚,他们也的确时常如此。

以明朝的第一个皇帝明太祖(1368—1398年在位)为例,他本是平民,以叛乱运动领袖的身份登上皇帝宝座。他粗通文字,据说极其不信任——并且嫉妒——学识渊博的士大夫阶级。1380年,明太祖怀疑自己的丞相阴谋推翻他,便废除了中书省——这是政府的核心行政机构——个人接管并直接控制了政府的几乎全部职能。儒家士大夫的意见毫无分量。那些得罪他的官员被他在朝堂众目睽睽之下以廷棍杖打(往往致死)。在明太祖治下,仁慈和家长式统治被残酷、有时甚至野蛮的暴政取代了。

天启帝(1620—1627年在位)是个懒政的统治者,他宁愿当个木匠,花时间制作精美家具,也不愿治理国家。他对国事的忽视——简直是厌恶——让太监魏忠贤趁机控制了政府。魏忠贤很快就用他的投机分子亲信们填补了掌权的职位,对民众征收剥削性的税款,并残酷清洗了数百名胆敢反对他的士大夫。简而言之,天启帝对帝国政事的漠不关心导致了臭名昭著的恐怖政权,王朝从那时起就再也没能恢复。魏忠贤掌权后不到二十年,明朝就崩溃了。

这些事例时有极端,但都说明(因为没有宪章的制约)当政府的最高层人士不接受儒家思想时,后果可能会非常严重。然而在大部分时间里,即便统治者和官员并未充分体现儒家的理想,他们也完全胜任,能够监督国事,捍卫王朝的利益。

儒家思想与家庭

正如本书第二章所述,孔子在《论语》中举了一个例子来说明家庭在中国社会中奠基性的重要意义,并认为它是道德-伦理同化的核心。个人正是在这里学习如何成为"中国人",认识了让中国人有别于"野蛮"世界的其他人的价值观、习俗和做法,也正是在这里开始接受规范的社会等级制度:前辈优先于晚辈;老者优先于幼者;男人优先于女人。

家族是父子相传的,意思就是家族的血脉可以通过男性追溯到创建家族的一个男性祖先。子女虽然是父母的共同后代,却是从父亲那一方继承了家族成员的身份。因此,只有家族继续产生男性后代,家族的血脉才会延续下去。正是因为这个原因,从中国历史的最初期开始,儿子的诞生就被看作"大喜",而生女则被认为只是"小喜"。儿子可以延续家族的血脉;女儿"外"嫁进丈夫的家族,主要责任便是确保他家族的血脉在下一代延续。孟子说过一句话,"不孝有三,无后为大"(《孟子·离娄上之二六》),对后世影响极为深远。

如果家族血脉断绝，后果如何？最令人痛苦的是无人照料祖先了。而祖先在中国文化中的重要性无论怎样强调都不为过。一个人能够存在，完全仰仗这些祖先。如果没有父亲、祖父，以及祖父之前的历代父辈，人就不会存在。他对于列祖列宗的感激将通过所谓的祭祖仪式，虔诚对待他们的灵魂来加以偿还。这些礼仪通过经典的《礼记》和《家礼》（理学思想家朱熹编纂）等著作传承下去，保持着对祖先的鲜活记忆，并让祖先一直存活在精神世界里。当这套礼仪不再继续，祖先的记忆和灵魂也会随之而去。

当然，在犹太-基督-伊斯兰教的西方，祖先也能得到供奉、感情和尊重。但这些亚伯拉罕①的西方传统与中国的儒家传统有着根本差别。在西方，人们认为那个一神论的上帝创造了过去和现在的一切。是上帝以亚当和夏娃的模样创造了人类；因此归根结底，上帝要对全人类的存在负责。奉行这些传统的人当然会尊重他们的家族血脉，但他们最高的敬畏与尊重都献给了起初创造他们家族血脉的上帝。在一个本土信仰中不存在创世神——而且外来的一神论信仰也未得到普及——的文化里，只有生物血脉才能解释一个人的存在，并应该得到个人的感恩与赞美。

与中国所有其他的规范关系一样，祖先和后代之间的关系也建立在互惠的原则上。正如父母和祖父母引导和保护幼者，祖先也继续为家族提供引导和保护。他们尽其所能地保佑家族福星高照、岁物丰成、儿孙满堂，反过来，在他们的生日及其他纪

---

① 指前面提到的三个有共同源头的一神教。如此称呼，皆因这三个宗教均给予《圣经·旧约》中的亚伯拉罕（阿拉伯语译作易卜拉欣）崇高的地位，且均发源于西亚沙漠地区，来源于闪米特人的原始宗教。

图8 家庭成员在祖宗牌位前敬拜祖先（这个家庭似乎在为摄影摆姿势，因为在正常情况下，他们应该面对牌位）

念活动中，整个家族致敬祖灵，在家里的供桌上摆放祖先生前喜爱的食物（例如橘子、猪肉、酒和糖果等）和物品（例如纸牌、书画卷轴、烟草、精美马车的纸质模型等）。如果是出自富裕宗族的家族（按照中国的说法，宗族包括可以追溯到同一个男性祖先的全部家族分支），这些祭品就会摆放在宗庙的祠堂里。人们认为，忘记祖宗会导致不幸——家人罹病、庄稼病害、生意失败。关注遭到忽视的祖先，按照礼仪尽职尽责地铭记他，则会使家族正在经历的麻烦得到一些缓解或改善。

这就提出了与西方传统的另一个明显差别。在西方，此世界与"彼世界"之间的鸿沟广阔无边。陌生而无形的上帝就住在"彼世界"里。上帝无所不能,不受互惠义务的约束。而上帝终究是不可知的,这也意味着上帝对人类的规划并非完全可知。因此,人们在祷告上帝,寻求超越现世的引导和希望时,得知自己必须有信仰。在中国传统中,住在彼世界的是冯二叔和冯祖[①]。对于冯家的后辈来说,二叔和老祖没有什么陌生感,也不算虚无缥缈。冯家的后辈自幼便接受他们的指导和建议。后辈子弟与他们共享食物,也了解他们最爱的菜式。他们全程参与过后辈的一切家族重要场合——冠礼、婚礼、葬礼以及祭礼。在后辈们年迈时,他们还会帮助照顾。冯家的后辈在望向彼世界时,坚信二叔和老祖的灵魂依然关注着家族的福祉,会尽其所能地恩泽家人,保护他们免受伤害。也就是说,在中国,"彼世界"既不是全然的"他者",也并非遥不可及。如此说来,我们大概最好把中国的灵性世界理解为家族所在世界的连续统一体的一部分,而不是一个"他界"。

无论是在家里的小供桌上还是在宗庙的大祠堂里举行的祭祖仪式,都有着多重作用。它们表达了家族对先辈所做的一切充满感恩,其中最重要的当然是生命本身;它们保存了对祖先的记忆,维持着他们在灵魂世界里的活力;它们减轻了对死亡的恐惧,向生者表明**他们**离别这个世界后,也将继续在家族生活中发挥作用;它们还通过把成员们聚集起来纪念共同的祖先,巩固了家族的纽带,改善了家族的共同形象。

重视祭祀和向祖先表达崇敬,并不是说中国人不信仰神灵。自然世界有主管河、山、风以及四季等的神灵。也有神灵向道

[①] "冯氏"家族为作者杜撰的人物,作者虚构出这个家族的故事,作为中国典型家族的替身。

教、佛教，以及各种民间教派的修行者提供帮助和慰藉。但祖灵信仰——以及向他们展示的礼仪尊重——在中国社会占据主导地位，无论社会或经济地位如何，几乎所有的人都普遍认同这种信仰（包括自认为是道教徒和佛教徒的人）。

儒家思想与妇女

孔子说："唯女子与小人为难养也。"（《论语·阳货第十七之二三》）尽管若干个世纪以来，很多诠释者试图削弱这句话的尖刻，却无法回避它贬低所有女性的事实。实际上，《论语》或其他典籍中没有一处表明，儒家的修身和道德完善计划同样适用于妇女。孔子的教义——以及他后来的追随者们的学说——似乎都是为男性考虑的。

儒家认定女人的道德潜力无法与男人相比，这就意味着在儒家看来，社会生活中没有女人的位置——这种偏见一直持续到20世纪。女人从来没有可能担任官职，也从未获准进入科场。她们的责任被局限在"家中"，负责打理家事。

这并不是说女人没有行使过政治权力。但她们所行使的权力并非来自她们自己合法的、制度化的权威，而是源于接近有权力的男性。中国历史上充满了这样的例子，作为地方行政长官、大臣和皇帝的配偶、妃嫔及母亲的女人拥有相当的政治影响力。我们只需想一想在19世纪的整个下半叶控制清廷的慈禧太后（1835—1908），她先是作为同治帝（1862—1874年在位）的母亲，然后作为光绪帝（1875—1908年在位，由她本人扶上皇位）的姨妈，最后从1898年开始，成为事实上的统治者。实际上，这个规则有一个真正值得注意的例外——唐朝的武后（690—

705年在位）。690年，已贵为唐高宗（649—683年在位）皇后的武后登基，宣称自己是"天子"。她是中国漫长历史上的第一位——也是最后一位——女性天子。

虽然她们也许永远不能参加考试或成为士大夫，但在精英家庭里长大的女孩们通常都会学习阅读《论语》《孟子》《诗经》《孝经》，以及汉朝的班昭所著的《女诫》等儒家入门读物和典籍。人们认为，接触这些著作及其教义可以帮助她们成为品行端正的儒家模范妇女。人们还认为，家中女孩的文化水平能够提高家庭的地位，表明这个家庭有资源和文化投资来像对待儿子那样教育女儿。但向女孩们提供教育还有另一个驱动力：可以让她们更适于结婚，也就是说，对于寻找新娘的家庭更有吸引力——作为这些家庭的母亲，她们可以担负起教导幼子学习儒家基础读物的角色。平民家庭的女孩很少会受教育。相反，她们会学习做家务，在余生的大部分时间里，这些都是她们的工作：缝补、纺织、做饭、打扫，或许还有种地。

对于女孩来说，婚姻就是人生大事。在结婚的那一天，通常不到20岁的新娘会离开自己的家，去新郎家与公婆、新郎尚未嫁人的姐妹、他的兄弟及其妻子儿女同住。到达新郎房舍或宅院的大门时，她会向新郎家族的长辈鞠躬行礼，并行礼缅怀家族的祖先。从此以后，她就是他家族的一员了；而他的祖先也就成了她的祖先。她祭祀致敬的将会是他们，而不是自己原生家族的祖先。她本人现在也属于新郎的家族血脉了。

对于很多人来说，搬去与丈夫全家同住带来的身份丧失一定是很大的心灵创伤。试想一下：成婚那天可能不仅是新娘第一次看到她丈夫的大家族，还是她第一次见到丈夫本人。她根本不认识他,也从未参与过与他结合的安排。这种结合是双方父母基于符合两家共同利益的一致意见,也许有媒人的协助。这绝对**不是**妻子和丈夫自由订立的爱情契约。

于是我们看到,这位非常年轻的女性进入一个她不熟悉的家庭,有一大堆新的关系需要处理。有公公婆婆、叔伯兄弟、姑子妯娌、侄儿侄女,更不用提还可能有仆人、女佣、姨太太、厨子之流。如今住在同一个屋檐之下,与他们相处融洽对她来说至关重要——唯有如此,她的新生活才会容易一些。

年轻的新娘从娘家和班昭在《女诫》中的教诲中学到,要在新家取得"成功",最为必要的是:孝敬公婆,听从他们的每一个吩咐。公公和婆婆如今就是她的父母。她的主要责任就是千方百计地取悦他们,特别是婆婆。她在《女诫》中读道:

> 放弃个人观点的服从是最好的做法。只要婆婆说,"不要那样做",如果她说得对,儿媳当然应该顺从。只要婆婆说,"那样做",哪怕她说得不对,儿媳也应绝对服从命令。女人在是非上不要违背公婆的愿望和意见;不要和他们争辩对错。这种(温顺)可以被称作放弃个人观点的服从。①

作为进入这个家庭的外人,儿媳一定要让自己的意愿从属于家庭的意愿。唯有这样,随着时间的推移,她才会被这个家庭欣然接受。

某些婆家也许会对新娘更加宽容、温和、友好,而某些婆家

---

① 固莫尚于曲从矣。姑云不尔而是,固宜从令;姑云尔而非,犹宜顺命。勿得违戾是非,争分曲直。此则所谓曲从矣。见班昭:《女诫·曲从第六》。

则更严苛一些。但所有的家庭对这个外人的期望全都一模一样：她怀上丈夫的孩子，延续家族的血脉——如今也是她的血脉。当然，生身父母也早就教育她懂得，这是她嫁人之后的义务。所以她一进入自己的新家，就知道对她的期望是什么；也知道她越早满足他们的要求，她作为家庭外来者的命运就可能越快得到改善。并且因为生育继承人是改善命运的最佳方法，她也和公婆一样希望能生个男孩。他们的"大喜"就是她的"大喜"。

　　生儿育女不止会改善她在新家的命运。她"出嫁"时，把对自己原生家族的充沛情感都抛在身后；进入丈夫的家族后，她在某种意义上不过是个尚在试用期的陌生人。同样，她在那里的生活基本上得不到情感上的满足和真正的爱情。如今有了自己的孩子，她的人生在情感上丰富了许多——也不再寂寞了。在婆家那个规模更大的父系家族中，她建起了自己联系紧密的"母系家庭"——某些人类学家如此命名——在这个小家庭里，她总算可以指望享受情感上一定程度的亲密。（她或许还会想象自己有朝一日也会成为儿媳的婆婆，享受她本人的婆婆曾经享有的权威、尊敬和特殊待遇。）

　　她身为母亲，要给幼年的子女提供指导。她就是他们的第一个老师。9世纪的一部概述"妇道"的著作《女论语》主张："大多数的家庭都有儿子和女儿。……教育他们的责任完全属于母亲。"①母亲的教导所采取的形式是树立良好的行为典范，以及讲述传授儒家道德的故事、历史事件和传统掌故。此外，有文化的母亲会为自己的孩子们大声吟诵《论语》《孟子》《孝经》及

---

① 大抵人家，皆有男女。……训诲之权，亦在于母。见宋若莘：《女论语·第八之训男女》。

图9　引自《吴友如画宝》(1908年出版,1983年重印)的一幅平版印刷插图,一个母亲在教儿子写字

其他主要著作。这种吟诵有两重目的:它有助于孩子们的道德培养,并把家族希望他们(特别是男孩)有朝一日能够掌握的经典著作介绍给孩子们。

因此,妇女在家庭范围内起到了顺从的儿媳和道德女教师的作用。但她还扮演着另一个角色,这个角色非常重要,在学术文献中却很少被提及——家务管理人。《女论语》说:

> 操持家务的女子应当节俭、勤劳。她勤劳,家庭就会兴旺;她懒惰,家庭就会衰落。她节俭,家庭就会富裕;她浪

费,家庭就会贫穷。①

在精英阶层的家庭里,与操持家务相关的责任可能会非常艰巨,可能还包括:记录家庭的财务情况;在各个儿子及其妻子们之间维持秩序;分配他们每个月的零用钱;管理家里的用人并按月付"薪水"给他们;监督厨房,意思是要负责所有食物的采购,以及所有家庭成员的伙食;如果是个地主家庭,她还要负责从佃户那里收租。在这样的家庭里,丈夫不屑于做跟金钱有关的事务和琐碎的家务这类不体面的事,很可能会躲进书房,把所有这些俗事都留给妻子。他还有可能离家去当官、经商,或者只是去城市的某个地方享受一番。

妇女的婚姻被看成终生承诺,婚姻关系延续到她丈夫过世之后——无论他是寿终正寝还是未能及冠便夭折了。儒家学说把再婚看作一种耻辱,把二婚的妇女比作服侍两位君主的大臣。她结婚时,不仅与新郎建立了关系,而且与他的全家都产生了关联。因此,他的死不能结束她对这个家庭的责任。如果公婆还在世,她侍奉公婆的责任也持续存在;并且如果子女或者子女的子女都生活在这个家中,她养育和教导他们的责任也持续存在。儒家的传统——以及《女论语》等相关著作——要求忠贞的妻子至死不渝地保持贞洁。国家支持并提倡这种理想,建造了石制牌坊来纪念那些赢得了贞节美名的寡妇(其中的一些幸存至今)。

如果我们只读写给妇女的那些规范性著作——像班昭的《女诫》和《女论语》等书籍——就很容易以为,女人都是被动而

---

① 营家之女,惟俭惟勤。勤则家起,懒则家倾,俭则家富,奢则家贫。见宋若莘:《女论语·第九之营家》。

顺从的人，先是严格服从父母，后又要毫无怨言地服从丈夫和公婆的要求。然而在家庭内部，她们也是一股支配的力量。著名政治家曾国藩（1811—1872）的女儿曾纪芬（1852—1942）在19世纪为妇女撰写的指导手册中有一个段落，雄辩（不过也许有些自私）地论证了妻子在中国儒家家庭的命运中所起到的核心作用：

> 那么，管理家庭成员的责任属于谁呢？我说属于妻子。……妻子是管理家庭内部之人。整个家庭里，无一事不与妻子密切相关。这些事情不能委托给丈夫。丈夫为何不能管理家庭？我说，他没有闲暇。另外，他的雄心无所不在，唯独不在家里。无论士农工商，丈夫都希望把全部天赋用于在家外谋生。他殚精竭虑，积累财富，依靠妻子的管理，并为了家庭而持之以恒。因此，家庭命运的兴衰完全依靠妻子是否有德。

尽管极富争议性，但这段话确实提醒我们不要妄下结论，看到有记录的有关中国社会控制妇女行为的规则强调了她们的从属地位，便以为前现代中国的女人就没有权力或权威了。某些妇女能够在政治领域施加影响，甚至主宰国家，这让儒家的清议派颇感困扰。更切中要害的是，在家庭这个中国社会的基本单位内部，妇女作为母亲、教师和家务管理人，被赋予了合法的权威地位。

后记：
20世纪和21世纪的儒家思想

儒家学说对前现代中国的政治、社会和思想的影响无远弗届，到20世纪初期却遭到了五四运动的民族主义领袖们的严厉谴责。一个世纪以来，经过西方帝国主义列强和日本对中国主权的冲击，以及中国新成立的共和政府（1912—1949）软弱无能，从1919年5月4日开始，中国的学生和工人发起了大规模抗议。这些五四改革者致力于建设一个强大的，首先是"现代的"中国，能够跻身世界强国之林。为了建设这个现代中国，他们首先要寻找这个国家羸弱的根源。他们认为，根源就是儒家思想。

在1910年代末和1920年代，他们发起了对儒家传统的正面进攻，坚称如果中国真正希望成为一个强大而健康的社会，就必须放弃"孔夫子"及其过时的习俗和信念。他们高喊着要"打倒孔子"，"砸烂孔家店"。全新的秩序亟待建立；关于这种新的世界秩序应该采取怎样的具体形式，胡适（1891—1962）等自由派和陈独秀（1879—1942）等马克思主义者的观点或许不能统一，但他们一致认为，是时候抛弃孔夫子，支持"德先生"和"赛先生"了。

1918年，鲁迅（1881—1936）——他或许是20世纪最伟大的中国作家——发表了短篇小说《狂人日记》，呼吁同胞甩掉儒家文化的桎梏。他讲了一个彻夜读史的狂人的故事，这部历史的每一页上都写满了"仁义道德"，但随着夜色褪去，狂人继续阅读，"才从字缝里看出字来，满本都写着两个字是'吃人'"。《狂人日记》是对儒家传统的强烈谴责。伪装成仁义虔诚的儒家思想实际上是吃人和毁人的；其宣扬孩童要孝顺，女人地位次要，下级服从上级的等级结构，剥夺了人的自主权和生命力，粉碎了人的精神。

19世纪的历史事件在很大程度上造就了陈独秀和鲁迅等知识分子的态度。中国自1839年起就饱受帝国主义列强的重创，一个世纪以来，中国被迫向外国人开放了所谓的通商口岸；承认在中国的外国人拥有根据自己国家的法律接受审讯的权利（即所谓的治外法权）；向一系列帝国主义国家支付巨额赔偿；还向英国人和日本人割让领土。中国人越来越强烈地感到自己作为一个民族和一个国家，主权受到了外国侵略者的严重侵犯。

19世纪末、20世纪初的政治家和知识分子原则上一致认为，如果中国想要应对西方列强和日本的挑战，改革是十分必要的。但要找到一个让他们一致认可的合乎逻辑的改革方案，就要困难得多了。主要的分歧就在于采用西方技术和学问与维护传统儒家价值观之间所要达到的具体平衡。由于这类冲突、宫廷内斗和帝国主义压力的加剧，改革的努力付之东流。1912年，在很大程度上由于这类努力的失败，清朝灭亡，结束了中国长达两千年的帝国统治史。

五四运动的领袖们对于国家如今需要走哪条道路毫不含糊。为了建立新的强大秩序，中国必须彻底摆脱儒家的传统。对于这次运动的某些参与者而言，抛弃儒家思想就意味着要在他处寻找可以在20世纪为中国服务的智识传统和政治意识形态。五四运动的领袖陈独秀和李大钊（1888—1927）转向了1917年的俄国革命和马克思的著作。作为北京大学的教师，他们在校园里组织了非正式的马克思主义学习小组，其中某些人成为日益了解和致力于马克思主义学说的知识分子核心。1921年，陈独秀和李大钊在上海成立了中国共产党（CCP）。因此，五四运动关于彻底与本土文化传统决裂的劝诫，为中国共产党的成立奠定了必要的基础。

　　当然，并不是所有的中国人都如此决绝地渴望丢弃儒家思想。一些知识分子继续在儒家传统中寻找意义。例如，梁漱溟（1893—1988）在《东西文化及其哲学》（1921）中反驳了五四运动的参与者，坚称中国传统文化，特别是儒家思想，可以——实际上必然会——有助于在20世纪重建中国。而在远离改革和革命风起云涌的中心城市的腹地，很多人仍然拥护和实践儒家的价值观和礼仪；那里的很多孩子在学习新式学校课程的"现代"教科书的同时，仍继续阅读"四书"。

　　蒋介石（1888—1975）领导的国民党也在继续寻找儒家思想的价值。1934年，蒋介石发起了"新生活"运动，号召国家和民众重整道德。他呼应了孔子的一个基本前提，即只有道德高尚的民众才会建设出军事、经济和道德上的强国。"新生活"运动特别提倡与儒家传统密切相关的四德：礼、义、廉、耻。1934年，蒋介石在为该运动揭幕的演讲中说道：

> 故"礼义廉耻"者,乃发民德以成民事,为待人、处事、持躬、接物之中心规律;违反此规律者,无论其个人、国家、与民族,未有不为之败亡者。①

但"新生活"运动命不久长,因为它未能引起它所针对的主要来自城市的人群的兴趣或支持。在短短几年内,人们就大多把它忘了。

蒋介石领导的国民党与毛泽东(1893—1976)领导的中国共产党之间二十年的内战在1949年结束。10月1日,毛泽东站在天安门上,宣布成立中华人民共和国(PRC)。

1978年,邓小平(1904—1997)成为中国的最高领导人,中国走上了经济和政治改革的道路。自2000年以来,北京的领导层渴望提升经济繁荣,促进社会稳定,他们引用《论语》中的段落"和为贵"(《论语·学而第一之十二》),开始宣扬实现"和谐社会"的目标。曲阜的孔子建筑群翻修一新,如今是每年九月底孔子诞辰的庆祝活动场地。近年来,全国各地的大学——北京大学、曲阜师范大学、人民大学、陕西师范大学,以及山东大学等——都成立了儒家学术研究中心。在2008年奥林匹克运动会的开幕式上,北京奥林匹克委员会欢迎从世界各地来到北京的客人,"有朋自远方来,不亦乐乎?"以及"四海之内,皆兄弟也",这些问候语都出自《论语》。

很多观察家认为,中国政府对儒家思想的这种"认可",旨在促进稳定、秩序与和谐。在21世纪的第一个十年里,中国人似

---

① 见蒋介石:《新生活运动纲要》。

乎对接受古代圣人的学说产生了真正的兴趣，特别是中产阶级的城市居民。2006年，北京师范大学一位鲜为人知的大众传媒教授于丹受邀在公共电视节目《百家讲坛》中，讲授七集有关儒家思想的讲座。她以非学术界人士可以接受的方式，解释了《论语》对今天日常生活的重要性，因此一夜成名。中国人对她的讲座产生了共鸣。

于丹的成功只是对本土儒家传统重新产生兴趣的一次表达。从3岁到12岁的孩童周末学习记诵"四书"的私立儒家学校在全国各地涌现。对于这种21世纪大众对儒家传统兴趣的"复兴"，观察家们解释这是多种因素综合作用的结果。至关重要的是，不断上升的民族情绪激发了人们在**本土传统中**寻找意义——并抵消西方贪图享乐和物质主义的恶性影响——的渴望。

因此，孔子在20世纪和21世纪的中国扮演了各种各样的角色。时而受到赞美，时而遭到污蔑，他既是好人又是坏人。但无论好坏，他一直都在舞台上。如今，孔子似乎在民众中再次受到了欢迎。但他和他的学说的前景仍然难以预测。可以肯定的一点是，孔子的深远影响仍将继续。

索 引

（条目后的数字为原书页码，
见本书边码）

A

Ai, Duke 哀公 35
Analects《论语》3—4, 8, 11, 14—15
    East Asia, influence in 在东亚的影响 8
    family 家庭 30, 100
    government 政府 40—43
    heaven 天 13—14, 45
    learning 学习 19—22, 80, 91
    Mandate of Heaven (*tianming*) and 天命与 45
    modern-day applications of 在现代的应用 118, 119
    morally superior man 道德君子 18, 22, 25, 42
    opening passage of 开篇段落 17*f*
    rectification of names 正名 57
    ritual (*li*) 礼 13, 22, 25—26, 27—28
    ruler 统治者 34, 39, 43
    true goodness (*ren*) 仁 22—25, 42
    women 妇女 104—105, 108；参见 *Analects for Women*
    Xunzi, comparison with 与《荀子》的比较 50
    Yu Dan on 于丹讲《论语》116
    Zhu Xi and 朱熹与 80—82
Analects for Women《女论语》108, 109, 110

ancestors 祖先
    Chinese culture 中国文化 97, 101—104
    importance in the family 在家庭里的重要性 101, 102*f*, 102—104
    marriage 婚姻 106
    ritual practice 礼 26, 27, 28, 102*f*, 102—104
ancestral rites 祭礼 101—104, 102*f*
"Announcement to the Prince of Kang, The"《尚书·康诰》38

B

ba (hegemon, strongman) 霸，见 hegemon
"backing the book," memorization "回课"，记忆 91, 91*f*
Ban Zhao 班昭 105, 107, 108, 110
Beijing Normal University 北京师范大学 116
Beijing Olympic Committee 北京奥林匹克委员会 116
Beijing University 北京大学 114, 116
Bible《圣经》48, 81
Book of Changes《易经》4, 6, 81
Book of Filial Piety《孝经》105, 108
Book of History《尚书》4, 5, 6, 10, 13, 20, 38, 44—47, 60, 81
Book of Odes《诗经》4, 5, 6, 10, 13, 20, 29, 38, 46—47
Book of Poetry《诗经》60, 81, 105
Book of Rites《礼记》4, 5, 6, 25, 26, 27, 28, 30—31, 81, 101
Bo Yi 伯夷 11
Buddhism 佛教 8, 71, 84, 104

C

capping 冠礼 26, 103
Cemetery of Confucius 孔林 117
cheating techniques 作弊技巧, 见 civil service examination
Chen Duxiu 陈独秀 112, 113, 114
Cheng, King 成王 45
Cheng Hao 程颢 72
Cheng Yi 程颐 72
Chiang Kai-shek 蒋介石 114—115
Chinese Communist Party (CCP) 中国共产党 114, 115
Chosŏn dynasty 朝鲜王朝 8
Christianity 基督教 48, 101
civil service examination 科举
    "backing the book," memorization "回课", 记忆 91
    cheating techniques 作弊技巧 94—95, 94f
    compound in Canton 广州科场 93f
    jinshi status 进士出身 92, 93
    juren status 举人出身 92
    objections to system 对制度的反对意见 95—96
    shengyuan status 生员出身 92
    and the state 与国家 88—89
    system 制度 90—96
Cixi, Empress Dowager 慈禧太后 105
Communist Party of China 中国共产党 114, 115
Confucian Classics 儒家经典 7, 8, 16, 72, 80, 94f
"Confucian Way for women" (*fudao*) 妇道 108
Confucianism 儒家思想
    assumptions 假设 12—13
    and common people 与平民 96—98
    East Asia, influence in 在东亚的影响 7—9
    empathy 恕 23—24
    family 家庭 29—32, 100—104
    government 政府 33—44
    hierarchial ranking of occupations 职业等级排序 88—89
    institutionalization of 制度化 88—89
    learning 学习 10—12, 19—22, 59—61
    Mencian 孟子的 49—58, 65—66, 68—69
    music 音乐 20, 28—29, 38, 60
    Neo-Confucianism, comparison with 与理学的比较 70—71, 73—77, 80, 82—85
    rectification of names 正名 57
    rise in China 在中国的兴起 4—7
    ritual (*li*) 礼 4, 8, 10, 13, 16, 22—23, 25—29, 30, 31, 36—39, 51—52, 61—62
    rulers 统治者 33—47, 54—58, 64—65, 98—100
    self-cultivation 修身 18—32, 51—54, 58—62
    state orthodoxy 国家的正统 88—89
    true goodness (*ren*) 仁 22—25, 42, 51—54, 58, 63, 64, 65—66
    varieties of 各种变体 48—49
    Western religions, comparison with 与西方宗教的比较 13, 48, 88, 101—104
    women 妇女 104—111
    Xunzi 荀子 49—50, 58—65, 66—69

Confucius 孔子 70, 85
    Analects《论语》3—4, 14—15, 17f
    learning 学习 10—12, 19—22
    portrait of, Tang dynasty 唐代的画像 2f
    ritual (*li*) 礼 25—29
    self-cultivation 修身 18—32
    true goodness (*ren*) 仁 22—25, 42
    vision 理想 10—14, 49
Cultures of East and West and Their Philosophies, The (Liang Shuming)《东西文化及其哲学》(梁漱溟) 114

D

Dao 道, 见 Way
Daodejing, Daoist classic 道教经典《道德经》14
Daoism 道教 6, 14, 39, 84, 104
daoxue (Learning of the Way) 道学 70
Daxue (*Great Learning*)《大学》, 见 *Great Learning*
de (inner virtue) 德, 见 inner virtue
Deng Xiaoping 邓小平 115
"Diary of a Madman" (Lu Xun)《狂人日记》(鲁迅) 113
"divine right of kings" "君权神授" 47
dushufa (hermeneutics) 读书法 (解经原则) 82, 83

E

education 教育; 参见 learning
    children by mothers 母亲对儿女 108—109
    civil service examination system 科举制度 90—96; 参见 civil service examination
    classroom, nineteenth century 19 世纪的课堂 91f
    of common people 普通人 96—97
    women 妇女 105—106
    Zhu Xi's program of learning 朱熹的学习计划 80—84
"Erudites of the Five Classics" "五经博士" 6
examination 考试, 见 civil service examination
examination compound, Canton 广州科场 93f

F

family 家庭
    altar 牌位 102f, 104
    ancestors 祖先 101—104, 102f
    Confucianism and 儒家思想与 29—32, 100—104
    in-law families 姻亲家庭 106—108
    marriage 婚姻 106—110
    moral cultivation of the individual, role in 在个人道德修养中的作用 29—32
    mothers 母亲 90—91, 106, 108, 109f
    women 妇女 90—91, 104—111, 109f
Family Rituals (Zhu Xi)《家礼》(朱熹) 101
filial piety 孝

and common people 与普通人 96

Confucian vs. Chinese 儒家与中国人 97—98

family 家庭 30—31

filial son, painting of (Li Gonglin) 孝子图（李公麟）29f

Mencius《孟子》55, 101

ritual practice 礼 23, 29f

Five Classics "五经" 4, 6—7, 81—83, 85, 88, 90, 95

five relationships 五伦 16, 26

Four Books "四书" 81—83, 85, 90, 92, 95,

"four shoots" of true goodness, righteousness, propriety, and wisdom 仁、义、礼、智 "四端" 52

fudao 妇道，见 "Confucian Way for women"

G

Gao Yao 皋陶 39

Gaozong (Tang emperor) 唐高宗 105

Gaozu (Han emperor) 汉高祖 5, 6

Gate of Heavenly Peace (Tiananmen) 天安门 115

God 上帝 13, 47, 101—102, 103

goodness (in man)（人之）善，见 true goodness (*ren*)

government 政府

    laws and punishments, role in governing 法律和惩罚在治理中的作用 6, 36—37, 38—39

Mandate of Heaven 天命 44—47

official caring for people, woodblock print of 官员关怀民众的福祉，木刻版画 41f

officials, characteristics of 官员的特点 40—42

recruiting civil officials 招募文官 89 (参见 civil service examination)

ruler as exemplar 作为典范的统治者 33—39, 40, 56

taxation 税赋 43

and the well-being of the people 与民众的福祉 39, 40, 42—44, 54—56

Great Learning (*Daxue*)《大学》16, 77—78, 81, 85, 86, 91

Guangxu emperor 光绪帝 105

Guan Zhong 管仲 11

H

Han dynasty 汉朝 5, 6, 9, 88, 105

heaven (*tian*) 天 13—14, 65—67

He Yan 何晏 40

hegemon (*ba*) 霸 65

Huan of Qi, Duke 齐桓公 11

Huan Tui 桓魋 14

Hui of Liang, King 梁惠王 56

human nature 人性

    Mencius on 孟子论 51—54

    Xunzi on 荀子论 58—62

    Zhu Xi on 朱熹论 76—77

human realm 人间 13

hundred schools of thought 诸子百家 5

Hu Shi 胡适 112

I

Imperial Academy 太学 6, 88
in-law families 婆家 106—108
inner virtue (*de*) 德 33
Islam 伊斯兰教 48, 101

J

Japan 日本 7, 8—9, 86
Jiang Jieshi 蒋介石, 见 Chiang Kai-shek
Jie, King 桀王 57, 67—68
Ji Kangzi 季康子 33, 34, 35
Jin dynasty 金朝 71
jinshi ("presented scholar" degree) 进士 92, 93
Judaism 犹太教 48, 101
junzi (superior man) 君子, 见 superior man (*junzi*)
Jurchen tribe 女真部落 71
juren (degree status) 举人 92

K

Koguryŏ, Korean kingdom 朝鲜高句丽王国 8
Korea 朝鲜 7, 8, 9, 86
Koryŏ kings 高丽国王 8

L

laws 法律, 见 government
learning 学习 19—22, 59—61, 77—84
"Learning of the Way" "道学", 见 Neo-Confucianism
Legalism 法家 6
Lessons for Women (Ban Zhao)《女诫》(班昭) 105, 107, 108, 110
li (principle) 理, 见 principle (*li*)
li (ritual) 礼, 见 ritual (*li*)
Liang Shuming 梁漱溟 114
Li Dazhao 李大钊 114
Li Gonglin 李公麟 29f
Liu Bang 刘邦 5
Liuxia Hui 柳下惠 11
li yi fen shu ("principle is one, its manifestations are many") 理一分殊, 见 "principle is one ..."
lizhi (to establish or fix the will) 立志 80
Lu Jia 陆贾 5—6
Lunyu《论语》, 见 *Analects*
Lu Xun 鲁迅 113

M

Maintaining Perfect Balance《中庸》81, 91
Manchus 满族人 47
Mandate of Heaven (*tianming*) 天命 44—47
Mao Zedong 毛泽东 115
marriage 婚姻, 见 women
Marxism 马克思主义 112, 114, 120
Marxism-Leninism 马列主义 120
May Fourth movement 五四运动 112, 114

Mencius 孟子 5, 49—50, 101
  "four shoots" of true goodness, righteousness, propriety, and wisdom 仁、义、礼、智"四端" 52
  Heaven 天 65—66
  human nature and self-cultivation 人性与修身 50, 51—54
  and Neo-Confucianism 与理学 70, 73, 75, 77, 79, 84—85
  Ox Mountain story 牛山的故事 53—54
  popular revolution 人民革命 57—58
  rectifcation of names 正名 57
  rulers 统治者 54—58
  Xunzi Confucianism, comparison with 与荀子的儒家思想的比较 50—51, 58—61, 65—66, 68—69
Mencius《孟子》16, 49—50, 66, 81, 91, 101, 105, 108
merchants, social class 商人，社会阶级 88—89
metaphysics(Neo-Confucianism) 形而上学(理学) 70, 73—77
Ming Dynasty 明朝 86, 99—100
moral principle 礼, 见 principle (*li*)
mothers 母亲, 见 women
music, rituals 礼乐 28—29
"Mysterious Learning" (*xuanxue*) "玄学" 84

N

Nationalist Party 国民党 114—115
Neo-Confucianism 理学

(classical) Confucianism, comparison with 与(经典)儒家思想的比较 70—71, 73—77, 79, 80, 82—85
  emergence of 兴起 71—72
  metaphysics 形而上 70, 73—77
  principle (*li*) 理 75—76, 77, 78—80, 83—84
  qi (material force, matter-energy, vital energy, psychophysical stuff) 气 73—77
  "neo" in "新" 84—85
  self-cultivation 修身 77—80, 82
  Zhu Xi 朱熹, 见 Zhu Xi
  after Zhu Xi 朱熹之后 85—86
  Zhu Xi's program of learning 朱熹的学习计划 80—84
New Life movement "新生活"运动 115
non-action (*wuwei*), ruling by 无为而治 39

O

officials 官员, 见 government
Ox Mountain story, Mencius 孟子的牛山故事 53—54

P

People's Republic of China (PRC) 中华人民共和国 115
Plato 柏拉图 10
politics 政治, 见 government
principle (*li*) 理 75—76, 77, 78—80, 83—84
"principle is one, its manifestations are many" (*li yi fen shu*) 理一分殊 75

Q

qi (material force, matter-energy, vital energy, psychophysical stuff) 气 73—77

Qing dynasty 清朝 47, 105

Qu Boyu 蘧伯玉 42

Qufu Normal University 曲阜师范大学 116

R

Ran Qiu 冉求 43

realm of heaven and earth 天地间 13

Records of the Historian (Sima Qian) 《史记》(司马迁) 5

ren (true goodness) 仁, 见 true goodness (*ren*)

Renmin University 人民大学 116

Republic (Plato) 《理想国》(柏拉图) 10

ritual (*li*) 礼
    ancestors 祖先 26, 27, 28, 101—104, 102f
    Book of Rites 《礼记》 4, 5, 6, 25, 26, 27, 28, 30—31, 81, 101
    dress 服装 26—27
    eating 用餐 27
    government 政府 38—39
    learning and, in shaping nature 学习与礼在塑造天性上的作用 59—62
    mourning 哀悼 26, 27
    music 音乐 28—29
    in self-cultivation 修身中 25—28
    and true goodness (*ren*) 与仁 22—23, 27

rulers 统治者

Confucian ideas, receptiveness to 对儒家思想的接受 1, 3, 5—7, 13—14, 42
    in Confucianism 儒家思想中 4, 11, 33—47, 54—58, 64—65, 98—100
    Mandate of Heaven (*tianming*) 天命 44—47
    as moral exemplars 作为道德的典范 33—39, 56
    and the well-being of the people 与民众的福祉 54—56

Russian Revolution of 1917 1917 年俄国革命 114

S

Sage 圣人, 见 Confucius

School 学派, 见 education; learning

self-cultivation 修身
    Confucius on 孔子论 18—32
    family, role in 在家庭中的作用 29—32
    learning, role in 在学习中的作用 19—22, 59—61, 77—84
    Mencius on 孟子论 51—54
    moral perfectibility 道德完善 22, 50—51, 54, 63—64, 105
    ritual (*li*), role in 在礼中的作用 22—23, 25—29, 61—62
    and the superior man (*junzi*) 与君子 18, 19, 21, 24, 30, 40
    Wang Yangming 王阳明 85—86
    women 妇女 105
    Xunzi on 荀子论 58—64
    Zhu Xi on 朱熹论 77—84

self-realization 自我实现 33, 72, 82, 86;

参见 self-cultivation
Seventeen Article Constitution《十七条宪法》8
Shaanxi Normal University 陕西师范大学 116
Shandong University 山东大学 116
Shang dynasty 商朝 44—47, 57, 98
shengyuan candidates 生员考生 92
Shintō 神道教 8, 9
Shôtoku, Prince 圣德太子 8
Shun, sage-king 圣王舜 11, 28, 39, 67
Silla kingdom 新罗王国 8
Sima Qian 司马迁 5, 6
small man (*xiaoren*) 小人 18, 38, 104
Song dynasty 宋朝 71—72
Spring and Autumn Annals《春秋》4, 6, 60, 81
Spring and Autumn period 春秋时期 4, 5
Sui dynasty 隋朝 90
superior man (*junzi*) 君子 18
   and family 与家庭 28—32
   in government 政府里 40, 42
   learning and 学习与 19—21
   ritual practice and 礼与 22—23, 25—29
   as virtuous ruler 作为贤德的统治者 36—37

T

Taizu (Ming emperor) 明太祖 99—100
Tang dynasty 唐朝 2f, 90, 95, 105
Thirteen Classics 十三经 81
Three Character Classic (Confucian primer)《三字经》(儒家启蒙读本) 91
Three Dynasties 三国 60
tian (heaven) 天, 见 heaven
tianming (Mandate of Heaven) 天命, 见 Mandate of Heaven
Tianqi emperor 天启帝 100
Tokugawa period 德川时代 8—9
Tongzhi emperor 同治帝 105
true goodness (*ren*) 仁
   Confucius on 孔子论 22—25, 42
   Mencius on 孟子论 51—54, 65—66
   Xunzi on 荀子论 58, 63, 64
   Zhu Xi on 朱熹论 73, 76

V

Vietnam 越南 9
vision of Confucius 孔子的理想 10—14, 49

W

Wang Yangming 王阳明 85—86
Warring States period 战国时期 4, 5
Way (Dao) 道
   Confucius 孔子 18, 22, 24, 25, 26, 34
   Daoist 道家 14
   women 妇女 (见 "Confucian Way for women")
   Xunzi 荀子 60—61
   Zhu Xi 朱熹 72, 77—78, 79, 81, 83
Wei Zongxian 魏忠贤 100
Wen, King 文王 11, 46—47
wind-grass metaphor 风与草的比喻

34, 35
women 妇女
   Confucianism and 儒家学说与 104—111
   education 教育 105—106
   educating children 教育儿童 108—109, 109f
   managing household 持家 109—110
   marriage 婚姻 106—110
Wu, Empress 武后 105
Wu, King 武王 11, 44, 57
Wu (Han emperor) 汉武帝 6, 88
wuwei (non-action), ruling by 无为而治，见 non-action, ruling by

X

Xia dynasty 夏朝 57
xiaoren (small man) 小人，见 small man
Xinyu (Lu Jia)《新语》(陆贾) 6
Xuan of Qi, King 齐宣王 57
xuanxue (Mysterious Learning) 玄学，见 Mysterious Learning
Xunzi 荀子 5, 50
   human nature and self-cultivation 人性与修身 58—64
   man and heaven 人与天 65—69
   Mencian Confucianism, comparison with 与孟子的儒家思想的比较 50—51, 58—61, 65—66, 68—69
   moral perfectibility 道德完善 63—64
   Neo-Confucianism, comparison with 与理学的比较 73, 84—85
   ritual (*li*) 礼 61—62

   on rulers 论统治者 64—65
   true goodness (*ren*) 仁 58, 63, 64
Xunzi《荀子》50, 59

Y

Yan Hui 颜回 14, 21, 24
Yao, sage-king 圣王尧 11, 67
yin and *yang* 阴与阳 67, 68, 73, 74
Youzi 有子 30
Yu, sage-king 圣王禹 11, 44, 63, 67
Yu Dan 于丹 119

Z

Zeng Guofan 曾国藩 111
Zeng Jifen 曾纪芬 111
Zengzi 曾子 24
Zhang Zai 张载 72, 73—74
zhi (will) 志 20, 80
Zhou, Duke of 周公 11, 45, 47
Zhou, King 周王 44—45, 57
Zhou Dunyi 周敦颐 72, 74
Zhou dynasty 周朝 1, 4, 10—12, 13, 14, 18, 26, 38, 44—47
Zhu Xi 朱熹 72, 90; 参见 Neo-Confucianism
   human nature 人性 76—77
   intelligence 智慧 79
   metaphysics 形而上 70, 73—77
   program of learning 学习计划 80—84
   self-cultivation 修身 77—84
   true goodness (*ren*) 仁 73, 76
Zigong 子贡 3, 20, 21, 23, 36, 42
Ziyou 子游 31

索引

Daniel K. Gardner

CONFUCIANISM

A Very Short Introduction

Acknowledgments

My sincerest thanks go to Cynthia Brokaw of Brown University. She listened attentively to my ideas, read drafts of chapters, and urged me forward when I was dragging. Every writer should be so fortunate to have a colleague—and friend—like her.

Cynthia Read, my editor at Oxford University Press, and her assistant, Charlotte Steinhardt, were unfailingly supportive of this project from the start. Anonymous readers for the Press provided especially thoughtful and thorough reviews of the manuscript. This book owes much to their professional generosity. Kristina Johnson assisted in the final stages of the editing process. I am thankful for her sharp set of eyes and sound judgment.

Contents

List of illustrations ii

Chronology iii

1 Confucius (551–479 BCE) and his legacy: An introduction 1

2 The individual and self-cultivation in the teachings of Confucius 16

3 Government in Confucian teachings 33

4 Variety within early Confucianism 48

5 The reorientation of the Confucian tradition after 1000 CE: The teachings of Neo-Confucianism 70

6 Confucianism in practice 87

Epilogue: Confucianism in the twentieth and twenty-first centuries 112

References 119

Further reading 123

List of illustrations

1. A portrait of Confucius **2**
   Werner Forman Archive/The Bridgeman Art Library

2. The opening passage of the *Analects* **17**
   Author's collection

3. A painting of a filial son **29**
   The Art Archive at Art Resource, NY

4. A dutiful Confucian official **41**
   Author's collection

5. A nineteenth-century Chinese classroom **91**
   © The British Library Board, 2354.f.1

6. The examination compound in Canton in ca. 1873 **93**
   Reprinted courtesy of the Library of Congress

7. An examination "cheat shirt" **94**
   Courtesy of The East Asian Library and The Gest Collection, Princeton University. Photograph by Heather Larkin, 2004

8. A family pays respect to ancestors **102**
   © Bettmann/Corbis

9. A Chinese mother teaches her son to write **109**
   Author's collection

Chronology

Shang Dynasty, ca. 1600 BCE–ca. 1045 BCE
Zhou Dynasty, ca. 1045 BCE–ca. 256 BCE
   Western Zhou, ca. 1046 BCE–771 BCE
      King Wen *(11th c. BCE)*
      King Wu *(11th c. BCE)*
      Duke of Zhou *(11th c. BCE)*
   Eastern Zhou, 771 BCE–256 BCE
     Spring and Autumn Period, 722–481 BCE
      Confucius (551 BCE–479 BCE)
     Warring States Period, 403 BCE–221 BCE
      Mencius (4th c. BCE)
      Xunzi (3rd c. BCE)
Qin Dynasty, 221 BCE–206 BCE
Han Dynasty, 206 BCE–220 CE
   Western Han, 206 BCE–9 CE
      Confucianism established as state teaching under Emperor Wu (r. 141 BCE–87 BCE)
   Wang Mang interregnum, 9–23
   Eastern Han, 25–220
Six Dynasties, 220–589
Sui Dynasty, 581–618
      Civil service examinations implemented countrywide
Tang Dynasty, 618–907
Five Dynasties, 907–60
Song Dynasty, 960–1279
   Northern Song, 960–1127

Major Neo-Confucian thinkers:
  Zhou Dunyi (1017–73)
  Zhang Zai (1020–77)
  Cheng Hao (1032–85)
  Cheng Yi (1033–1107)
Southern Song, 1127–1279
  Neo-Confucian synthesis:
    Zhu Xi (1130–1200)
Yuan Dynasty, 1279–1368
Ming Dynasty, 1368–1644
  Wang Yangming (1472–1522) School of Neo-Confucianism
Qing Dynasty, 1644–1912
  Civil service examinations system abolished (1905)

Chapter 1
Confucius (551–479 BCE) and his legacy: An introduction

Confucius (孔子) lived in the sixth century BCE. Given a choice, however, he would have preferred to live five hundred years earlier, at the dawn of the Zhou dynasty (1045?–221 BCE). It was, he imagined, a golden age, a time when rulers governed through moral example, people practiced time-honored rituals, and social harmony prevailed throughout the land. Much had changed since. No longer was China unified under a virtuous and powerful Zhou king. By 700 BCE the country had splintered into small, independent, and often warring states, ruled over by feudal lords whose authority was maintained not through moral behavior and genuine concern for the welfare of the people but through laws, punishments, and force.

Confucius's preoccupation with the early Zhou was lifelong. If good government, proper social relations, and respectful treatment of one's fellow human beings—all expressed through correct ritual performance—had prevailed then, he was confident that they could be made to prevail again in his own lifetime. To that end, he traveled from one feudal state to another, hoping to find a receptive ruler who, sharing his views, would appoint him to a position of authority where he could put his sociopolitical vision into practice. But his travels were in vain; he never won meaningful employment.

1. A Tang dynasty (618–907) portrait of Confucius carved on a stone stele

Rulers of the day apparently found his ideas impracticable. After all, warfare among the competing states was constant in the sixth century; the message that governing by moral example could triumph in the face of tens of thousands of enemy troops stationed at the borders probably held little persuasive power. It is likely, too, that the Master's personality did not readily win over the feudal rulers. As his teachings in the *Analects* indicate, he could at times be complimentary, sympathetic, tolerant of mistakes, and humorous, but he would often be critical, uncompromising, sarcastic, and harsh.

Confucius, however, never entirely gave up the hope that some ruler somewhere would appreciate the true value of his political teachings. His disciple Zigong once asked, "'If you possessed a piece of beautiful jade, would you hide it away in a locked box, or would you try to sell it at a good price?' The Master [as he is known] responded, 'Oh, I would sell it! I would sell it! I am just waiting for the right offer'" (9.13). Forever disappointed that the right offer never came, Confucius turned his life's work from politics to the teaching of his disciples, men he hoped would embrace his political ideals and go on to succeed in official life where he himself had failed. Traditional accounts put the number of Confucius's serious disciples at seventy-two.

It is a tribute not only to his success as a teacher but, equally, to the dedication of his disciples and later generations of followers that his name holds the place in history that it does. For it is their records of Confucius's sayings and conversations that form the basis of the *Lunyu* (論語), the *Analects*, our main source for Confucius's thought. A text in twenty brief, so-called books—we might understand them better as chapters—totaling roughly five hundred passages or "verses," the *Analects* is a collection of the Master's teachings as recorded by his disciples and edited over the course of generations. It was only in the second century BCE, three centuries after Confucius's death, that the text of the *Analects* achieved its present form.

Any study of the thought of Confucius should begin with this relatively short text. But Confucius came to be closely associated with other early texts in the Chinese tradition as well, especially the *Book of Changes*, the *Book of Odes*, the *Book of History*, the *Book of Rites*, and the *Spring and Autumn Annals*. Beginning in the second century BCE, the Master's followers would claim that Confucius had a role in writing, editing, or compiling each of these five texts (all compiled sometime between roughly 1000 BCE and 200 BCE). Although this claim has not stood up under critical scrutiny, these texts, known as the Five Classics, have been regarded as canonical in the Confucian tradition ever since. Confucians revere them as works that convey principles of sage government, descriptions of proper ritual practice, beliefs about the organization of the cosmos and humankind's relationship to it, and lessons from the history of the Spring and Autumn period (722–481 BCE), perfectly in accord with the Master's teachings.

The rise of Confucianism in China

To say that Confucius gathered around him a group of devoted disciples is not to say that his teachings won universal acclaim immediately. In the highly unstable centuries of the Zhou dynasty known as the Spring and Autumn era and the Warring States period (403–221 BCE), many thinkers, with a wide range of agendas, rose to address the urgent problems of the day. The teachings of Daoists, Legalists, Yin-Yang cosmologists, Diplomatists, Military Strategists, Agriculturalists, Moists (followers of Mozi), and Logicians, among others, all asked: What makes for an effective ruler? What makes for an effective government? What is the ideal relationship between the government and the people? How can China achieve the unity, stability, and prosperity it once knew? What are the responsibilities of the individual, to his family, his community, his state? What is man's place in the cosmos?

Of course, not every thinker gave equal weight to all of these matters. But these were the general concerns that preoccupied what have come to be known as the "hundred schools of thought" that flourished during the Spring and Autumn era and the Warring States period. Vigorous intellectual debate marked these centuries, as thinkers representing the different schools vied to persuade rulers and the intelligentsia of the rightness of their respective teachings. Although Confucianism had especially lively and prominent representatives during these centuries, most notably Mencius (孟子) (fourth c. BCE) and Xunzi (荀子) (third c. BCE), we need to be reminded that Confucian teachings were not yet strongly favored over the teachings of any other thinkers.

That would change by the second century BCE, as Han (202 BC–222 CE) rulers lent increasing support to Confucian teachings. At the dynasty's outset, however, the prospects for these teachings did not appear bright. The Han founder, Liu Bang, was contemptuous of Confucianism. The *Records of the Historian*, written in the first century BCE by Sima Qian, describes the future ruler's early hostility toward the learning of Confucians: "Whenever a visitor wearing a Confucian hat comes to see him, he immediately snatches the hat from the visitor's head and pisses in it, and when he talks to other people, he always curses them up and down."

Having established the Han dynasty, however, Liu Bang (now Emperor Gaozu, r. 202–195 BCE) eventually found it expedient to soften his attitude. In meetings with his principal advisor, Lu Jia, Lu repeatedly urged him to look to the Confucian teachings found in the great classical texts, the *Book of Odes* and *Book of History*, for guidance in governance. One day, clearly tiring of Lu's too frequent admonitions, the emperor responded brusquely: "All I possess I have won on horseback! Why should I bother with the *Book of Odes* and *Book of History?*" Persevering, probably at considerable personal risk, Lu answered:

Your Majesty may have won the empire on horseback, but can you rule it on horseback?... Qin [the short-lived dynasty replaced by the Han and notorious for its harshness] entrusted its future solely to punishments and law, without changing with the times, and thus eventually brought about the destruction of its ruling family. If, after it had united the world under its rule [in 221 BCE], Qin had practiced benevolence and righteousness and modeled its ways upon the sages of antiquity, how would Your Majesty ever have been able to win possession of the empire?

Gaozu was sufficiently intrigued that he asked Lu Jia to write a book (*Xinyu*, New Discourses) expanding on these ideas. Sima Qian writes that "as each section was presented to the throne, the emperor never failed to express his delight and approval, and all those about him cried, 'Bravo!'"

But it was not until half a century later, during the long reign of Emperor Wu of the Han (r. 141–87 BCE), that Confucian scholars were able, decisively, to promote the teachings of their school and give Confucianism a privileged status at the court, a status that (with some ups and downs) it held until the early years of the twentieth century. Urged by his ministers to elevate Confucianism and abandon the two other major teachings of the day, Daoism and Legalism, the emperor in 141 BCE decreed that all non-Confucians, especially those with Legalist orientations, be dismissed from office. A few years later, in 136 BCE, he established the institution of the "Erudites of the Five Classics," a group expert in the five texts that scholars of the Confucian school had begun to regard as their canonical works—the *Book of Changes*, the *Book of Odes*, the *Book of History*, the *Book of Rites*, and the *Spring and Autumn Annals*. These erudites served as his advisors, drawing on the teachings and principles in the Five Classics in counseling him. In 124 BCE, these same erudites would become the teaching staff at the newly created Imperial Academy. Students who performed well there—who passed examinations demonstrating expertise in one or more of the Five Classics—would win appointment to the official bureaucracy.

The significance of these steps, which will be taken up in some detail in chapter 6, can hardly be overstated. From this time on, Confucianism served as the essential ideological prop of the imperial Chinese state. Rulers would rely on Confucian teachings for guidance and legitimacy, and recruit their bureaucracy through Confucian-based examinations. And, as a consequence of the ideological dominance of Confucianism in government, education in imperial China would center on mastery of Confucian writings. The great prestige—and economic rewards—associated with government service ensured that those who could afford schooling devoted their efforts to the mastery of those texts that would earn them examination success and thus official position. Boys from the age of six or seven would be expected to devote themselves to the study and memorization of primers incorporating Confucian values and then the Confucian Classics. The result: virtually all literate Chinese, particularly during the millennium leading up to the end of imperial China in 1912, were Confucian-schooled and Confucian-socialized. Thus the lives and work of almost all educated Chinese, not just officials but poets, essayists, novelists, artists, calligraphers, historians, scholars, teachers, and the small percentage of literate women were shaped, to one degree or another, by the beliefs and ideals embodied in Confucian texts.

The influence of Confucianism in East Asia

The influence of Confucianism did not stop at China's borders. Although this short introduction focuses on the role of Confucianism in China, we should appreciate that over the course of the centuries, Korea and Japan would find in Confucianism teachings and ideals that, with adaptation, would speak to their social, political, and spiritual needs.

As early as 372, the Korean kingdom of Koguryŏ set up a Confucian academy where the sons of the nobility would be instructed in the Confucian Classics. A few centuries later (682), the Silla kingdom, following Koguryŏ's precedent, established a national Confucian academy for the training of officials; and in 788 it instituted a rudimentary examination system based on the Confucian classics. Under the Koryŏ (918–1392) kings, the examination system expanded; examinations to recruit officials were held more regularly, and the requirements for them now included not only the Classics themselves but also mastery of Chinese commentary on the Classics.

The growing influence of Confucianism peaked in the Chosŏn dynasty (1362–1910). Urged by Confucian reformers, the founders themselves embarked on the task of creating a model Confucian society by restructuring the value system and social practices inherited from the Koryŏ. They set up a nationwide Confucian-based school system and recruited as officials only those who had succeeded in the examination system, which served as the foundation of the Chosŏn Confucian state.

Korea also played an important role in the transmission of Chinese texts to Japan. Korean scholars began bringing these texts, including the *Analects* of Confucius, to Japan as early as the fifth or sixth century. In 604 Prince Shôtoku issued Japan's first "constitution," the so-called Seventeen Article Constitution. Confucian influence is apparent throughout. Article 1 begins by citing directly from the *Analects* (1.12), "Harmony should be valued," and article 4 exhorts ministers and officials to practice proper ritual behavior (*li*, 禮), reminding them that should they abandon the rites, the people will be disorderly. Throughout much of Japanese history the teachings of Buddhism and Shintō would overshadow those of the Confucian school. But in the Tokugawa period (1603–1868), the Confucian school prospered as never before. Japanese scholars, exposed to strains of

Confucianism that had developed in China between the eleventh and sixteenth centuries (see chap. 5, "The Teachings of Neo-Confucianism"), now opened up academies and schools to instruct others. And they lectured to Tokugawa shoguns, urging them to embrace Confucian teachings, which, they argued, could serve as the moral basis of Japanese government and society.

Although Confucianism was promoted as the state learning by the Tokugawa shoguns, it never quite became the exclusive orthodoxy it had been in Chosŏn Korea or China since the tenth century. It may be that in Japan, where a civil service examination system never developed, there was simply more intellectual freedom and space for Buddhism, Shintō, and other currents of thought to flourish. Still, Confucian teachings enjoyed enormous popularity and success in the Tokugawa period, and did much to reshape Japanese ethics and social relations.

Vietnam, too, felt the influence of Confucianism. In 111 BCE, during the Han dynasty, China annexed the region of northern Vietnam, ruling over it for more than a millennium until 939 CE, when Vietnam finally gained its independence. During these many centuries, Chinese culture—in the form of the Chinese writing system, Confucian texts and rituals, and Chinese-style administration—infiltrated Vietnamese life. As part of the Middle Kingdom, the region was also introduced to the Confucian-based Chinese civil service examination system (see chap. 6, "Confucianism in practice"). Even after winning independence in the tenth century, Vietnamese dynasties continued to rely on Confucian examinations to recruit court officials until the 1910s. The prominence of the examination system ensured that into the twentieth century (1) Confucian texts would be the core of the country's educational curriculum; and (2) the educated and political elite would champion values and practices associated with Confucian teachings.

The vision of Confucius

Confucius imagined a future where social harmony and sage rulership would once again prevail. It was a vision of the future that looked heavily to the past. Convinced that a golden age had been fully realized in China's known history, Confucius thought it necessary to turn to that history, to the political institutions, the social relations, the ideals of personal cultivation that he believed prevailed in the early Zhou period, in order to piece together a vision to serve for all times. Here a comparison with Plato, who lived a few decades after the death of Confucius, is instructive. Like Confucius, Plato was eager to improve on contemporary political and social life. But unlike Confucius, he did not believe that the past offered up a normative model for the present. In constructing his ideal society in the *Republic*, Plato resorted much less to reconstruction of the past than to philosophical reflection and intellectual dialogue with others.

This is not to say, of course, that Confucius did not engage in philosophical reflection and dialogue with others. But it was the past, and learning from it, that especially consumed him. This learning took the form of studying received texts, especially the *Book of Odes* and the *Book of History*. He explains to his disciples: "The *Odes* can be a source of inspiration and a basis for evaluation; they can help you to get on with others and to give proper expression to grievances. In the home, they teach you about how to serve your father, and in public life they teach you about how to serve your lord" (17.9). The frequent references to verses from the *Odes* and to stories and legends from the *History* indicate Confucius's deep admiration for these texts in particular and the values, the ritual practices, the legends, and the institutions recorded in them.

But books were not the sole source of Confucius's knowledge about the past. The oral tradition was a source of instructive ancient lore for him as well. Myths and stories about the legendary sage kings Yao, Shun, and Yu; about Kings Wen and Wu and the Duke of Zhou, who founded the Zhou and inaugurated an age of extraordinary social and political harmony; and about famous or infamous rulers and officials like Bo Yi, Duke Huan of Qi, Guan Zhong, and Liuxia Hui—all mentioned by Confucius in the *Analects*—would have supplemented what he learned from texts and served to provide a fuller picture of the past.

Still another source of knowledge for Confucius, interestingly, was the behavior of his contemporaries. In observing them, he would select out for praise those manners and practices that struck him as consistent with the cultural norms of the early Zhou and for condemnation those that in his view were contributing to the Zhou decline. The *Analects* shows him railing against clever speech, glibness, ingratiating appearances, affectation of respect, servility to authority, courage unaccompanied by a sense of right, and single-minded pursuit of worldly success—behavior he found prevalent among contemporaries and that he identified with the moral deterioration of the Zhou. To reverse such deterioration, people had to learn again to be genuinely respectful in dealing with others, slow in speech and quick in action, trustworthy and true to their word, openly but gently critical of friends, families, and rulers who strayed from the proper path, free of resentment when poor, free of arrogance when rich, and faithful to the sacred three-year mourning period for parents, which to Confucius's great chagrin, had fallen into disuse. In sum, they had to relearn the ritual behavior that had created the harmonious society of the early Zhou.

That Confucius's characterization of the period as a golden age may have been an idealization is irrelevant. Continuity with a "golden age" lent his vision greater authority and legitimacy, and such continuity validated the rites and practices he advocated. This desire for historical authority and legitimacy—during a period of disrupture and chaos—may help to explain Confucius's eagerness to present himself as a mere transmitter, a lover of the ancients (7.1). Indeed, the Master's insistence on mere transmission notwithstanding, there can be little doubt that from his study and reconstruction of the early Zhou period he forged an innovative—and enduring—sociopolitical vision. Still, in his presentation of himself as reliant on the past, nothing but a transmitter of what had been, Confucius established what would become something of a cultural template in China. Grand innovation that broke entirely with the past was not much prized in the pre-modern Chinese tradition. A Jackson Pollack who consciously and proudly rejected artistic precedent, for example, would not be acclaimed the creative genius in China that he was in the West. Great writers, great thinkers, and great artists were considered great precisely because they had mastered the tradition—the best ideas and techniques of the past. They learned to be great by linking themselves to past greats and by fully absorbing their styles and techniques. Of course, mere imitation was hardly sufficient; imitation could never be slavish. One had to add something creative, something entirely of one's own, to mastery of the past.

Thus when you go into a museum gallery to view pre-modern Chinese landscapes, one hanging next to another, they appear at first blush to be quite similar. With closer inspection, however, you find that this artist developed a new sort of brush stroke, and that one a new use of ink-wash, and this one a new style of depicting trees and their vegetation. Now that your eye is becoming trained, more sensitive, it sees the subtle differences in the landscape paintings, with their range of masterful techniques and expression. But even as it sees the differences, it recognizes that the paintings evolved out of a common landscape tradition, in which artists built consciously on the achievements of past masters.

Assumptions behind the vision

In forging his vision of a perfectly harmonious society and sage government, Confucius brought with him, as all major thinkers do, a set of assumptions—a worldview that he had been born into and that did much to condition his vision. At its core, Confucius believed, the universe comprised two realms: the human realm and the realm of heaven and earth (the natural realm). In contrast to the human realm, where he assumed order must be actively created and nurtured by human agency (through the practice of ritual), the realm of heaven and earth has an inherent rhythm and harmony that maintain—spontaneously—a perfect balance among its parts. A sort of organic interconnectedness of all being exists. Indeed, one important function of ritual practice in the *Analects* is to ensure that human activity and activity in the realm of heaven and earth are mutually responsive and sustaining.

Thus in Confucius's cosmological outlook, there is no God—that is, there is no monotheistic creator deity, nor any being or entity responsible for the creation of the universe or for its ongoing operation. The cosmos operates on its own, automatically, as it were, and so it has since the beginning of time. It is not that a spirit world populated by nature deities and ancestors does not exist for Confucius and his contemporaries; various spirits could assist human beings in controlling rivers and fields, villages and cities, and families and lineages. But there is no ultimate, omnipotent spirit or deity responsible for the creation of all that is and was. In fact, nowhere in the indigenous Chinese tradition is there textual or archaeological evidence of a belief in what might be called a creator deity. The contrast here with dominant Western monotheistic beliefs is sufficiently striking that some scholars speak about a "cosmological gulf" separating Chinese civilization from Western civilization.

While there is no God or monotheistic creator deity in the *Analects*, the text does make reference to *tian* (天), a concept appearing earlier in the *Book of History* and *Book of Odes*, where, most scholars believe, it refers to a sort of sky-god or a deified ancestor of the Zhou people. The term has come to be conventionally translated as "heaven." The Master, in remarks to disciples, speaks of this *tian* or heaven as understanding him, as recognizing his special qualities—even as rulers of his day might not (14.35); as protecting him when he is briefly imprisoned by the men of Kuang (9.5) and again when Huan Tui attempts to assassinate him (7.23); and as abandoning him when his favorite disciple, Yan Hui, dies (11.9). Thus in most of its appearances in the *Analects*, heaven, although not the all-powerful creator God we find in the West, is an entity possessed of a consciousness and invested in the affairs of the human world. That this heaven can also offer moral guidance to man is clear in 2.4, where the Master comments that at the age of fifty he had finally come to understand "heaven's decree."

The cosmos, Confucius thus assumed, operated of its own, effortlessly achieving a balanced (and moral) harmony among its parts. It was the human realm that needed active regulation. Politics and morality had by his time fallen into a wretched state. The normative sociopolitical order of the early Zhou—what Confucius and his followers called the Dao (道) or Way—had given way to chaos and disorder. Daoists also speak of the Dao or Way, but Confucians and Daoists imbue the term with different meanings. For Daoists, the Way is much grander than the sociopolitical order; indeed, for them it subsumes the sociopolitical order—even heaven and earth. The first chapter of the Daoist classic, the *Daodejing*, refers to it as "the mother of all things." But, although the good order no longer prevailed, it was Confucius's deepest hope and fervent belief that it could be made to prevail again. The Way, he assumed, could be restored, but the restoration project would require the effort of good and righteous men.

Conclusion: Reading the *Analects of Confucius*

Reading the *Analects* for the first time can be challenging, as there is no apparent surface logic to it. After all, the *Analects* is not a sustained text the Master put to writing in his study but rather a collection of his sayings edited over generations by others. The reader thus can find a comment by Confucius on ruling by virtue followed by one about how a child should behave toward his parents, which in turn can be followed by one that speaks to the equal importance of studying and thinking. But, however disparate-seeming they may be, I would suggest that all five hundred or so passages, directly or indirectly, address one of two concerns: (1) what makes for a good man; and (2) what makes for good government. These are for Confucius inseparable matters. Government can be good, as he understands "good," only if good people serve in it. At the same time, it is government by virtue and moral example that leads those it governs to goodness and harmonious human relations. If the reader keeps in mind these two overarching, related concerns—what makes for a good person and what makes for a good government—the coherence underlying the text and the Master's teachings should become clear.

Chapter 2
The individual and self-cultivation in the teachings of Confucius

> There is a common saying among the people: "The empire, the state, and the family": the foundation of the empire lies with the state; the foundation of the state lies with the family; the foundation of the family lies with the person.
> (*Mencius* 4A.5)

A moral vanguard of individuals is called for by Confucius and his followers. These individuals move others to proper behavior through the power of their example. By practicing the rituals and respecting the mutual responsibilities required to sustain the so-called five relationships—father–son, ruler–subject, husband–wife, older brother–younger brother, and friend–friend—they provide a model for those around them to follow and thereby bring harmony to family, community, and empire.

The prominent role played by the individual in creating the good sociopolitical order explains why Confucian teachings, throughout the ages, give such profound attention to the process of self-cultivation. Each and every human being is urged to engage in a process of moral refinement, as each and every human being has the capability to exercise a beneficial moral force over others. The *Great Learning*, one of the Confucian classics, puts it straightforwardly: "From the Son of Heaven on down to

論語卷之一　　　朱熹集註

學而第一 此篇乃入書之首篇故所記多務本之意乃入道之門積德之基學者先務也凡十六章

子曰學而時習之不亦說乎 說悅同○學之為言效也人性皆善而覺有先後後覺者必效先覺之所為乃可以明善而復其初也習鳥數飛也學之不已如鳥數飛也說喜意也既學而又時時習之則所學者熟而中心喜說其進自不能已矣又程子曰學者將以行之也時習之則所學者在我故說○謝氏曰學者將以行之也時習之則所學者無時而不習坐如尸坐時習也立如齊立時習也

有朋自遠方來不亦樂乎 樂音洛○朋同類也自遠方來則近者可知又曰程子曰說在心樂主發散在外

人不知而不慍不亦君子乎 慍紆問反○慍含怒意君子成德之名尹氏曰學在己知不知在人

commoners, all without exception should regard self-cultivation as the root." Confucian teachings, then, oblige all followers, irrespective of social, political, and economic status, to take self-cultivation as the starting point in their pursuit of the true Way. It is the basis, "the root" of the devoted Confucian's endeavor to regenerate civility, harmony, and ritual elegance in Chinese society.

The goal for the individual in undertaking the self-cultivation process is to become a *junzi* (君子). *Junzi* is a term that by Confucius's time already had a long history. Made up of two characters, it meant literally, "ruler's son," and referred traditionally to the aristocratic nobility of the Zhou. To be a *junzi* was to be born into the sociopolitical elite; it was a hereditary status, a matter of bloodline. Confucius appropriated the term, giving it a decidedly new twist. In his usage, it came to refer to a person of moral—not sociopolitical—nobility. A *junzi* for Confucius is the *morally* superior person who, by according with the ritual code of the tradition, treats others with respect and dignity, and pursues virtues like humility, sincerity, trustworthiness, righteousness, and compassion.

Throughout the *Analects*, Confucius contrasts this morally superior man with the *xiaoren* (小人), "small man." The small man is one who does not abide by the conventions of decorum and does not choose to follow the moral path. He is *morally* small. On one occasion Confucius baldly distinguishes between the two: "The Master said, 'The superior man [*junzi*] understands righteousness; the small man [*xiaoren*] understands profit'" (4.16). An important shift is taking place in the *Analects* with Confucius's recharacterization of the *junzi*. Whereas earlier a person could not strive to become a *junzi*—one was born into *junzi* status or not—now anyone, at least theoretically, could attain the status through successful self-cultivation. Here Confucius lays down a novel challenge to his contemporaries: through effort, any one of you can *become* a noble person.

The role of learning

Foundational to the self-cultivation process, to becoming a *junzi*, is learning. This perhaps explains why the very opening line of the *Analects* exclaims, "The Master said, 'To learn something and rehearse it constantly, is this indeed not a pleasure?'" (1.1). In comments scattered throughout the rest of the *Analects,* Confucius remarks autobiographically that if there is anything that differentiates him from others it is simply his fondness for learning: "The Master said, 'In a hamlet of ten households, there are sure to be those who in loyalty and trustworthiness are my equal, but none who are my equal in love of learning'" (5.28). This devotion to learning is precisely what separates him from others and makes him a moral example for them.

Consistent with his view that anyone could become a *junzi*, Confucius argues that learning should be open to all. There are to be no social or economic barriers: "In instruction there are to be no distinctions of status" (15.39). Of his own teaching he remarks: "Never have I refused instruction to one who of his own accord comes to me, though it be with as little as a bundle of dried meat." It is the Master's conviction that any person possessed of a genuine eagerness to learn, regardless of status, can hope to improve morally, even to attain "superior man" status.

Scholars have been quick—and right—to point out that while Confucius may have advocated that learning be open to all, in practice few people in his day could have entertained the prospect of receiving the sort of education he proposed. It was simply too costly for much of the Chinese population, most of whom were peasants living close to subsistence. Few families could afford to give up a son's pair of hands around the family plot; if they could, they would next be obliged to pay for supplies—brushes, ink, paper, and texts available at that time only in editions written out laboriously by hand at considerable expense; finally, since education was not sponsored by the state, merely becoming literate typically necessitated the services of a teacher, who required "gifts" or payments from each pupil to support himself.

The Master's willingness to teach anyone who presents himself requires one important qualification: the student has to be genuinely determined (*zhi*, 志) to learn. In thinking back on his own moral trajectory, Confucius marks the starting point of his quest for moral perfection at the age of fifteen when he tells his disciples, "I set (*zhi*) my mind-and-heart on learning." For Confucius to take on a student he must sense a similar passion and commitment: "Those not excited I do not instruct; those not eager I do not enlighten. If I raise up one corner and they do not come back with three corners, I do not continue" (7.8). Confucius presumably is drawing on his own experience. Learning, he knows, can be difficult and the path long. Success demands desire and perseverance. It also demands true engagement and intellectual initiative.

Learning, for Confucius, is learning about the past, about the ancients and their ritual practices, their music, their social and political institutions, and their normative relationships. This past is a reservoir of historical experience in which the "empirical data" for what makes a good order—and what does not—can be found. Because he himself has been so inspired, so deeply affected, by the *Book of History* and the *Book of Odes* in particular, Confucius makes them the basis of his instruction, urging his disciples to read them with the utmost care (e.g., 1.15, 2.2, 2.21, 14.40, 16.13, 17.9, 17.10).

Learning, Confucius cautions, must never become simply a matter of accumulating knowledge: "The Master said, 'Si [disciple Zigong], you think I am the kind of person who learns many things and remembers them, do you not?' He replied, 'Yes, I do. Is that not the case?' The Master replied, 'No, it is not the case. I have one thread that runs through it all'"(15.3). Learning about rituals, music, institutions, proper relationships, and history can easily produce nothing but a list of details and facts. One needs a comprehensive framework that gives coherence to everything one has learned. The particulars acquired through learning hold little significance unless bound together by a totalistic vision, the "one thread."

The good student is therefore expected to build on his learning inferentially, from bits of knowledge to a more comprehensive understanding. Take, for example, Confucius's favorite disciple, Yan Hui. It is, in part, Yan Hui's exceptional inferential powers that explain Confucius's special affection for him: "The Master said to Zigong, 'Of you and Hui, who is the better?' He responded, 'Me? How could I dare compare myself to Hui? Hui hears one matter and understands ten; I hear one matter and understand two.' The Master said, 'No, you are not his equal. Neither of us is his equal'" (5.9). Further, the good student should know how to apply his inferential knowledge. "The Master said, 'Imagine a person who can recite the three hundred poems by heart but when entrusted with matters of governing cannot carry them out, or when sent on a mission to one of the four quarters is unable to exercise his own initiative. No matter how many poems he might have memorized, what good are they to him?'" (13.5). The message here is that book learning that devolves into mere memorization is sterile and useless and not the true learning that will enable self-transformation and the betterment of society.

By "learning," then, Confucius means moral learning, the study and embodiment of the values that will make one a *junzi*, a superior man. He laments that in his own day learning has been reduced to nothing more than a means to worldly success or acclaim: "In ancient times those who learned did so for the sake of bettering themselves; nowadays those who learn do so for the sake of impressing others" (14.24). His aim is to get men back on the right track, to make learning once again about moral self-improvement.

The Master's insistence that the Confucian responsibility to pursue moral perfection, or sagehood, must be rooted in a steadfast commitment to learning is in large part based on his own life experience. In the famous "autobiographical" passage in the *Analects*, he states:

> At fifteen, I set my mind-and-heart on learning. At thirty, I stood on my own. At forty, I had no doubts. At fifty, I knew heaven's decree. At sixty, my ears were in accord. At seventy, I followed the desires of my mind-and-heart without overstepping right. (2.4)

Though autobiographical, the remark is clearly intended to serve as a sequential template for all students of the Confucian school. The path to moral perfection, it counsels, must start with an unswerving commitment to learning. Through learning, a student, too, might become a sage—a man whose every action is instinctively in line with the Way.

Being a morally superior man: true goodness through ritual practice

Although the *Analects* does not offer up one neat definition of the morally superior man, it does in passage after passage introduce his various attributes. Most importantly, the morally superior man is a man of *ren* (仁). *Ren* is the highest virtue in the Confucian vision, the one that subsumes all others, including trustworthiness, righteousness, compassion, ritual propriety, wisdom, and filial piety. No translation quite captures the full significance of the term. It has been variously rendered as "benevolence," "humanity," "humanness," and the like; I translate it as "true goodness" here, hoping that this translation conveys something of *ren*'s overarching, paramount status in Confucius's teachings.

True goodness is not a quality that can be cultivated in seclusion, cut off from other human beings. True goodness exists only as it is manifested in relation to others and in the treatment of others.

It is in concrete behavior that true goodness, as a virtue, is achieved. A filial son, for instance, "enacts" his filial devotion by bowing before his father. True goodness is thus closely associated with ritual, for it is principally through the practice of ritual, the Master believes, that true goodness is given meaningful expression. For this reason, we find the Master dedicating much of his teaching in the *Analects* to a discussion of proper ritual. To be morally superior, Confucius argues, is to have a keen sense of ritual propriety.

On true goodness

As crucial as the concept of true goodness may be for Confucius, he never provides a synoptic explanation or definition of his supreme virtue. This frustrates his disciples, who dog him throughout the *Analects* with questions like: "What is true goodness?" "Is so-and-so a man of true goodness?" "Is such-and-such behavior a matter of true goodness?" The Master's answers are varied and appear to depend on to whom and about whom he is speaking. True goodness can be to love others (12.22), to subdue the self and return to ritual propriety (12.1), to be respectful, tolerant, trustworthy, diligent, and kind (17.5), to be possessed of courage (14.4), to be free from worry (9.29), or to be resolute and firm (13.27). What Confucius offers by way of explanation to his disciples are but glimpses or facets of true goodness. Aware of their frustration and eagerness for fuller disclosure, he remarks, "My friends, I know you think that there is something I am keeping from you. But I keep nothing from you at all" (7.23). True goodness, it would seem, is not fully expressible, fully definable. There is an ineffable quality to it.

It remains for us—as it did for his followers—to tease out of the *Analects* a deeper appreciation of this essential moral quality. A few passages in the text are especially revealing: "Zigong asked, 'Is there one word that can be practiced for the whole of one's life?' The Master said, 'That would be 'empathy' perhaps: what you do not wish yourself do not do unto others'" (15.24). True goodness lies in the direction of empathetic behavior. In dealing with others, we are obliged to treat them as we ourselves would wish to be treated. We need to put ourselves in their place, to plumb our own feelings, in order to judge the feelings of others; this is Confucian empathy. True goodness is realized when these feelings of empathy are successfully extended to others, when they are actualized in our relations with others: "The Way of our Master is being true to oneself and empathetic toward others, nothing more" (4.15).

It may be rather easy to be empathetic at any one particular moment or in any one particular encounter. The difficulty, Confucius suggests, lies in sustaining the feelings and the practice of empathy over the course of an entire day as we interact with a variety of people, from concerned student to grieving friend to demanding child to sickly neighbor to aggressive panhandler to distraught colleague to exhausted spouse. And if an entire day poses a challenge, more challenging still is an entire week or an entire month. This perhaps explains why Confucius resists describing anyone, including himself, as a man of true goodness (7.43). For the very moment one's empathetic feelings and practice lapse, so too does one's true goodness. Yan Hui does better than most at sustaining true goodness but even his success is limited: "The Master said, 'Hui! For three months his mind-and-heart would not lapse from true goodness. As for others, they might attain it for a day or for a month, but that is all'"(6.7). Thus it is important to recognize that true goodness is not an indwelling state that one achieves once and for all; it is a *behavior* involving mind and body that is ongoing and requires constant vigilance. This is why Zengzi, another of Confucius's foremost disciples, remarks, "A learned man must be broad and resolute, for his burden is heavy and the journey is long. He takes true goodness as his burden: Is that not indeed heavy? And only with death does he stop: Is that not indeed long?" (8.7). In the Confucian tradition, being a superior man, a man of true goodness, requires a lifelong commitment that ceases only with death itself.

The etymology of the Chinese character for true goodness is itself instructive. *Ren* (仁) is constituted of two components, one for "man" and the other for "two," indicating that a person can be *ren*—truly good—only in associating with others. True goodness in the Confucian tradition is not a quality that can be cultivated and expressed in isolation. There is no place in Confucianism for the Semitic tradition's "athlete of God," who sits atop a forty-foot pillar in the Syrian desert cultivating goodness and ridding himself of evil in the eyes of God. True goodness for Confucius is inter-relational, a virtue given realization only in a person's interactions with other human beings.

On ritual

Confucius insists in the *Analects* that the superior man's empathetic concerns are necessarily both guided by and expressed through a set of *li* (禮) (conventionally translated as rituals or ritual propriety, but rendered also as rites, ceremonies, prescriptions for proper behavior, rules of etiquette, and customs) handed down by the tradition and refined over the centuries. Yet, as in the case of true goodness, he does not attempt to define ritual for his disciples or offer a general explanation of its significance and function. Turning to the later *Book of Rites*, however, we find some helpful passages. For instance:

> Now, ritual furnishes the means of determining the observance towards relatives, as near and remote; of settling points that may cause suspicion or doubt; of distinguishing where there should be agreement and disagreement; and of making clear what is right and what is wrong. In practicing ritual, one does not seek to please others in an improper way or to be lavish in one's words. In practicing ritual one does not go beyond the proper measure, nor take liberties with others, nor presume an intimacy with others. To cultivate the self and put one's words into practice is what is called good conduct. Conduct that is cultivated, words that accord with the right Way—this is the substance of ritual.

It is the performance of ritual that "humanizes" or "civilizes" man and distinguishes him from beast:

> The parrot can speak, and yet is nothing more than a bird; the ape can speak, and yet is nothing more than a beast. Here now is a man who observes no rules of ritual propriety; is not his mind-and-heart that of a beast? But if men were as beasts, and without the principle of ritual propriety, father and son might have the same mate. Therefore, when the sages arose, they framed the rules of ritual propriety in order to teach men, and cause them, by their possession of them, to make a distinction between themselves and brutes.

Li, or ritual, offers guidance for people in their manifold dealings with others, and it is this guidance that makes social harmony possible. A father, in practicing proper ritual, behaves as a true father should; a son, in practicing proper ritual, behaves as a true son should. Ritual thus promotes the actualization of the normative five relationships. Confucius believes that the good order of the early Zhou had been built on these five relationships and that it is these relationships that constitute the basis of any good sociopolitical order. As the *Book of Rites* states, "Ruler and subject, father and son, husband and wife, elder brother and younger brother, and friend and friend: these five relationships constitute the universal Way of the world."

As a young child, a person begins to learn from family ceremonies how to pay reverence to ancestors, how to mourn the dead, and how to celebrate life's important transitions, like capping—the ceremony representing the coming of age—and marriage. He becomes familiar with how many and which particular ritual vessels to use in sacrificing to his grandfather, and which clothes to wear, prayers to say, and foods to eat during times of mourning. He even knows not to wear purple or mauve-colored adornments or use red or vermillion for informal dress and not to wear a black cap on condolence visits. But for Confucius, ritual practice is not limited to what we may think of as religious or ceremonial occasions; for him, all aspects of life, even the most mundane, are governed by a system of rituals. How we eat, how we speak, how we greet others, how we dress, and how we bear ourselves publicly and privately are matters determined by ritual expectations and tradition. Thus, about eating, the *Book of Rites* admonishes:

> Do not roll the rice into a ball; do not bolt down the various dishes; do not swill down the soup. Do not make noise in eating; do not crunch the bones with the teeth; do not put back fish you've been eating; do not throw the bones to the dogs; do not snatch at what you want. Do not spread out the rice to cool; do not use chopsticks in eating millet. Do not try to gulp down soup with vegetables in it, nor add condiments to it; do not keep picking the teeth, nor swill down the sauces.

To many in the West, these proscriptions may seem trivial—a matter of simple manners or etiquette rather than of moral development. But there is no doubt that Confucius saw them as rituals, the correct performance of which enabled man to nurture and give expression to true goodness: "The instructive and transforming power of rituals is subtle: they stop depravity before it has taken form, causing men daily to move towards what is good and to distance themselves from vice, without being themselves conscious of it."

Of course ritual would have this "instructive and transforming" power only if performed with utter sincerity. The Master worries lest students take ritual practice to be mere performance, gesture empty of meaning. For ritual to have genuine significance, the performance of it must be infused with the proper feeling: "Ritual performed without reverence, the forms of mourning observed without grief—these are things I cannot bear to see!" (3.26). Offerings of wine and food to ancestors must be accompanied by feelings of reverence and affection; bowing before an elder must be accompanied by feelings of respect; polite speech, dress, and meal manners must be accompanied by feelings of propriety and civility toward other human beings. Ritual practice is thus the means by which man gives expression to his most human qualities. It is the means by which his inner feelings and outer demeanor become one.

In the teachings of the *Analects*, ritual practice appears to be at once a means of manifesting our humanity and a means of nurturing within us the very qualities that make us human. Through sacrificial offerings we deepen our feelings of reverence for ancestors; through the act of bowing we deepen our feelings of respect for the elderly; through decorous speech, dress, and meal manners we deepen our feelings of propriety and civility toward others. For Confucius, the physical practice of the rites inculcates in the performer the emotions and feelings associated with those rites. Immersion in the rites, which is what Confucius calls for throughout the *Analects*, habituates man externally to good, normative social behavior, and this habituated behavior guides and reshapes his moral impulses. Once, when asked what constitutes true goodness, the Master replied simply: "If contrary to ritual, do not look; if contrary to ritual, do not listen; if contrary to ritual, do not speak; if contrary to ritual, do not act" (12.1).

For Confucius, ritual is closely linked to music. The capacity of music to inspire moral behavior had been realized long before by the ancients. As the *Book of Rites* states, "In music the sages found pleasure and saw that it could be used to make the hearts of the people good. Because of the deep influence that it exerts on a man, and the change that it produces in manners and customs, the ancient kings appointed it as one of the subjects of instruction." Confucius thus assumes that his followers should study music—or, more precisely, certain types of music he finds morally uplifting—as an essential part of the ritual matrix of the past. He especially recommends Shao music (i.e., the court music of the sage-king Shun), remarking that it has a powerful effect even on himself (3.25, 7.14, 15.11). Music's importance—and its close association with ritual in Confucian teachings—is summed up neatly in this simple exhortation to his disciples: "Find inspiration in the *Book of Odes*, take your place through ritual, and achieve perfection with music" (8.8).

The family as the crucible of virtue

Family clothes and shelters us, but its most important function in Confucian teachings is to set us on the path to virtue. Family is a microcosm of society, the locus for learning about human relationships and the norms that govern them. It is here that, ideally, we are inculcated in those values and practices that make a harmonious Confucian society possible: obedience and respect for authority, deference to seniority, affection and kindness toward the young and infirm, and so forth.

3. A copy (fourteenth century?) of a painting by Li Gonglin (ca. 1041–1106) of a filial son bowing before his parents

The second passage of the *Analects* speaks to the essential role of family in shaping the moral individual and promoting a peaceful and stable social and political order. Youzi, expressing the views of his Master, remarks:

> One who is filial and fraternal but at the same time loves defying superiors is rare indeed. One who does not love defying superiors but at the same time loves sowing disorder has never existed. The superior man attends to the root. When the root is established, the Way issues forth. Filial piety and fraternal respect—are they not the root of true goodness? (1.2)

Moral cultivation of the individual thus begins in the family. This is where a person is introduced to filial piety, fraternal respect, and deference for elders; this is where a person is instructed in the nomenclature of ritual etiquette. The lessons learned here apply readily in the world out there. A good son will naturally be obedient to the ruler; a good younger brother will naturally be respectful to elders; a good daughter and wife will naturally be submissive to men. The pressure on the family to provide the right moral environment is considerable, for a wayward son—one who is disobedient to the village elders or the ruler—brings disrepute not only on himself but on his entire family, especially his father and mother. His failure is theirs; as parents they did not engender moral purpose and proprietary awareness in their son, and it is the community that now suffers the consequences.

Of the virtues to be learned in the family, filial piety is the most fundamental. The essence of filial piety is obedience to parental authority: to respect their wishes and to care for their well-being. The *Book of Rites* summarizes the responsibilities associated with this cardinal virtue:

> A filial son, in nourishing his aging parents, seeks to make their hearts glad and not to go against their will; to make their ears and eyes glad and bring comfort to them in their bed-chambers; and to

support them wholeheartedly with food and drink—such is the filial son to the end of life. By "the end of life," I mean not the end of his parents' lives, but the end of his own life. Thus what his parents loved he will love, and what they reverenced he will reverence. He will do so even in regard to all their dogs and horses, and how much more in regard to the men whom they valued.

In Confucian thinking, filial obligations do not cease with the death of the parents. True filiality requires that the child behave throughout his entire life just as his parents would wish and in a fashion that would reflect well on the family's good name:

> Although his parents be dead, when a son is inclined to do what is good, he should think that he will thereby transmit the good name of his parents, and carry his wish into effect. When he is inclined to do what is not good, he should think that he will thereby bring disgrace on the name of his parents, and must not carry his wish into effect.

Filial respect thus does not play out within the web of family relations alone but gets actualized in the larger network of social relations as good, virtuous conduct.

What is true of ritual generally is equally true of filial piety more particularly: the feeling behind the form is essential. This message is repeated over and over in Confucian teachings, as in the Master's pointed response to disciple Ziyou's query about filial piety: "Nowadays to be 'filial' means simply to be capable of providing parents with nourishment. But even dogs and horses get their nourishment from us. Without the feeling of reverence, what difference is there?" (2.7). As he does with all ritual practice, Confucius insists that outer filial behavior be the faithful expression of a genuine inner feeling.

The family, in the Confucian vision, is of central importance in sustaining the Chinese sociopolitical order, for it is here, in the family, that the child becomes conditioned to the dominant assumptions and values of Chinese society. From the family the child learns that the world is naturally hierarchical; that hierarchy works effectively when there exist clear status differentiations and clear roles; that each status has set, normative responsibilities attached to it (e.g., there are behavioral norms for being a good son or daughter); that, enmeshed in a hierarchical network, a good person is one who carries out the responsibilities associated with his status; and that harmony of the whole results from each person within the hierarchy conscientiously fulfilling the duties demanded by his defined role.

Chapter 3
Government in Confucian teachings

> Ji Kangzi [the de facto but illegitimate ruler of the state of Lu] asked Confucius about governing. Confucius responded, "To govern (*zheng*, 政) means to correct (*zheng*, 正). If you lead by correcting yourself, who would dare to remain incorrect?" (12.17)

The ruler as exemplar

The cultivation of the individual has as its aim moral self-realization. But, as this remark suggests, self-realization of the individual is by no means an end itself. Self-realization, Confucius believes, results in the self-realization of others, which, ripple-like, can result in the moral transformation of society at large. This, of course, is why the presence of a moral vanguard is so crucial to Confucian teachings—and why Confucius dedicates the time he does to explaining what it means to be good, to be moral, and to become a superior man. Social harmony comes about less through the instrumentation of government than through the power of example set by a moral elite. At the apex of this moral elite, at least ideally, sits the exemplary ruler, who, in his utter correctness, serves as a model for all.

The Confucian ruler possesses an inner virtue (*de*, 德). This inner virtue exerts a spiritual-ethical power over others. People are drawn to it and to him. Confucius offers a comparison to the natural world: "One who practices government by virtue may be compared to the North Star: it remains in its place while the multitude of stars turn toward it" (2.1). The people's submission to the good Confucian ruler clearly is not submission to some coercive power but rather to a fixed, reliable moral authority that radiates throughout the realm. This moral authority is a force capable of guiding others in their movements, of setting them in the right direction. The theme of instructing and ruling the populace through moral suasion runs throughout the *Analects* as well as other classical Confucian texts; indeed, it is one of the distinguishing features of Confucian political philosophy.

Ji Kangzi, cited above, returns to the subject of government on a number of occasions: "Ji Kangzi asked Confucius about government, saying, 'Suppose I were to kill the Way-less in order to promote those possessed of the Way. What would you say?'" With no little hint of impatience and even disdain for the usurper Ji Kangzi, Confucius answered, "You are governing; what need is there for killing? If you desire the good, the people will be good. The virtue of the superior man is wind; the virtue of the small person is grass. When wind passes over it, the grass is sure to bend" (12.19). Ji Kangzi just does not get it. Harsh government that relies on punishment and physical force is ineffective and represents "misgovernment" in Confucius's view. All that is necessary for good government is moral leadership. Morality breeds morality. The wind–grass metaphor that brings the exchange with Ji Kangzi to its conclusion is easily one of the most famous in the Chinese tradition. The people are susceptible to the moral suasion of their ruler. And his influence on them is presented as altogether "natural," just as wind naturally bends the grass. Note here that just as a moral ruler will move the people in the direction of goodness, a ruler lacking in moral authority will move the people in the direction of immorality. Thus in the Confucian tradition, a ruler without virtue poses a serious threat to the entire moral-social order.

So strong is his confidence in the transformative power of virtue, in its ability to win others over to a moral life, that when Confucius once expressed a desire to settle among the Nine Barbarian Tribes of the East and was asked, "But what about their crudeness?" he matter-of-factly replied, "If a superior man were to settle among them, there would be no crudeness" (9.14). With correct moral leadership even "barbarians" would become correct.

A good ruler, Confucius tells Ji Kangzi, simply desires the good himself. He must model the morality he would like his subjects to cultivate. Conversely, when disorderly behavior prevails in a state, the ruler must look within and consider his own culpability: "Ji Kangzi was having trouble with burglars. He asked Confucius what he should do. Confucius answered, 'If only you were free from desire, they would not steal even if you rewarded them for it'" (12.18). If thievery abounds in the state of Lu, the responsibility, Confucius maintains, falls on Ji Kangzi. It is, after all, from the ruler that the people learn morality. If the ruler is good and without avarice, the people, too, will be good and without avarice. That being the case, there is nothing that could induce them to steal. A ruler thus can bring Confucian harmony to his state and people only if he is without selfish desire himself.

If good government depends upon the existence of a moral vanguard, then the responsibility falls to the ruler to identify those individuals whose moral character qualifies them for official service. Choosing the right men is essential: "Duke Ai asked, 'What can be done so that the people will be obedient?' The Master responded, 'Raise up the straight, place them over the crooked, and the people will be obedient; raise up the crooked, place them over the straight, and the people will not be obedient'" (2.19). This passage speaks to a familiar theme: the power of example, the power that the blowing wind naturally exercises over blades of grass. The straight in office will bring correctness to those whom they oversee. But it speaks to another, related point as well. If the ruler is unprejudiced in the selection of his officials, if he bypasses the unqualified and the corrupt and promotes only the good, his commitment to the well-being of his people will be apparent. Observing his dedication to their well-being, the people in turn will continue to offer him their trust and support.

It is this trust, Confucius goes on to say, that is the basis of the state and of the ruler's legitimacy:

> Zigong asked about government. The Master said, "Let food be sufficient, let military preparations be sufficient, and let the people have trust in you." Zigong said, "If you have absolutely no choice but to give up one of the three, which should go first?" He said, "Let the military preparations go." Zigong said, "If you have absolutely no choice but to give up one of the remaining two, which should go first?" "Let the food go. Since ancient times, nobody has escaped death; but if the people lack trust, the government has nothing on which to stand." (12.7)

The implication here is that a people with confidence in their ruler, persuaded that he puts their welfare above all else, will be willing to endure all manner of hardship. His genuine concern for their well-being will be rewarded with their loyalty and support, even when their very lives are at risk.

The good, virtuous ruler is the consummate superior man, always comporting himself as he should. He is the perfect model, according effortlessly with the prescriptions for proper behavior. It is through his charismatic moral example that he instructs and guides his people, and sets them on the right path. In this ideal of rulership, Confucius argues, laws, edicts, and punishments—the routine tools of government—are inessential. It is not to say they are altogether unnecessary, but for the Master, the less dependence on them—and the greater dependence on the person of the ruler, his moral light, and his ritual modeling—the better. Laws and punishments imposed from above may indeed promote a superficial social order among the people, but they do little to inculcate in them a sense of right and to lead them to moral betterment. And they do little to promote a true spirit of community, a mutual commitment by the people to the creation of a harmonious society. Of all the Master's remarks, this one best sums up Confucius's view on the basis of good government:

> Guide them by edicts, keep them in line with punishments, and the common people will stay out of trouble, but will have no sense of shame. Guide them by virtue, keep them in line with ritual and they will, besides having a sense of shame, reform themselves. (2.3)

Moral reformation of the individual, as well as social harmony, do not result from the external threat and coercion of laws and punishments. Instead, they result from the people, inspired by the ruler's model to re-create in the community and state, through ritual practice, the fluid, normative relationships that have formed their familial life since childhood.

Culture and tradition, Confucius suggests here, are more effective, stronger tools in shaping the behavior and ideals of the people than legal and penal codes. Through example and moral suasion, the good ruler promotes a system of shared values and practices, which effectively regulates the conduct of the people and, importantly, binds each person to the community and its norms. Violating these norms has real and sometimes long-lasting consequences, Confucius assumes. A person who uses his fingers rather than chopsticks to eat yellow fish, or curses his elderly father in public, or wears lavish clothing during the mourning period for a parent will likely be branded by others as uncouth and uncivilized. He has failed, after all, to learn what it means to be truly Chinese and now risks being marginalized by his fellow villagers. While no formal laws mete out fines or other penalties for this sort of "misbehavior," the threat of punishment is nonetheless substantial. This is why Confucius is confident that in a society governed by shared culture the people will not be quick to transgress the boundaries of customary behavior and will develop a keen sense of shame.

In leading by ritual, the ruler assumes the role as standard-bearer of the culture, thus enhancing his legitimacy; at the same time, he serves as instructor, exemplifying for the people the beliefs and practices they are expected to embrace as well. Confucius's faith in the efficacy of rule by ritual is evidenced repeatedly in conversations with his disciples: "The Master said, 'If a person is capable of governing the state with ritual and humility, what difficulties will he have? If he is incapable of governing the state with ritual and humility, what does he have to do with ritual?'" (4.13). But ritual is effective *only* if the ruler's practice of it is informed by the proper feeling, the spirit of humility or deference. It is this feeling that gives the ruler's ritual performance authenticity and endows that performance with the power to guide and "reform" (2.3) the people.

It would be a mistake, however, to conclude that Confucius sees no place for law and punishment in government. Despite his appeal for rule by virtue and ritual, he regards penal law as a routine part of the apparatus of government. He says of the superior man, for example, that he "cherishes a respect for the law," in contrast to the small man, who "cherishes lenient treatment" (4.11). And in an exchange with Zilu, he remarks, "If rituals and music do not prosper, punishments and penalties will not be correct; if punishments and penalties are not correct, the people will have no place to put hand or foot" (13.3). Indeed, both the *Book of History* and *Book of Odes*, which Confucius holds so dear, speak of the righteous application of laws and punishments by the virtuous rulers of the early Zhou (e.g., "The Announcement to the Prince of Kang"). He likely appreciates that in order to maintain social order, occasional recourse to laws and punishments is unavoidable. Still, it is clear that he would like their use to be minimized. When he remarks, "In hearing lawsuits I am just like others. What is necessary is to see to it that there are no lawsuits" (12.13), the

Master is stating a central tenet of Confucian teachings: the best government is the one that relies on law least.

The picture of the ideal ruler that emerges from the *Analects* is of a man whose inner virtue radiates outward as a powerful, charismatic, moral force that moves people toward true goodness and the practice of ritual propriety, thus producing social harmony. This force is non-coercive, and its effects seem natural, like grass bending in the direction of the blowing wind. The ideal ruler thus need not even govern actively: "The Master said, 'Ruling through non-action (*wuwei*, 無為), is this not Shun! For what did he do? Assuming a reverential pose, he faced due south and nothing more'" (15.5). Commentators understand this passage to mean that so great, so abundant was the sage-ruler Shun's virtue that he transformed his people effortlessly without taking action; it is an echo of analect 2.1, where the ruler is likened to the North Star "that remains in its place while the multitude of stars turn toward it." Daoists, too, use the term "non-action" to suggest that "action" or "doing" should be spontaneous, not purposeful or in any way contrary to the natural course of things. Commentators distinguish Confucius's use of the term here by giving it moral significance, explaining that "non-action" in Shun's case was possible only because his inner virtue was exceptionally powerful. In other words, "non-action" was a direct consequence of his moral condition. We need also to remember, however, that Shun's "non-action" in the concrete, daily affairs of government was possible only because as a virtuous ruler and in his compassion for the people, he had chosen upright and good men like Gao Yao to carry out the administration of government (12.22).

The good ruler is necessarily a good judge of character and selects as officials only those men who share his commitment to Confucian principles and the well-being of the people. Here we get a hint of why the famous Chinese civil service examination system will take on the importance it does for more than two millennia beginning in the second century BCE.

Government and the well-being of the people

In the Confucian vision, then, the well-being of the people is dependent largely on the moral character of the ruler. The responsibility of actualizing his benevolence in the administration of the realm is shared by him and his appointed officials. Like the ruler himself, the ideal official is expected to be a good man; he is a man who, having undergone the process of self-cultivation, is steeped in learning and dedicated to becoming a morally superior man (*junzi*). Indeed, we have seen that the *Analects* is, in part, an attempt by the Master to teach his students the way of being moral, in the hope that they might succeed where he himself had failed—in achieving official position. Only good people, he believes, can make good officials, and it is only good officials who can make the government good.

A good official is not a person who exercises a particular skill or fulfills a particular function. Indeed, Confucius's terse remark, "The superior man is not a utensil" (2.12), speaks to this ideal. The traditional commentary on this passage by He Yan (fl. third century CE) states: "As for utensils, each is of circumscribed usefulness. But when it comes to the superior man, there is nothing he does not do." The reason that "there is nothing he does not do" is that he embodies virtue. In embodying virtue, he is fully compassionate and benevolent and unfailingly extends himself to others. Through his finely honed empathetic skills, he is poised to deal with the whole gamut of affairs confronting state and society. This is not to say that he might not be especially expert in certain areas, such as irrigation control or taxation or techniques of administration; rather, such specialized skills are not what make him a good official. It is his readiness to improve the lot of the people, to see to their needs as they arise, that makes him a good official.

4. (*Opposite*) **A woodblock print of an official caring for the well-being of his subjects, as his Confucian duty demands. The caption reads, "Open the granaries and provide relief to the distressed." From** *Zhongguo gudian wenxue banhua xuanji*, **ed. by Fu Xihua (1981)**

開倉賑濟

Confucian teachings oblige the superior man to serve government, to assist the ruler in implementing the Way throughout the country. True goodness, after all, lies in serving and bettering others. Yet there are times, according to Confucius, when the superior man can refuse to serve. Of Qu Boyu, a minister in the state of Wei who resigned his post in 559 BCE, the Master exclaims: "A superior man indeed was Qu Boyu! When the Way prevailed in the state, he served it; when the Way did not prevail in the state, he was able to roll up his principles and hide them away" (15.7). And, similarly but more abstractly, the Master says: "When the Way prevails in the world, show yourself; when it does not, hide yourself" (8.13).

Remarks like these seem at odds with the leitmotif running through the *Analects*—that it is the responsibility of the superior man to transform a wayward society and give it moral redirection. How can Confucius permit the superior man to "hide himself" at the very time his presence is most required? Consider too that Confucius is living in a time when the Way certainly does not prevail, and yet, as we have seen in the exchange with Zigong cited earlier (see chap. 1), he still anxiously awaits the "right offer" (9.13). Never does he doubt his own ability to set a benighted ruler and society on the right path, given the opportunity: "The Master said, 'If there were someone to employ me, in the course of but twelve months we would be doing well, and within three years we would achieve success'" (13.10). Serving a ruler, then, is what is *ordinarily* expected of the superior man. But in passages like the ones above, the Master sounds a cautionary note, suggesting that occasionally a state and its ruler may be so hopelessly depraved that they simply are not susceptible to the morally transforming influences of the superior man. In such a state, the superior man has no room or license to act on his principles. In fact, any insistence on doing so will merely invite the ruler's wrath and result in severe punishment. Faced with a ruler hostile to moral reform, the superior man would do better to "roll up his principles and hide them away."

Since good government in the Confucian vision depends largely on the virtue of the ruler and those he appoints to serve him, the teachings of the Master do not offer much in the way of plans for the organization of government or division of governing powers—as one finds, for example, in the U.S. Constitution—or of specific measures or policies the government should adopt. The Master assumes that a moral ruler, out of compassion and benevolence, will do what is right and will take the appropriate steps to address the needs of his subjects.

Still, it is possible to deduce a few general policy suggestions from some passages of the *Analects*. For instance, the Master says, "To guide a state of one thousand chariots, be respectful in your handling of affairs and display trustworthiness; be frugal in your expenditures and cherish others; and employ the common people only at the proper seasons" (1.5). The ruler, according to Confucius, has a responsibility to the people for their material well-being. A government that spends too much is one that is bound to tax too much; government must be fiscally sensitive, mindful of the heavy burden taxation places on the people. Government must be mindful, too, not to draw on the people's labor for public work projects during the agricultural seasons. To interfere with the people's agricultural activities cannot but reduce their agricultural productivity, the basis of their livelihood.

In an exchange with his disciple Ran Qiu, Confucius suggests why the material well-being of the people is a critical concern for the government:

> The Master traveled to Wei, with Ran Qiu as his carriage driver. The Master remarked, "How numerous the people of this state are!" Ran Qiu asked, "Since the people are already numerous, what next should be done for them?" The Master said, "Enrich them." Ran Qiu said, "Once they have become rich, what next should be done for them?" The Master said, "Instruct them." (13.9)

The implied claim here is that only when the people's material needs have been satisfied will they be susceptible to moral instruction. In this view, the receptivity of the people to the ruler's charismatic influence depends on socioeconomic conditions, for which the ruler is accountable.

Confucius praises the legendary sage-king Yu for dedicating himself to projects intended to benefit the people's agriculture. The Master says of Yu, "He lived in a mean hovel expending all of his energies on the construction of drainage ditches and canals. I can find no fault with Yu" (8.21). By attempting to tame the constant flooding and improve field irrigation, Yu's government was doing just what government is supposed to do: to promote, to the best of its ability, the agricultural prosperity of the people (cf. 14.5). Agricultural prosperity had long been the concern of Chinese rulers. Indeed, in oracle bone inscriptions from the Shang dynasty (ca. 1600 BCE–ca. 1045 BCE), which represent the earliest recorded history in China, dynastic rulers rarely stop dancing, praying, and performing sacrifices to coax the rain and to ensure bountiful harvests.

The mandate of heaven

The ideal of rule by virtue is by no means new with Confucius. It is a major theme wending its way through many of the early Zhou documents preserved in the *Book of History*.

These documents tell of a Shang dynasty that began virtuously with wise and benevolent rulers. Over time, however, the character of the rulers changed, and men given to great lewdness, debauchery, and wickedness came to occupy the throne. The last of the Shang rulers, King Zhou, was especially depraved, and the descriptions of him in the documents are unrestrained in their contempt for him. In rallying his troops for the Zhou attack on the Shang forces, King Wu, the founder of the Zhou, says:

Now Zhou, the great king of the Shang, does not reverence heaven above and inflicts calamities on the people below. He has been abandoned to drunkenness and reckless in lust. He has dared to exercise cruel oppression. Along with criminals he has punished all their relatives. He has put men into office on the hereditary principle. He has made it his pursuit to have palaces, towers, pavilions, embankments, ponds, and all other extravagances, to the most painful injury of you, the myriad people. He has burned and roasted the loyal and the good. He has ripped up pregnant women. August heaven was moved with indignation, and charged my deceased father Wen reverently to display heaven's majesty, but he died before the work was completed.

King Zhou was not a "good" man and thus not a "good" ruler. Under him, the *Book of History* goes on to say, people lived in abject misery. And so, "wailing and calling to heaven, they fled to where no one could reach them." Heaven, in its compassion, took pity on the people and withdrew the Mandate it had given earlier rulers of the Shang, bestowing it anew on the Zhou.

It is here, with the *Book of History*, that the concept of the Mandate of Heaven (*tianming*, 天命) is first introduced in Chinese history. Attributed to the Duke of Zhou, the righteous regent of the young King Cheng, the Mandate of Heaven would serve as the basis of Chinese political ideology from the Zhou dynasty until the early years of the twentieth century. Curiously, however, though Confucius insists throughout his teachings that virtue alone makes for the good ruler, he does not use the term *tianming* in the sense of the Mandate of Heaven in the *Analects*. It may be that the term did not have especially wide currency yet; conversely, it may have had sufficiently wide currency that he simply assumed his disciples to understand that much of his discussion with them was a sort of commentary on it. Whatever the case, it is certain that his teachings subscribed to and promoted the ideals embodied in the Mandate of Heaven.

The theory of the Mandate, on the face of it, is simple enough. A concerned heaven, a heaven invested in the well-being of the people (see chap. 1), confers a mandate to rule on virtuous and benevolent men who, like heaven, are committed to the people's welfare. Such had been the case with the early rulers of the Shang, according to the *History* documents. To maintain the Mandate, these men—and their successors—must never abandon virtue. If they do, if the rulers go bad, they forfeit the right to rule, and heaven withdraws its Mandate.

What is essential to note here is that heaven does not act on its own; heaven responds to the wishes and will of the people. In "wailing and calling to heaven," the people voice *their* displeasure and discontent with the ruler and with the conditions prevailing in the state. Heaven, to be sure, is a vital force—and a powerful sanction—in the political dynamic, but it is something of an agent operating on behalf of the interests of the people. A justly famous line from the *Book of History* neatly captures this important point: "Heaven sees as the people see; heaven hears as the people hear." In doing the bidding of the people, heaven is not a willful or arbitrary force. It does not bestow and withdraw its Mandate capriciously as it alone pleases.

It should be clear, then, that there is nothing "fated" about the Mandate. Rulers win it through virtuous and benevolent rule; they lose it by abandoning virtuous and benevolent rule. It is not a matter of heaven's whimsy. A poem in the *Book of Odes* warns the successors of King Wen, the illustrious founder of the Zhou, that retaining the Mandate or losing it is in their hands:

> The Mandate is not easy to keep;
> may it not end in your own persons.
> Display and make bright your good fame,
> and consider what heaven did to the Yin [i.e., the Shang].
> The doings of high heaven

have no sound, no smell.
Make King Wen your pattern,
and all the states will trust in you.

The message here is emphatic: be virtuous and the Mandate is yours; abandon virtue and lose the Mandate. In the end, it is the ruler's relationship with, and treatment of, his people that decides the fate of the Mandate, not heaven. The Mandate of Heaven thus stands in rather sharp contrast to the European doctrine of the "divine right of kings," where rulers are granted the right to rule directly from God and are accountable for their actions to God alone. Not subject to the will of the people, their authority is absolute.

It was on the occasion of the Zhou conquest of the Shang in the mid-eleventh century BCE that the principles of the Mandate of Heaven were first articulated by the Duke of Zhou. If the theory of the Mandate was brilliant propaganda—serving to legitimize the Zhou conquest of the Shang—it could, nonetheless and just as readily, serve to legitimize the conquest of the Zhou by others. This is why poems in the *Odes* and documents in the *History* implore the Zhou leaders to dedicate themselves to the cultivation of virtue as the basis of their legitimacy. The Mandate is precarious: it can be won, and it can be lost.

So ingrained would become this notion of the Mandate of Heaven that when the foreign, "barbarian" Manchus entered the city of Beijing in 1644 and proclaimed the establishment of the Qing dynasty (1644–1912), the first edict the leaders issued, inviting the Chinese populace to welcome Manchu rule, invoked the spirit and language of the Mandate of Heaven:

> The empire is not an individual's private property. Whosoever possesses virtue holds it. The army and the people are not an individual's property. Whosoever possesses virtue commands them. We now occupy the empire.

Chapter 4
Variety within early Confucianism

In considering the success of the Confucian tradition, its ability to endure over the course of a couple of millennia—even into the twenty-first century—we must be mindful of this simple fact: Confucianism was ever changing. This is hardly surprising, as all major systems of belief are sustained by change and variety. Few, after all, would assume that the Christianity of Thomas Aquinas was the Christianity of St. Paul, or that the Christianity of Ignatius of Loyola was the Christianity of John Calvin. The different theological outlooks of these men, to be sure, all emerged from the general vision outlined in the Hebrew Bible and in the New Testament and thus share certain core beliefs. But at the same time, these thinkers from different ages and places naturally brought to their reflection on the foundational teachings a range of social and religious priorities, which resulted in "Christianities" with different, sometimes widely different, emphases. This ability of Christianity to keep itself relevant to different people and changing times and places is what has enabled it to survive and remain vital.

What is true of Christianity—and Judaism and Islam as well—is equally true of Confucianism. Yet in much of the West, until the early years of the twentieth century, Confucianism was regarded as some sort of unchanging monolith, a stagnant tradition that had undergone little change since the time of its founder and was responsible for China's "backwardness" in the nineteenth and twentieth centuries. Whether this view was born of ignorance of the Confucian tradition or of Western self-satisfaction with its version of material progress in these same centuries, it has since given way in the twentieth and twenty-first centuries to a much richer understanding of the vibrancy of Confucianism in the history of East Asia generally and of China in particular.

The vision outlined by Confucius lent itself to a variety of interpretations. These interpretations, though anchored in a set of shared foundational beliefs, could nonetheless evolve, as did Christianity, into quite distinctive "Confucianisms." Students of China speak of classical Confucianism, Mencian Confucianism, the Confucianism of Xunzi, Han Confucianism, Song Confucianism, Neo-Confucianism, utilitarian Confucianism, Wang Yangming Confucianism, and so on. The reader need not fear: I have no interest in cataloguing all the various schools within Confucianism here or elaborating on their major differences. My aim is simply to show how the Master's vision could unfold differently in the hands of different interpreters. The focus will be on his most prominent earlier followers—Mencius (fourth c. BCE) and Xunzi (third c. BCE)—whose "competing" interpretations of Confucius's vision would endure throughout imperial Chinese history. (Chapter 5 will treat the influential "Neo-Confucian" reinterpretation of Confucianism—the standard interpretation of Confucian teachings in the later imperial period.)

We do not have precise dates for either Mencius or Xunzi, but we can comfortably place Mencius in the heart of the fourth century BCE and Xunzi in the very late fourth but mostly third century BCE. Mencius hailed from the small state of Zou in northeast China. From Zou, he set out to find a ruler sympathetic to his views and, as the text in his name indicates, had audiences with a few of them. But he failed to gain the sympathetic ear he had hoped and thus, like Confucius before him, turned to teaching. The text of the *Mencius*, in seven "books," is said to be a record of conversations compiled by disciples between Mencius and rulers of the day, his disciples, and philosophical interlocutors.

Xunzi was a native of Zhao in the central part of north China. He spent much of his later life as an academician of the Jixia Academy, a center of lively intellectual debate at the court of Qi in northeast China. His eponymous text, the *Xunzi*, in thirty-two chapters or sections, is different from both the *Analects* and the *Mencius*: it is not a record of conversations or aphorisms but a set of self-contained essays thought to be written by Xunzi himself. Hence what we find in the *Xunzi* is sustained argumentation, a text far less fragmentary in composition than either the *Analects* or the *Mencius*.

Both Mencius and Xunzi fully embraced the Master's core beliefs: (1) that man can become a sage; (2) that moral goodness results from self-cultivation; (3) that learning is a part of the self-cultivation process; (4) that a vanguard elite is essential in promoting morality among the people; and (5) that good governance depends on the virtue of the ruler, who creates the right conditions whereby the people can become good and society can become harmonious.

Yet there were fundamental disagreements between the two great thinkers, most especially over the source of man's moral perfectibility. Mencius locates that source internally in human nature, asserting that man is born with a nature that naturally tends toward goodness, just as water naturally tends to flow downhill (6A.2). Man must learn to develop this innate goodness—in the face of external forces that might lead him astray—in order to achieve moral perfection. Xunzi strongly objects, unambiguously proclaiming: "Man's nature is evil" (sec. 23, "Man's Nature is Evil"). To find the moral resources that will enable him to redirect his recalcitrant human nature, man needs to look externally, to his environment and culture. With such starkly different assumptions about man's inherent nature—and consequently about where the source of man's morality is to be found—it is unsurprising that the particular paths Mencius and Xunzi propose for achieving moral perfection diverge as well, especially in the important areas of self-cultivation and learning.

Mencius

1. On human nature and self-cultivation

In stating that human nature is good just as water flows downhill, Mencius is not arguing that all men *are* good—but rather that by the nature endowed in them they are all *inclined toward goodness*. Not everyone actualizes this goodness, just as water does not *always* flow downhill (consider, Mencius says, water that has been dammed or forced uphill). The goodness of human nature is an inherent potential that must be developed or nurtured. As Mencius explains, goodness in human nature is like shoots that must be given the opportunity to grow:

> All people have a mind-and-heart that cannot bear to see the suffering of others.... Here is why I say that all men have a mind-and-heart that cannot bear to see the suffering of others: today, no matter the person, if he suddenly comes upon a young child about to fall into a well, his mind-and-heart fills with alarm and is moved to compassion. It is not because he wishes to ingratiate himself with the parents of the young child; nor is it because he seeks renown among villagers and friends; nor is it because he would hate the bad reputation. From this we can see that to be without a mind-and-heart of compassion is not to be human; to be without a mind-and-heart that is ashamed of evil in oneself and hates it in others is not to be human; to be without a mind-and-heart of humility and deference is not to be human; to be without a mind-and-heart of right and wrong is not to be human. The mind-and-heart of compassion is the shoot of true goodness (*ren*); the mind-and-heart that is ashamed of evil in oneself and hates it in others is the shoot of righteousness; the mind-and-heart

of humility and deference is the shoot of ritual propriety; the mind-and-heart of right and wrong is the shoot of wisdom. People have these four shoots just as they have the four limbs.... All of us have these four shoots within us; if we know to develop and bring each to completion, it will be like a blaze catching fire or a spring finding a path. He who is able to bring them to completion is capable of preserving all within the four seas; he who doesn't complete them is incapable of caring for his parents. (2A.6)

For Mencius, each and every human being is born with the four shoots of true goodness, righteousness, ritual propriety, and wisdom. To be without these shoots "is not to be human"; they are no less a part of man's normal, natural make-up than are man's four limbs. To persuade us of the rightness of his belief he asks us, his readers, to imagine encountering a young, defenseless child about to fall into a well. That every one of us, he argues, would *instinctively* be moved to compassion is evidence that the shoot of compassion is within each of us.

The astute reader may have noticed, however, that nowhere in this passage does Mencius go on to say that having been moved to compassion, we would *all* actually rush to rescue the child. This is not mere oversight on Mencius's part. It is essential to his philosophical position and speaks to his belief that there exists a gap between the "four shoots" endowed in us at birth and their maturation into true goodness, righteousness, ritual propriety, and wisdom. There are some who, when they encounter the child facing almost certain death, may pause to assess, "Will I benefit from rescuing the child?" "Will I suffer injury in the rescue process?" or "Will I be held liable for the child's death?" These people, Mencius asserts, are no different in their human nature from other people; they too possess the shoots of true goodness, righteousness, ritual propriety, and wisdom. But, unlike those who rush to save the child without calculation or concern for their safety, their shoots of morality have not been nurtured to maturity. This is where self-cultivation plays an essential role.

To illustrate what happens if man's moral shoots are left uncultivated, Mencius tells the story of Ox Mountain. In this story, Mencius also suggests—without being as explicit as we might like—that the source of man's evil is the back-and-forth of everyday life. His daily needs for sustenance and his competition with others for limited resources put him at great risk of losing hold of his innate goodness:

> The trees on Ox Mountain were once quite luxuriant. But as they were just on the outskirts of the capital, axes chopped them down one by one. Could they remain luxuriant? And yet, given the renewal that goes on day and night and the nourishment that rain and dew bring, shoots and buds never fail to sprout. But then cattle and sheep come to graze. This is what accounts for the bald appearance of the mountain. When people see its baldness, they assume it was never wooded. But could this really be the nature of the mountain?
>
> The same is true of what belongs to a person: can he really be without the mind-and-heart of true goodness and righteousness? His letting go of his originally good mind-and-heart is like the axe chopping down the trees: if day after day it is chopped away, can it remain luxuriant? And yet, given the renewal that goes on day and night and the restorative vital energy that accompanies the dawn, his likes and dislikes will still bear some small resemblance to those of other people. But what he does during the day will fetter and destroy it [the originally good mind-and-heart] completely. If it is fettered repeatedly, the restorative vital energy of the nighttime will be insufficient to sustain it. And if the restorative vital energy of the nighttime is insufficient to sustain it, he will become little different from a beast. When others see a beast, they will assume that it never had a natural disposition for goodness. But could this really be the natural tendency of the man? Thus if it receives nourishment, there is nothing that will not grow; if it does not receive nourishment, there is nothing that will not decay. Confucius said, "Hold on to it and you preserve it; let go of it and you lose it...." Isn't it of the mind-and-heart that he speaks? (6A.8)

This passage underscores the point that all human beings, no matter how depraved-seeming, are born with precisely the same good human nature. Even a serial killer is so endowed, though simply by looking at him we would hardly know it. Just as the constant lopping of trees by axmen and the eating of young shoots and buds by sheep and cattle rob Ox Mountain of any semblance of its natural vegetation, forces external to a man's nature can cut down his shoots of morality and rob him of any semblance of humanity. This is why "holding on" to the original mind-and-heart is so urgent; for it is here, in this mind-and-heart, that the four shoots of virtue are located.

Holding on to the mind-and-heart is thus what distinguishes the morally superior man from others. It is this mind-and-heart, Mencius says, that enables man to think and reflect; and only by thinking and reflecting is man capable of keeping to the right path—of warding off the perils and lures of the external world—thereby giving his four inborn shoots of true goodness, righteousness, ritual propriety, and wisdom the opportunity to grow to maturity—to develop fully. It is such growth that results in man's moral perfection.

2. On the ruler

It is the explicit responsibility of the ruler, Mencius argues, to assist his subjects in their efforts to keep to the right path. To this end, the ruler is enjoined, in what is an especially eloquent passage in the text, to provide for the material well-being of his people:

> If the people lack a constant livelihood it follows that they will lack a constant mind-and-heart. And if they lack a constant mind-and-heart, they will become reckless and depraved, and there is nothing they will not do. To lead them into crime and then follow it up with punishment is to entrap the people. Is it possible that a truly good man in a high position would entrap the people? For this reason, an enlightened ruler supervises the livelihood of the people, making sure that they can adequately serve their parents above and children

below, and that in good years they are abundantly full and in bad years escape death. Only afterward does he urge them on toward goodness (*shan*, 善); in this way, the people will find it easy to follow him. (1A.7)

Confucius, too, had suggested that only when their basic material needs have been satisfied will the people be susceptible to moral instruction. But Mencius goes on at much greater length, proposing specific and concrete measures that a good ruler should take in promoting the people's well-being:

> Do not interfere with the farming seasons, and the crops will be more than can be consumed; do not let finely meshed nets be cast in ponds and lakes, and the fish and turtles will be more than can be consumed; let axes enter the mountain groves only at the appropriate time, and the timber will be more than can be used. When crops and fish and turtles are more than can be consumed, and timber is more than can be used, the people will nurture the living and mourn the dead in contentment. Their nurturing of the living and the mourning of the dead in contentment: such is the beginning of the kingly way. Let mulberry trees be planted in households of five *mu*, and fifty-year olds can wear silk; do not let the times for breeding chickens, pigs, dogs, and hogs be neglected, and the seventy-year olds can eat meat. In fields of one hundred *mu*, do not deprive them of the seasons, and families of several mouths will never go hungry. Be attentive to instruction in the village schools and set forth the principles of filial piety and fraternal respect, and those with graying hair will not be on the roads carrying heavy loads on their backs and heads. It is impossible in a state where seventy-year olds wear silk and eat meat, and the black-haired people suffer from neither hunger nor cold, for the ruler not to be regarded as a true king. If pigs and hogs eat the food meant for the people and you know not how to restrain them, and if there are famished dying on the roads and you know not how to distribute aid from the granaries, and then say, "It is not me, it is just a bad year," how is this any different from mutilating

and killing a person and then saying, "it is not me, it is the weaponry." Let the king not put blame on a bad harvest, and all under heaven will come to him. (1A.3; cf. 1A.5 and 1A.7)

Such are the policies and practices of a "true king."

Mencius criticizes the rulers of his day, claiming that they are concerned more with profit and wealth for themselves than with the welfare of their people. The very first passage of his text conveys Mencius's displeasure with King Hui of Liang:

> Mencius went to see King Hui of Liang. The king said, "Sir. You've come here from a very great distance. Surely you've brought something that will be of profit to my state?" Mencius responded, "Why must Your Majesty use the word 'profit'? Surely, it is true goodness and righteousness alone that matter. If the king were to say, 'what will be of profit to my state?' and the high officials were to say, 'what will be of profit to my family?' and gentlemen and commoners were to say, 'what will be of profit to myself?' then everyone above and below would turn to attacking one another for profit, and the state thereby would be put in grave danger.... Let Your Majesty say, 'It is true goodness and righteousness alone that matter.' Why must Your Majesty use the word 'profit'?" (1A.1)

A ruler who speaks of profit prompts his people as well to speak of—and pursue—profit, which not only leads them astray, away from attending to their moral shoots, but ironically does nothing to profit the ruler or his state. The ruler's job, as Confucius stated earlier, is to be a moral exemplar: "When the prince is truly good, everyone else is truly good; when the prince is righteous, everyone else is truly righteous" (4B.5). In short, for Mencius, good government is one that provides food and shelter and sets a moral example for the people, thereby creating an environment, material and moral, in which the innate sprouts of true goodness, righteousness, ritual propriety, and wisdom can grow naturally and without impediment.

Mencius goes so far as to assert that only a ruler who practices this sort of benevolent government, who places the people first (7B.14), is a true ruler. According to tradition, Jie, the last king of the legendary Xia dynasty, and Zhou, the last king of the Shang dynasty, were cruel tyrants. Thus, when King Xuan of Qi asked,

> "Is it the case that Tang banished Jie and King Wu cut down Zhou?" Mencius responded, "So it says in the records." King Xuan said, "Is it permissible for a minister to murder his sovereign?" Mencius said, "A thief of true goodness is called 'thief'; a thief of righteousness is called 'criminal.' Thieves and criminals are called good-for-nothings. I have heard of the punishment of the good-for-nothing Zhou; I have not heard of the murder of a sovereign." (1B.8)

In arguing that a sovereign is to be called a sovereign only when he comports himself as a "true" sovereign should, Mencius is associating himself with his Master's call for the "rectification of names": the belief that names and reality must be brought into perfect accord (*Analects* 13.3). Killing Zhou, in Mencius's judgment, is not a matter of regicide, but rather a matter of killing a good-for-nothing who abandoned the proper way of a ruler and so abandoned being a real ruler. Mencius's point here, which will resonate powerfully throughout imperial Chinese history, is that a ruler who does not behave as a true sovereign, caring for the people with benevolence and righteousness, may be deposed.

While rulers may be deposed, there is no call here for popular revolution, as it is the ministers alone who have the right to depose an evil ruler (cf. 5B.9). Still, with this passage, the ruler's responsibility to care for the welfare of the people—to provide an environment where the people's shoots of virtue might develop—is backed up by a powerful sanction—the removal of the ruler by force. Over the centuries, this passage has sometimes been cited—though not entirely accurately, as I have indicated—as support for the right to popular rebellion.

Xunzi

1. On human nature and self-cultivation

On the question of human nature, our two philosophers could hardly be in more conspicuous disagreement. If for Mencius human nature contains the shoots of true goodness, for Xunzi it is the very source of man's immorality and waywardness. Taking direct aim at his predecessor, Xunzi declares, "Mencius states that man's nature is good (*shan*), but I say that this view is wrong" (sec. 23, "Man's Nature is Evil"). In the opening to a chapter devoted entirely to the proposition that "man's nature is evil," Xunzi explains:

> Man's nature is evil; goodness is the result of deliberate action. The nature of man is such that he is born with a fondness for profit. If he indulges this fondness, it will lead him into wrangling and strife, and all sense of courtesy and humility will disappear. He is born with feelings of envy and hate, and if he indulges these, they will lead him into violence and crime, and all sense of loyalty and good faith will disappear. Man is born with the desires of the eyes and ears, with the fondness for beautiful sights and sounds. If he indulges these, they will lead him into license and wantonness, and all ritual principles and correct forms will be lost. Hence, any man who follows his nature and indulges his emotions will inevitably become involved in wrangling and strife, will violate the forms and rules of society, and will end as a criminal. (sec. 23, "Man's Nature is Evil")

Xunzi insists that man has to turn away from his nature in order to become good. And so—like Mencius before him—he attaches great importance to the cultivation process. But for Xunzi the aim is not the nurturing of man's inborn nature; it is the restraint and redirecting of man's natural impulses.

Given his view of human nature and the need to "reform" it, Xunzi places considerably more emphasis on the role of learning and ritual principles in the cultivation process than does Mencius. Learning and rituals are essential tools in acculturating man, in reshaping his recalcitrant nature. For Mencius, who assumes human nature to be naturally inclined toward the good, these tools are simply less necessary. It is not that Mencius entirely dispenses with them, but they are not given the same prominence in his thinking that they are in Xunzi's, where gentle nurturing of the emergent shoots within is more essential.

The essential role that learning plays in Xunzi's variety of Confucianism is revealed in the very first passage of the *Xunzi* text:

> Learning should never cease. Blue comes from the indigo plant but is bluer than the plant itself. Ice is made of water but is colder than the water ever is. A piece of wood as straight as a plumb line may be bent into a circle as true as any drawn with a compass, and even after the wood has dried, it will not straighten out again. The bending process has made it that way. Thus if wood is pressed against a straightening board, it can be made straight; if metal is put to the grindstone, it can be sharpened; and if the gentleman studies widely and each day examines himself, his wisdom will become clear and his conduct without fault. (sec. 1, "Encouraging Learning")

Learning is endowed here with the enormous power to take the raw, unruly, and selfish stuff of man's nature and mold—indeed, *force*—it into morally sensitive tissue.

As we have seen, Mencius, by contrast, does not view learning as the forceful reshaping tool it is for Xunzi for the simple reason that for him man's moral "shoots" need but gentle cultivation, not an aggressive bending, dying, or grinding, to produce true goodness. Thus, while Mencius may encourage man to "learn widely" (4B.15), as Confucius did (e.g., 6.27, 9.2), and may urge true kings to establish schools for illuminating proper social relations, as rulers during the glorious Three Dynasties did (3A.3), learning in the sense of disciplined study or schooling does not hold the urgency for him that it does for Xunzi and consequently receives far less systematic attention from him.

If, for Xunzi, learning is to be an effective tool of transformation, it has to be the *right* learning. For this reason he lays out a model curriculum, one to be followed throughout a lifetime:

> Where does learning begin, and where does it end? I say that as to program, learning begins with the recitation of the Classics and ends with the reading of the ritual texts; and as to objective, it begins with learning to be a man of breeding and ends with learning to be a sage. If you truly pile up effort, you will enter into the highest realm. Learning continues until death, and only then does it cease. Therefore, we may speak of an end to the program of learning, but the objective of learning must never for an instant be given up. To pursue it is to be a man, to give it up is to become a beast. (sec. 1, "Encouraging Learning")

Xunzi offers further curricular direction, prescribing the subjects and the "textbooks" to be covered—and even suggesting the sequence in which they should be taken up:

> The *Book of History* is the record of government affairs, the *Book of Poetry* the repository of correct sounds, and the rituals are the great basis of law and the foundation of precedents. Therefore, learning reaches its completion with the rituals, for they may be said to represent the highest point of the Way and its power. The reverence and order of the rituals, the fitness and harmony of music, the breadth of the *Poetry* and the *History*, the subtlety of the *Spring and Autumn Annals*—these encompass all that is between heaven and earth. (sec. 1, "Encouraging Learning")

This passage represents the earliest effort in the long Confucian tradition to establish a coherent curriculum for students of the Way.

Rituals, as should be evident, are at the heart of Xunzi's learning program. It is through the guidance of ritual, Xunzi argues, that man's proclivity for evil can be restrained and that, over time, his behavior can become habituated to doing good:

> A straight piece of wood does not have to wait for the straightening board to become straight; it is straight by nature. But a warped piece of wood must wait until it has been laid against the straightening board, steamed and forced into shape before it can become straight, because by nature it is warped. Similarly since man's nature is evil, he must wait for the ordering power of the sage kings and the transforming power of ritual principles; only then can he achieve order and conform to goodness. (sec. 23, "Man's Nature is Evil")

Xunzi ends this passage with what is a refrain throughout his writings—the purposeful, mindful effort to reform or redirect our unruly inborn nature: "From this it is obvious, then, that man's nature is evil, and that his goodness is the result of deliberate action."

For Mencius, as we might expect, ritual does not have the same "straightening" or restraining effect since restraint is not called for in his view of the innate goodness of human nature. In Mencius's understanding, correct ritual practice—like true goodness, righteousness, and wisdom—is but the natural realization of man's good nature; it is, in his words, an "adornment" of true goodness and righteousness (4A.27; cf. 7A.21), not an instrument for producing these virtues.

For Xunzi, though, rituals are an essential part of self-cultivation. They do, as he explains in the passage cited above, serve to "straighten," but they also nurture man emotionally and psychologically. Proper ritual practice allows man to give expression to his emotions without risk of disrupting the social order. By moderating or "civilizing" his unruly innate emotions and desires, rituals enable man to harmonize his affective world with the larger world around him: "Rituals trim what is too long and stretch out what is too short, eliminate excess and remedy deficiency, extend the forms of love and reverence, and step-by-step bring to completion the beauty of proper conduct" (sec. 19, "A Discussion of Rites"). Ritual thus makes possible man's emotional fulfillment, even while it restrains his most anarchic emotional impulses. Xunzi remarks, "All rituals begin in simplicity, are brought to fulfillment in elegant form, and end in joy. When rituals are performed in the highest manner, then both the emotions and the forms embodying them are fully realized" (sec. 19, "A Discussion of Rites"). Performed well, then, ritual has a powerful beauty, an aesthetic appeal that uplifts man and contributes to his emotional well-being.

Finally, ritual also serves the important function of demarcating the various statuses in society—a function Confucius himself would surely have endorsed. Xunzi comments:

> Where ranks are all equal, there will not be enough goods to go around; where power is equally distributed, there will be a lack of unity; where there is equality among the masses, it will be impossible to employ them.... If men are of equal power and station and have the same likes and dislikes, then there will not be enough goods to supply their wants, and they will inevitably quarrel. Quarrelling must lead to disorder and disorder to exhaustion. The former kings abhorred such disorder, and therefore they regulated the principles of ritual in order to set up ranks. (sec. 9, "The Regulations of a King")

Rituals reinforce the hierarchy of society. They lend cohesion and stability to that hierarchy, encouraging all—"rich and poor," "eminent and humble"—to play their roles as they should.

2. The mind and moral perfectibility

We should not let Xunzi's rather dark view of human nature obscure an essential point: he believes as fervently as Mencius does in the moral perfectibility of men. He writes:

> The man in the street can become a Yu [the sage king].... Any man in the street has the essential faculties needed to understand true goodness, righteousness, and proper standards, and the potential ability to put them into practice. Therefore, it is clear that he can become a Yu. (sec. 23, "Man's Nature is Evil")

It is, in short, because man is born with a faculty for knowing, for discriminating right from wrong, that he is able to come to understand morality from his environment. If in Mencius it is man's nature that distinguishes him most starkly from beasts, in Xunzi it is man's capacity to know and to put into practice what he knows, through conscious activity, that separates him most clearly from other creatures.

But while man may be capable of understanding morality, why should he want to? Why would man, born evil with "natural" selfish desires, love of profit, and feelings of envy and hate, have any impulse to turn toward the good? In other words, why would he of evil nature choose to submit to the straightening tools of learning and ritual in the first place? Xunzi's explanation is fascinating:

> Every man who desires to do good does so precisely because his nature is evil. A man whose accomplishments are meager longs for greatness; an ugly man longs for beauty; a man in cramped quarters longs for spaciousness; a poor man longs for wealth; a humble man longs for eminence. Whatever a man lacks in himself he will seek outside. But if a man is already rich, he will not long for wealth, and if he is already eminent, he will not long for greater power. What a man already possesses in himself he will not bother to look for

outside. From this we can see that men desire to do good precisely because their nature is evil. (sec. 23, "Man's Nature is Evil")

It is expressly because of the selfish desires and feelings of envy and jealousy with which we are born that we aggressively seek to possess the goodness we do not yet have. Here man does not pursue goodness for the sake of goodness, at least initially, but rather to satisfy his longing for what is not his. The pursuit of morality, ironically, is thus born of selfishness and avarice.

But it is not man's selfish nature alone that explains his impulse to seek out good. It is also the mind's realization that if he gives free expression to his unruly inborn tendencies, "chaos and mutual destruction" result (sec. 23, "Man's Nature is Evil"). Concluding that chaos and mutual destruction are not in his self-interest, that they do not ultimately enable him to satisfy his desires, the mind looks to restrain his innate tendencies and turns to ritual principles and classical teachings for guidance.

3. On the ruler

The responsibility of the ruler, according to Xunzi, is to establish order among people innately averse to it. The ruler understands that the people's inborn passions and desires must be restrained if social order and harmony are to be achieved. Through routine ritual instruction, he ventures to curb these passions and desires, and thus acculturate the people to a pattern of socially appropriate behavior.

Xunzi recognizes, however, that there are some subjects for whom the relatively gentle force of ritual will be insufficient, men whose impulses are so unruly that other, more assertive means of control are required. For this reason, he argues that the ruler should also employ law and punishment as means of keeping order. Xunzi's ideal is a society in which order and harmony are created and maintained largely through the transformative influence of ritual practice; when ritual fails, however, the ruler must rely on the more coercive instruments of law and punishment.

This ideal society can be realized only under a "true king." It is the good and righteous ruler alone who is capable of taking the true measure of his people and of determining how best to suppress their self-interest. He is a keen and fair judge, knowing unerringly when to guide by ritual and when to compel through law and punishment. Because he is caring and kind in his treatment of them, the people willingly lend him their support.

Xunzi is quite realistic in his assessment of the likelihood that a "true king" would actually come to power in his own day. Unlike Mencius, who spends much of his life trying to persuade contemporary rulers to strive to become true kings, Xunzi acknowledges that perhaps the best that could be hoped for is a ruler capable of imposing order—whether it be through law and punishment or military might—on his state. The age of the sage rulers, he concludes, is long past; needed now is a hegemon or strongman (*ba*, 霸) who can at least ensure a stable government and an ordered social hierarchy, if not a population morally perfected and harmonized through ritual.

Man and heaven in Mencius and Xunzi

In the fourth century BCE Mencius argues that heaven is an ethical entity. A short century later, Xunzi characterizes heaven as a naturalistic entity, operating according to its own internal rhythms and without any ethical impulses; heaven, for him, approximates "nature" or the "natural order." Given these different views, it is quite natural that the two philosophers understand the role that heaven plays in the life of man differently as well.

A close ethical connection exists between man and heaven, according to Mencius:

> There are honors bestowed by heaven, and there are honors bestowed by man. True goodness, righteousness, conscientiousness, trustworthiness, unflagging delight in the good—these are honors bestowed by heaven. (6A.16)

Heaven is responsible for what is moral in man. For it is from heaven that man receives his shoots of virtue. If he is to become fully good, fully human, it is his obligation to develop these shoots. By developing them, he is conforming with—and satisfying—heaven's ethical plan for him. In a sense, then, heaven is dictating, biologically, man's norms of behavior.

In a passage in the *Mencius* that is rather unique in its cosmic scope and suggestion of cosmic unity, the philosopher states:

> For a man to give full realization to his mind-and-heart is for him to understand his own nature, and a man who knows his own nature will know heaven. The retention of his mind-and-heart and the nurturing of his nature are the means by which he serves heaven. (7A.1)

Mencius means here to impress on his followers the binding ethical connectedness between man and heaven. If heaven is the author of man's morality, of the moral potential embedded in man's mind-and-heart, the realization of this morality yields insight into heaven's design. This is to know heaven. Fulfilling the task heaven imposes on us at birth, carrying out the ethical responsibilities it seeds in us, is to serve heaven. The term "serve" reminds us too that ultimately we are subordinate to the morally legislative force of heaven.

Xunzi's understanding of heaven could hardly be more different. For him, heaven is naturalistic, without intent, and thus has no ethical connection to humankind. In fact, Xunzi is highly critical of the widespread contemporary belief that heaven communicates with man, signaling its approval and disapproval of him through omens and portents:

> When stars fall or trees make strange sounds, all people in the country are terrified and go about asking, "Why has this happened?" For no special reason, I reply. It is simply that, with the changes of heaven and earth and the mutations of the *yin* and *yang*, such things once in a while occur. You may wonder at them, but you must not fear them. (sec. 17, "A Discussion of Heaven")

Heaven here is the natural order. Its manifestations are nothing but the spontaneous "mutations of the *yin* and *yang*" of the universe. This is not an interested or willful heaven "communicating" with or responding to human activity. Xunzi's writings are insistent in their rebuke of those who believe that heaven is an entity responsive to their entreaties: "You pray for rain and it rains. Why? For no particular reason, I say. It is just as though you had not prayed for rain and it rained anyway." And, he reminds them, "heaven does not suspend the winter because men dislike the cold" (sec. 17, "A Discussion of Heaven"). His insistence indicates how pervasive he regards the "superstitious" practices and beliefs of the day to be. And the message he hopes to convey is emphatic: Heaven is unconcerned with man!

It is because there is no ethically connected or concerned heaven that human beings must look to the sages and the rituals they created for moral guidance. Heaven offers no moral endowment, no moral assistance. Indeed, in Xunzi's view, what made the sages of the past—Yao, Shun, and Yu—deserving of reverence and praise is that they alone grasped that man requires a set of ritual principles and teachings to give him moral direction.

When all goes well for man, when all goes well for society, it is entirely man's doing. Man must come to realize that his lot is not a matter of heaven's will or fate, as many would believe:

> Are order and disorder due to heaven? I reply, the sun and the moon, the stars and the constellations, revolved in the same way in the time of Yu as in the time of Jie. Yu achieved order; Jie brought

disorder. Hence order and disorder are not due to heaven. (sec. 17, "A Discussion of Heaven")

Man's lot depends simply on man's efforts.

Although heaven does not exist for the purpose of providing for man, Xunzi acknowledges that in its "mutations of *yin* and *yang*," heaven does have powerful effects on man. Xunzi exhorts man to be alert to these effects and to make the best possible use of them.

> Is it better to exalt heaven and contemplate it,
> Or to nourish its creatures and regulate them?
> Is it better to follow heaven and sing hymns to it,
> Or to take hold of what heaven mandates and make use of it?
> Is it better to look ahead to the seasons and await what they bring,
> Or respond to the seasons and exploit them?
> Is it better to wait for things to increase of themselves,
> Or to develop their capacities and transform them? (sec. 17, "A Discussion of Heaven")

For Xunzi, heaven is separate and other, without interest in the human world or in man's well-being; yet through the conscious effort described here, man can find in the effects of heaven's ever-mutating *yin* and *yang*, in its constancy of change, much that benefits human life.

To conclude: Mencius and Xunzi, the founders of the two major branches of early Confucianism, agree: (1) that man is morally perfectible; and (2) that to achieve moral perfection man must undertake a self-cultivation process. But for Mencius, the source of man's moral potential is internal, found in man's nature itself; for Xunzi, it is to be found externally, in the culture, especially in the body of ritual created by the sages of antiquity. For Mencius, consequently, self-cultivation is largely a process of gentle nurturing, of keeping the growing inner goodness shielded from the harmful and corrupting influences of society; for Xunzi, the process is necessarily more expansive and aggressive, and looks directly to society for tools capable of "straightening" or reshaping man's inborn twisted nature. For Mencius, the ideal ruler is responsible for creating the right environment—moral and material—for his subjects, one in which man's moral potential can develop naturally and without impediment; for Xunzi, the ruler is more of a presence, actively guiding the behavior of his subjects and acquainting them with an array of cultural tools—ritual, law, punishment—necessary to curb their reckless impulses and become accustomed to a goodness foreign to their nature.

Xunzi's faith in the transformative power of learning and ritual has had an indelible influence on education and social practices throughout Chinese history. But Mencius's influence has been greater still: thinkers responsible for the grand reformulation of the Confucian intellectual tradition a millennium later would reject Xunzi's view of human nature and embrace Mencius's sunnier outlook that man is born with the shoots of perfect goodness within him.

Chapter 5

The reorientation of the Confucian tradition after 1000 CE: The teachings of Neo-Confucianism

Confucius, Mencius, and Xunzi would set the philosophical course for the Confucian tradition for more than the next one thousand years. But in the eleventh century there emerged a coterie of Confucian thinkers who began to rethink the teachings of their classical predecessors. Their "school" of Confucianism, known as *daoxue* (道學) or "Learning of the Way," and often referred to as Neo-Confucianism, would quickly come to dominate Chinese intellectual and political life. Indeed, by the thirteenth century, it had become the state orthodoxy—the statement of principles that ostensibly guided the Chinese imperial government and the foundation of the civil service examination systems—a status it would retain until the early years of the twentieth century.

Neo-Confucianism represents a reworking of the Confucian tradition. It upholds the values and ethics of classical Confucianism but reorients that Confucianism in two important ways: (1) it grounds the values and ethics of classical Confucianism in an elaborate system of metaphysics (that is, an explanation of the nature of being and knowing) generated over the eleventh and twelfth centuries; and (2) on the basis of this system of metaphysics, it creates a structured program of self-cultivation, a step-by-step template for "becoming a sage."

Why the emergence of Neo-Confucianism at this particular time? Looking around, Confucian scholar-officials of the Song period (960–1279) perceived their world to be in a state of crisis—politically, intellectually, and morally. Since the beginning of the dynasty in the tenth century, parts of the north China plain, the heartland of Chinese civilization, had been occupied by a string of non-Chinese tribes; in 1127 the last of these tribes, the Jurchen, captured the Song capital of Kaifeng and set up the Jin dynasty (1115–1234), forcing the Song court to flee south. The loss of the north was a terrible shock to Chinese scholar-officials. For them, it represented far more than just a straightforward military or political defeat; it meant that the Way was in steep decline. Had the Chinese emperor and his ministers been behaving as virtuous Confucian rulers and ministers should, the Way would have prevailed, and the north would not have been vulnerable to "barbarian" attack. What led these men to stray from the Confucian path of moral cultivation and virtuous government?

Many blamed another, earlier "barbarian" intrusion: Buddhism. This foreign teaching, introduced to China from India in the first century CE, became increasingly popular after the sixth century. Its allure was such that Confucians plaintively acknowledged, "Be they adults or children, officials, farmers, or merchants, men or women, all have entered the Buddhist fold." Even many scholars, the very men who were supposed to keep the Confucian Way alive and well, had been drawn to Buddhism over the years (especially to elite schools like Chan, more commonly known as Zen in the West), attracted by its philosophical exploration of human nature, the mind, ways of knowing, self-realization, and man's relation to the cosmos. Confucians viewed this popularity with dismay, fearful that Buddhism's preoccupation with the enlightenment of the individual was distracting people at all levels of society from their fundamental Chinese—and Confucian—obligation to better themselves morally for the purpose of serving society and promoting the welfare of others.

Beginning in the tenth and eleventh centuries, scholars who identified with the Confucian tradition, mindful of the challenges posed to the prominence of the Confucian Way, were given to deep reflection on how the challenges to their Way could be met. They turned to the canon of classical texts with an almost religious vigor, seeking in them those teachings—those truths—that would speak eloquently to the urgent issues of the day and thereby serve to resuscitate a Way in decline. Many men were involved in this tenth- and eleventh-century engagement with the canon, searching for its contemporary relevance. Among the most predominant of these thinkers were Zhou Dunyi (周敦頤) (1017–73), Zhang Zai (張載) (1020–77), Cheng Hao (程顥) (1032–85), and Cheng Yi (程頤) (1033–1107).

But this Song reflection on the meaning of the Confucian tradition would find its most influential voice in the next century with Zhu Xi (朱熹) (1130–1200), the great synthesizer of Song Neo-Confucianism. Based on the writings of these earlier Song thinkers, Zhu Xi's synthesis is given its full expression in a series of brilliant interlinear commentaries on the Confucian Classics. Zhu's genius rests on his presentation of a "new" Confucian philosophy that looks to and is justified by readings of what by his day were ancient—indeed archaic—texts. Deeply influenced by the ideas of his Song forerunners (and no doubt, too, by some of the concerns introduced and popularized by Buddhism), he constructs from the Classics, in the metaphysical language of his day, a systematic process of self-realization that, if followed scrupulously, was to lead the individual to sagehood. In true Confucian fashion, this morally perfected man—unlike the enlightened Buddhist—is fully committed to serving society and bringing harmony to the people. Through his efforts, and those of others like him, the once-great Way can be resuscitated.

Zhu Xi's Neo-Confucian metaphysics

The classical Confucian thinkers, Mencius and Xunzi, assume—albeit on different grounds—that man is capable of moral perfection. Zhu Xi, too, assumes that man is morally perfectible, but he develops a metaphysics that supports this assumption in new philosophical terms—or, rather, in old terms that he invests with new meanings. He embraces and provides ontological support for Mencius's belief that human nature is good, that all men are born with the beginnings of the four cardinal virtues: true goodness, righteousness, ritual propriety, and wisdom. Indeed, it is with Zhu Xi that the Mencian view of human nature triumphs over Xunzi's and becomes orthodox. But Zhu goes further to address the philosophical question left largely unresolved by Mencius: If men are born good, where and how does evil arise? And, having pinpointed the source of human evil, Zhu Xi then lays out a detailed, step-by-step program for eradicating evil and nurturing man's innate goodness.

The entire universe, Zhu Xi claims, is made up of *qi* (氣), translated variously as material force, matter-energy, vital energy, and psychophysical stuff (but in this volume will simply be left transliterated as *qi*). This *qi* is dynamic, circulating endlessly, coalescing in particular configurations to constitute particular things in the cosmos. However different the forms or shapes of things might be, they are all constituted of *qi*. In the words of his predecessor Zhang Zai:

> *Qi* moves and flows in all directions and in all manners. Its two elements [the primal forces of *yin* and *yang*] unite and give rise to the concrete. Thus the manifold diversity of human beings and things is produced. Through the ceaseless succession of these two elements of *yin* and *yang* the great meaning of the universe is established.

Qi is thus what binds everything in the universe together. This assumption of a shared, pervading cosmic *qi* has strong ethical implications for Zhu and his fellow Neo-Confucians. For if all things are constituted of *qi*, all things and people in the universe are interrelated. A well-known essay by Zhang Zai opens with the following lines:

> Heaven is my father, and earth is my mother, and even such a small creature as I finds an intimate place in their midst.
>
> Therefore that which extends throughout the universe I regard as my body and that which directs the universe I consider as my nature.
>
> All people are my brothers and sisters, and all things are my companions.

Related by a shared *qi*, people are to treat all other people as they would "brothers and sisters." This quasi-biological relationship among human beings helps to explain why, as Mencius suggested many centuries earlier, man spontaneously feels compassion toward others. Humankind, after all, is simply one big family.

This *qi* thus argues for the interconnectedness among all things in the universe, living and inanimate. But it is also this *qi* that accounts for the differences among the multitude of things. At birth different things receive different allotments of *qi*, varying in both quality and quantity. Human beings overall, Neo-Confucians explain, receive *qi* in its most clear and pure form, and it is precisely the quality of this *qi* that distinguishes them most sharply from other beings and things in the universe. Zhu's predecessor, Zhou Dunyi, writes:

> The interaction of the two *qi* [*yin* and *yang*] engenders and transforms the myriad things. The myriad things produce and reproduce, resulting in unending transformation. Human beings alone receive the most refined and spiritually efficacious *qi*.

He goes on to explain that it is because he is possessed of the "most refined and spiritually efficacious *qi*" that man, among all creatures, is singularly capable of moral discernment, or knowing the difference between good and evil. A tree receives the *qi* for a tree and consequently does not have a similar capability.

But *qi* is not the *source* of man's innate goodness. For just as all things in the universe are constituted of *qi*, all things are also possessed of *li* (理) or principle (sometimes translated "moral principle"). As Zhu Xi explains, "In the universe there has never been any *qi* without principle nor any principle without *qi*." If *qi* is what gives a thing its particular psychophysical form, the principle inhering in the thing is, in Zhu's words, "the reason why it is as it is and the rule to which it should conform." Every object, event, relationship, matter, and affair in the universe has principle. A boat has the attributes or normative properties of a boat, a cart the attributes of a cart, a tree the attributes of a tree, a human being the attributes of a human being, and the relationship between father and son the attributes of a relationship between father and son on account of principle. That man as a species is inherently good is owing to the principle inhering in man.

Thus principle is found in each and every thing and affair. Yet principle is ultimately one, Zhu insists. For him, the principle of the boat, the cart, the human being, the tree, and the father-son relationship is but a particular manifestation of the one universal principle. He frequently repeats the formula, "principle is one, its manifestations are many" (*li yi fen shu*, 理一分殊). "Principle," then, might best be understood as something like the underlying pattern or blueprint for the cosmos, encoded in each and every thing in the universe; the particular manifestation of principle designates the more particular role each thing is to play in the unified, cosmic plan. To rephrase Zhu's brief definition: each thing has its manifestation of principle, but the rule or pattern to which all things in the universe conform is ultimately one, as is the reason all things are as they are. Though without form or generative power, it is principle that provides coherence and order for a universe of ever-changing *qi*.

75

Following Mencius, Zhu Xi understood human nature to be precisely the same in each and every person, for each and every person is endowed at birth with the same four cardinal virtues. In wholeheartedly adopting the Mencian view of goodness of human nature, however, Zhu gives it a contemporary metaphysical grounding, arguing that human beings have the nature they have *because* human nature is identical with principle or *li* in man: "Human nature is simply this principle."

But if human nature is principle and thus always the same and always good, what accounts for "bad" people and "bad" behavior? Zhu Xi and his fellow Neo-Confucians look beyond Mencius (who never really answers this question satisfactorily) to elaborate an explanation of evil that is grounded in their understanding of *qi*. And what they conclude is that although man, relative to all other creatures in the universe, receives the highest-grade *qi*, each and every person receives a different allotment of *qi*; the quality and quantity of this allotment varies from one individual to another—in contrast to human nature, which is the same in everyone. Some *qi* is clearer than others, some more refined than others, and some less dense than others.

This allotment of *qi* gives each person his or her peculiar form and individual characteristics; it is what accounts for individuation among human beings. And it is this allotment of *qi* that, depending on its degree of clarity and density, either enables a person's innately good nature to shine forth or obscures it, preventing it from becoming manifest. Zhu Xi remarks to his disciples, "Human nature is principle. The reason that there are good and bad men is simply that each allotment of *qi* has its clarity and turbidity."

The particular endowment of *qi* that any individual receives at birth is fated. I happen to receive *this* quantity and quality of *qi*, and you happen to receive *that* quantity and quality of *qi*. But—and it is essential to understand this if we are to understand the Neo-Confucian project—our endowment of qi is malleable. It is because qi is dynamic and changeable, and because its change can be directed by human endeavor, that people can better themselves, even become sages. The clearest, most refined qi, if it is not properly tended to, can become turbid and coarse, but a turbid and coarse endowment can be nurtured into something more refined and clear. The challenge for each human being is to care for his allotment of qi, keeping or making it perfectly refined and clear so that the goodness, which is his nature, can reveal itself without obstruction.

This potential for perfection creates what is for Neo-Confucians *the* human moral predicament: man lives at all times with the capability to be fully moral and yet commonly finds himself falling short of moral perfection. He is possessed of an innate moral potential but a potential that must actively and consciously be given realization. To this end, his endowment of qi has to be nurtured, for it is the condition of his share of qi that determines whether his moral potential as a human being will be achieved. Zhu Xi thus shares with Mencius the view that man is perfectible; but by elaborating the meaning of the terms li, "principle," and qi, he and his fellow Neo-Confucians offer a detailed ontological explanation of *how* one can improve oneself.

Self-cultivation and the investigation of things

It is this moral predicament that explains the centrality of the self-cultivation process in the Neo-Confucian philosophical system. Self-cultivation is the conditioning process, the means by which the individual can refine his qi, thereby enabling the goodness that is in his human nature to be realized. In reflecting on the canon of texts in the Confucian tradition, Zhu Xi finds in the first chapter of the *Great Learning* (*Daxue*, 大學) what he regards as the basis of a Neo-Confucian program of self-cultivation for followers of the Confucian Way:

Those of antiquity...wishing to cultivate themselves, first set their minds in the right; wishing to set their minds in the right, they first made their intentions true; wishing to make their intentions true, they first extended knowledge to the utmost; the extension of knowledge lies in the investigation of things.

Self-cultivation thus rests on efforts to investigate things, a term that had for many centuries been a matter of debate.

In a chapter of commentary that Zhu writes on this passage in the *Great Learning*, he formulated what would become the orthodox interpretation of "the extension of knowledge lies in the investigation of things":

> What is meant by "the extension of knowledge lies in the investigation of things" is this: if we wish to extend our knowledge to the utmost, we must probe thoroughly the principle in those things that we encounter. Now every person's mind, with its intelligence, is possessed of the capacity for knowing; at the same time, every thing in the world is possessed of principle. To the extent that principle is not thoroughly probed, a person's knowledge is not fully realized. For this reason, the first step of instruction in the *Great Learning* teaches students that, encountering anything at all in the world, they must build on what they already know of principle and probe still deeper, until they reach its limit. Exerting themselves in this manner for a long time, they will one day suddenly become all-penetrating; this being the case, the manifest and the hidden, the subtle and obvious qualities of all things, will all be known, and the mind, in its whole substance and vast operations, will be completely illuminated. This is what is meant by "the investigation of things." This is what is meant by "the completion of knowledge."

The process proposed here is an inductive one. Man is required, whenever he encounters any thing, any affair, or any relationship, to look beyond its mere surface. He is to probe into and reflect on the particular manifestation of principle that inheres in it, in order to get at its underlying truth. With time and effort, his understanding of things will deepen and broaden, resulting in an ever-clearer apprehension of the world around him. Probing principle thus begins with the particular but yields to an understanding of the universal principle that gives coherence to all things.

The aim of this investigation, of course, is not an understanding of the world for understanding's sake, nor is it scientific inquiry that is being proposed. Rather, if a person genuinely understands the true nature of things and affairs, if he truly recognizes why things, affairs, and relationships are as they are, he will be capable of dealing with those things, affairs, and relationships he encounters in the world in a perfectly appropriate way. Getting at the various manifestations of principle leads to an enlightened understanding of the cosmic order, which, in turn, results in moral awareness of how one ideally is to comport oneself with respect to all things and affairs in that cosmic order.

According to Zhu, what makes the apprehension of principle possible for each and every man is that we are all born, as Xunzi suggested, with a mind capable of understanding—an intelligence capable of penetrating the underlying principle in things. Yet, he acknowledges, not everyone achieves the sort of total illumination that is the goal of self-cultivation. For while the mind is capable of realizing principle and arriving at a cosmic understanding, it can also be led astray from such realization by excessive human emotions or creaturely desires. Hence, echoing the words of Mencius, Zhu Xi frequently admonishes disciples "to hold on to the mind" or "to seek the lost mind." As he says on one occasion, "It's simply because man has let go of his mind that he falls into evil." Or on another, "If a person is able to preserve his mind so that it is exceptionally clear, he'll naturally be capable of merging with the Way." For Zhu, the mind, which is constituted of only the most refined *qi*, is the "root." It must be tended to and kept refined if man is to behave as he should, in accord with principle.

Helping to guide the mind in the right direction is *zhi* (志), the will, which Zhu explains as the intention or the inclination of the mind or, literally, "where the mind is headed." Man must strive to keep this will firmly fixed; for if it is strong and determined, the will is sure to lead the mind along the right path toward apprehension of principle and away from insidious desires. *Lizhi* (立志), "to establish or fix the will," significantly, is one of Zhu Xi's most common refrains in his discussions with his disciples. Of course, the central importance of the will was suggested long before by the Master himself, when, in his "autobiographical" remark in the *Analects* (2.4), he related that fixing his will on learning at the age of fifteen had been the first step on his journey to moral perfection.

Zhu Xi's program of learning

As Zhu Xi explains, principle can be investigated anywhere and in anything. An individual could find principle looking at the natural world and its phenomena, at a filial son, at historical events and persons, at personal experiences and relationships. Principle inheres in all things and affairs, after all. But Zhu worries that such a broad and undefined field of inquiry will prove overwhelming and discourage individuals from taking up the investigation of things seriously. He wishes to provide students with more focused direction, suggesting what "things" in particular are likely to yield clear and direct apprehension of principle.

For Zhu Xi, these "things" turn out to be the texts of the ancient sages, the Confucian Classics: "All things in the world have principle, but its essence is embodied in the works of the sages and worthies. Hence, in seeking principle we must turn to these works." Because the Classics had been written by the great sages of antiquity—men who themselves had in their own lives come to refine their *qi* and apprehend principle fully—principle would be most clearly and readily manifest in them. There might be other ways to investigate principle, but studying the writings of the sages is simply the most efficient.

To give followers of the Confucian Way still further direction—in the hopes of making the Way as accessible as possible to them—Zhu Xi develops a coherent, sequential program of classical learning. From the canon, which by the late eleventh century has expanded to the Thirteen Classics from the original Five Classics, he selects four—referred to commonly after the thirteenth century as the Four Books—that he has students read before all others: the *Great Learning*, the *Analects*, the *Mencius*, and *Maintaining Perfect Balance*. The "ease, immediacy, and brevity" of these four works gives them an accessibility that other texts in the canon lack. They are the very foundation of all Confucian learning:

> In reading, begin with passages that are easy to understand. For example, principle is brilliantly clear in the *Great Learning*, *Maintaining Perfect Balance*, the *Analects*, and the *Mencius*—these four texts. Men simply do not read them. If these texts were understood, any book could be read, any principle could be investigated, any affair could be managed.

Only after mastering these four texts are students to turn to the so-called Five Classics, the texts that had been, for a millennium and a half since the Han period, the focal works of the tradition: the *Book of Changes*, the *Book of Poetry*, the *Book of History*, the *Book of Rites*, and the *Spring and Autumn Annals*.

The shift in emphasis advocated here by Zhu, away from the Five Classics and toward the Four Books, underscores an obvious point but one that should be made explicit: much as the Christian Bible offers a range of teachings that invite readers to take away a variety of meanings, so too does the Confucian canon of Thirteen Classics include multiple writings with different contents and emphases. The Five Classics and the Four Books may share a fundamental moral, social, and political vision, but the expression of that vision takes rather different forms in the two collections.

To generalize, the Five Classics illustrate Confucian morality using examples and lessons from ancient history; identify ideal institutions and methods of governance drawn from the past; describe in detail how one should conduct oneself in life's varying circumstances; and prescribe at length the ritualistic practices for maintaining a well-ordered society. From the Five Classics the ruler learns how to rule, the minister learns how to administer the realm, father and mother learn how to parent, children learn how to express filial devotion, older and younger learn how to show mutual respect, and friends learn how to be friends.

The Four Books tend to be less historical, descriptive, and concrete. Concerned primarily with the nature of man, the inner source of his morality, and his relation to the larger cosmos, they introduce and explain general principles of proper conduct and action and do not require the detailed, and often abstruse, knowledge of ancient Chinese institutions and social practices that comprehension of the Five Classics requires.

A shift from the Five Classics to the Four Books is something more than a curricular shift; it represents a major philosophical reorientation in the Confucian tradition "inward" toward teachings in the canon that place considerably more emphasis on the inner realm of human morality—and on the all-important process of self-cultivation. From the thirteenth century on, these Four Books—with Zhu's interlinear commentary on them—would make up the "core curriculum" in the Confucian tradition, the gateway to self-realization and true understanding.

Thus in Zhu's program of learning, there is a right set of texts to be read, and there is a right sequence in which to read them. But, just as importantly, there is a right *way* to read them. Over the course of many years, Zhu develops for his students an elaborate hermeneutics (or, to use his own term, *dushufa* [讀書法]), a comprehensive theory and method of reading the canonical texts. Merely passing one's eyes over a text will not produce genuine understanding, he warns. For the writings of the sages to reveal their truths, the reader must approach them with a seriousness of purpose, with the proper mental attitude. He is to be fully attentive, free of all other concerns and distractions: "In reading, you want both body and mind to enter into the passage. Don't concern yourself with what's going on elsewhere, and you'll see the principle in the passage." To this end, Zhu advocates the practice of quiet-sitting or meditation, for it settles and clears the reader's mind, leaving it perfectly open and receptive to the message of the sages.

The reader is expected to recite the classical text over and over again until he no longer sees it as "other." This repeated recitation results in memorization of the text, but the process is anything but mechanical or "rote"; each reading-and-recitation produces a deeper, more subtle and personal understanding of it. There is no prescribed number of times a text should be read, Zhu says, commenting only, "when the number's sufficient, stop," but he acknowledges that in some instances fifty or a hundred readings may not be too many. Zhu Xi's hermeneutical goal is straightforward: the follower of the Way, through recitation and memorization of the Classics, is to internalize or embody the words of the sages. By truly making them his own, he himself can become sage-like.

It should be clear that for Zhu Xi, the study of the canon is important not principally as an intellectual exercise but as the intellectual means to a moral—even spiritual—end. Through the classical texts, especially the Four Books, the sensitive reader can apprehend the principle underlying the universe and hence, as Zhu writes, "practice the Way with all his strength, and so enter the realm of the sages and worthies." The investigation of things thus may be directed toward things in the world "out there," especially the Four Books, but it is a process that takes as its ultimate aim internal moral cultivation. By apprehending the principle that inheres in things, we awaken fully the principle that is our human nature, and thereby give full expression in our daily lives to the true goodness, righteousness, ritual propriety, and wisdom, endowed in each and every one of us at birth. Probing principle to "its limit" is simply to perfect oneself morally.

The "Neo" in Neo-Confucianism

A religious or philosophical tradition endures because of its ability to adapt and remain relevant over time. One that is unable to respond to a changing world necessarily becomes moribund. The famous longevity of the Confucian tradition is attributable in large degree to its elasticity, to its effectiveness in shaping its message to address the pressing issues of the day. The "Learning of the Way," or Neo-Confucianism, exemplifies the capacity of the Confucian school to engage in ongoing reinterpretation of its fundamental teachings. Eleventh- and twelfth-century reflection on the Confucian tradition and the revered canonical texts yields an understanding of that Confucian message that is meaningful and relevant to an eleventh- and twelfth-century audience. This is an audience, which following the introduction of other schools in the first millennium, such as "Mysterious Learning" (*xuanxue*, 玄學, once commonly rendered as Neo-Daoism) and Buddhism, has become accustomed to thinking about the metaphysical nature of the cosmos, man's place in it, and man's capacity for understanding and accessing the true reality of the universe.

A brief list of ways that eleventh- and twelfth-century "Neo"-Confucianism is "new" or different from classical Confucianism would include:

- the use of a language of metaphysics;
- the placement of man in the context of a universe of principle and *qi*;
- the introduction of "the investigation of things," probing principle as *the* basis of the Confucian self-cultivation process;
- a narrowing of focus with an emphasis on man's interior life;

- the establishment of a set program of learning, privileging the Four Books over the Five Classics.

The metaphysical cast of the Neo-Confucian system, in particular, can make it challenging to appreciate that this later school of Confucianism indeed shares classical Confucianism's most fundamental beliefs:

- that man is morally perfectible;
- that learning is key to moral improvement;
- that the sages of antiquity provide a Way to be moral and behave appropriately in society;
- that the morally superior man has a transforming effect on others (*Daxue*, ch. 4);
- that social harmony is the result of people fulfilling the moral responsibilities of their roles.

The Neo-Confucian school may thus incorporate a metaphysical terminology of principle and *qi* into its teachings, but the school ultimately reaffirms—and promulgates for a contemporary eleventh- and twelfth-century audience—the moral-ethical teachings that lie at the heart of the early Confucianism of Confucius, Mencius, and Xunzi.

Neo-Confucianism after Zhu Xi

Over the course of the thirteenth and fourteenth centuries, Zhu Xi's Neo-Confucian synthesis would establish itself as *the* Chinese intellectual and political orthodoxy. Challenges to his teachings did, however, emerge. Most notably, in the fifteenth century, Wang Yangming (王陽明) (1472–1529) developed a competing variety of Neo-Confucian thought. Initially a follower of Zhu Xi's teachings and program of self-cultivation, Wang concluded that Zhu's approach to moral perfection was too bookish and his process of investigating things too onerous. He proposed that "principle is identical with the mind," and *not* with human nature, as Zhu had insisted.

The implications were great. No longer was there a need for students to engage in the protracted study of the canon or to seek to apprehend principle in the world "out there." In Wang's understanding, the "extension of knowledge" from the *Great Learning* did not refer to the expansion of one's knowledge of principle through *external* investigation. Instead, it referred to the extension or application of one's *inborn* moral mind—one's innate faculty for knowing Confucian right from wrong—to every thing, affair, and situation one encounters. For Wang, to learn right from wrong, to conduct oneself properly in all of life's circumstances, did not depend on undergoing an arduous program of learning; rather, it required only that one be mindful in what one does, exercising the good moral—and Confucian—conscience with which every human being is born.

One obvious appeal of the Wang Yangming school was to make moral self-realization considerably more accessible than Zhu had, since canonical literacy and study were no longer essential. The Zhu Xi school maintained, in theory, that anyone could achieve moral perfection, but in practice its program of rigorous classical learning limited the field to those who had the good fortune, means, and leisure to devote themselves to study. In sum, Wang's teachings offered—at least in theory—the possibility of Confucian self-cultivation to the unlettered, or as Wang himself put it, to "ignorant" men and women.

The Zhu Xi school would be the dominant school of Neo-Confucianism in China through the early decades of the twentieth century; its doctrines and commentaries would serve as the foundations of the educational curriculum. But Wang's school would also achieve considerable popularity, especially in the later years of the Ming dynasty (1368–1644). And as their teachings made their way to Korea and Japan, both the Zhu Xi and Wang Yangming schools of Neo-Confucianism would find loyal and enthusiastic followers beyond the borders of the Middle Kingdom.

Chapter 6
Confucianism in practice

Thus far we have seen Confucius "transmit" an idealized sociopolitical vision from the early Zhou past; we have seen faithful followers elaborate on this vision and, in the process, give it different emphases and meanings; and we have seen thinkers more than a millennium after his death reorient this vision, explaining its significance in the context of a universe of principle and *qi*, philosophical terms that would have meant little to Confucius himself. Our focus has been mainly on the realm of ideas, looking at how the original vision of the Master has been given a variety of interpretive shapes over the centuries.

These teachings, however, did not remain confined to the realm of ideas. They played out in the ritual practice of the people, in the everyday life of the family, in the moral education of peasants and elite alike, and in the administration of the state. It may be an oversimplification to characterize premodern Chinese society and politics as "Confucian"—suggesting more of an exclusivity than is warranted—but to say they were heavily "Confucianized," informed and guided by principles of the Confucian persuasion, is entirely apt.

The "Institutionalization" of Confucianism

As early as the Han dynasty, Confucianism would be made an important ideological prop of the Chinese state. As we saw in chapter 1, Emperor Wu, upon ascending the throne in 141 BCE, decreed that all non-Confucians be dismissed from office; and a few years later, in 124 BCE he founded the Imperial Academy, which took as its core curriculum the Five Classics. Students at the academy who demonstrated their familiarity with one or more of the Classics through end-of-year examinations would become expectant officials, filling positions in the bureaucracy as they became vacant.

Until this time, Confucianism had been just one among many schools of thought. But with the measures taken under Emperor Wu, it assumed a central role in China's official ideology. By the tenth century or so, with the more regular use of the civil service examinations, it would become *the* dominant teaching, a sort of state orthodoxy. Thus beginning in the second century BCE, the Chinese state was increasingly a "Confucian" one—a state administered by a Confucian elite whose policies and principles of governance were rooted, at least ideally, in Confucian teachings. (Of course, as with Western Christendom, a considerable disjuncture frequently existed between the ideals of the Chinese state and its actual practices.)

In the view of Confucians, official service was society's highest and most important calling. This view was reflected in their hierarchical ranking of occupations, which (though never formally legislated) exercised profound influence over the course of Chinese history. In this ranking, the (Confucian) scholar-official held the top spot; next came the farmer whose labors fed the people; then came the artisan who provided products and tools for daily use; and finally came the merchant. The merchant's ranking at the very bottom was indicative of the Confucian view of the merchant as parasitic, making and doing nothing of his own but trading in the wares of the more productive "classes"—the farmers and artisans. This disparagement of merchants would persist through most of imperial Chinese history, as Confucian values became increasingly dominant in society. (Note also that the military man figures nowhere in this hierarchy, foreshadowing the culture's privileging of the civil service over military service and the generally low esteem in which military men and their pursuits were held in the later imperial period.)

Merchants, the least socially esteemed, might amass great wealth and live in luxury and comfort, while peasants typically struggled to survive. Indeed, merchants' wealth could easily exceed that of even the most prominent officials. Such wealth, however, would never confer on merchants the social status and prestige associated with officials, and it was perhaps for this reason that successful merchants often insisted that their sons study for the examinations rather than continue in their profession. Officials, it was believed, had won appointment to the civil service through extraordinary talent and moral character—talent and character so great that they had come to the attention of the emperor himself. Called to serve, they stood at the side of the imperial presence, assisting and advising him on how to bring peace and harmony to the empire. They were the elite of society, "the stars in heaven," as a popular saying put it.

Chinese governments employed a variety of methods for recruiting civil officials. The most common were: (1) recommendation, whereby local authorities would forward the names of outstanding individuals to the capital for appointment to the civil service; (2) "appointment by protection," a privilege held by officials of a certain status to nominate one or more of their sons, or other family members, for civil service; and (3) state-sponsored examinations, success in which would lead to official status in the civil service, if not always to official appointment. Of these, it was the civil service examinations that would become the major—and by far most prestigious—avenue of recruitment.

The civil service examination system

Rulers of the Sui dynasty (589–618) extended the use of examinations, administering them throughout the empire. The following dynasty, the Tang (618–907), continued and expanded the Sui practice, holding them more regularly and bringing in larger numbers of officials—though by no means the majority—through the examination process. But it was the later Tang practice of awarding those successful in the examinations with the highest offices that gave the examination system decisive momentum. By the ninth century, even those who might have won a civil appointment through hereditary privilege felt it necessary to sit for the examinations if they were ever to obtain a position of real importance. Henceforth, for a full millennium, until the early years of the twentieth century, the road to elite status in China was through the examination system.

From the time of its maturity in the late Tang to the early twentieth century, the examination system was based almost entirely on what had come to be identified as Confucian teachings; its purpose, after all, was to recruit officials who could assist in governing a state that defined itself as Confucian. The particular form that examinations would take, and the particular weighting given to different features of the examination (e.g., explications of the Classics, poetic composition, policy questions, prose style, calligraphy), might change over the centuries, but the knowledge tested on the examinations remained steadfastly Confucian. Prior to the thirteenth century, candidates were expected to demonstrate mastery of the Five Classics in particular; they were the core of the examination curriculum. In 1313, with the growing influence of the Zhu Xi school, the government decreed a change, announcing that the Four Books, and in particular Zhu Xi's understanding of the Four Books, would now serve as the basis of the examinations.

It is hard to exaggerate the influence that the examination system exercised in Chinese society. Children would begin their education

5. A nineteenth-century Chinese classroom. Students standing in front of the teacher's desk are "backing the book," that is, reciting the text aloud by rote.

in the home, typically under the tutelage of their mothers, with Confucian primers like the *Three Character Classic*. If they continued with their schooling—as only a very small percentage of Chinese children did due to limited family resources—by the age of seven or so they would embark on the study of the *Great Learning*, the *Analects*, the *Mencius*, and *Maintaining Perfect Balance* under a private tutor or a village teacher. The learning process would be arduous and not necessarily intellectually challenging or stimulating. Most time would be spent in rote memorization, in the exercise of "backing the book." In "backing the book," a pupil would approach the teacher's desk, and with his back to the teacher recite aloud, from memory, the line or lines the teacher had asked him to prepare. If his recitation was flawless, he would return to his desk and begin work on the next line in the text. But if he forgot a word or confused word order, then with the *thwack* of a bamboo rod, he would be ordered back to his seat to continue his memorization efforts. This learning regimen ensured that by the time he was fifteen he would "know" the Four Books; he would be capable of reciting each of them front-to-back, line-by-line, without error.

Come age fifteen, if his talent was deemed sufficient and if his family's resources were ample enough, he would likely continue with his education, focusing his aim now on the civil service examinations. The chances of winning the highest degree in the examinations, the *jinshi* (進士) or "presented scholar" degree, were slim indeed. A candidate first had to pass the prefectural-level examinations; success there would entitle him to sit for the provincial-level examinations, held triennially; success at the provincial level, in turn, permitted him to move on to the imperial capital and compete in the metropolitan examination, held triennially as well.

Studies indicate that less than 1 percent of those sitting for the district examinations would ultimately pass the metropolitan examinations. And yet, even in the face of such long odds, virtually all literate Chinese would start down the examination path. The most ambitious among them hoped to earn the *jinshi* degree, which almost guaranteed official appointment, wealth, and high status in late imperial Chinese society. Many others, aware that their chances of "hitting the bull's eye" (that is, gaining *jinshi* status) were quite slim, embarked on examination study because of other benefits the system offered. *Shengyuan* (生員) candidates who succeeded in the first major set of examinations at the prefectural level, although not yet eligible for office, were rewarded with certain privileges: exemption from corvée labor and corporeal punishment. In addition, holders of *shengyuan* status (and even more of *juren* [舉人] status, the next step up) could claim some degree of learning and knowledge of the great texts of the Chinese tradition, assets that would aid them in a variety of professions—teaching, business, and estate management among them—and in the forging of useful social networks.

The pressure to succeed in these examinations was as great as their allure. Candidates had given years, even decades, to examination preparation. Many had failed the provincial or metropolitan examinations repeatedly, only to return again for the next round. Indeed, among those successful in winning a *jinshi* degree at the capital the average age was in the mid-thirties. The onerous years dedicated to examination life by persevering candidates became fertile material for Chinese satirists and fiction writers. And no matter how well prepared or how deep and genuine their knowledge of Confucian teachings, candidates knew all too well their meager statistical chances. Not surprisingly, many would look for a competitive edge—and that edge was not necessarily always on the up-and-up.

6. The examination compound in Canton in ca. 1873. On entering the compound the candidate would be assigned a "cell" number in one of the marked rows. This compound contains 7,500 cells.

Candidates might resort to one of any number of common cheating techniques, including (1) wearing undergarments with the text of the Classics or exemplary examinations essays inscribed on them; (2) wrapping cheat-sheets in their food and bedding; (3) hiring an "impersonator"—an experienced, more accomplished essayist—to assume their identity and take their place in their assigned cell; (4) buying the examination question in advance from an official examiner; (5) bribing an examiner; and (6) arranging for someone inside or outside the compound to compose an answer to the question once it had been announced and pass that answer to them in their cell. Measures were constantly introduced by the state to prevent against these abuses and the many others that grew up around the system. But candidates could be resourceful, and given the rewards that

7. An undergarment with hundreds of model examination essays written in tiny characters. "Cheat shirts" like this, inscribed with the text of the Confucian classics or model essays, might be sewn into the lining of a candidate's robe and "consulted" during the examinations.

were sure to come with success, the temptation to boost their chances proved too great. Corruption was a constant throughout the system's history. The irony here is profound: in an examination system whose explicit purpose it was to seek out those in the empire with the best understanding of Confucian moral-ethical teachings, cheating would become epidemic.

Still, it was this system that fostered the transmission of the moral ideals and practices associated with Confucianism throughout Chinese society. As I have suggested, most education in China was geared toward examination learning and, consequently, reinforced the values promoted in the examinations. School children, whether they lived in Beijing, Xi'an, or Guangzhou, read the same Confucian primers and the same Four Books and Five Classics; and in reading the Four Books and Five Classics, they all read the commentary declared orthodox by the state. Similarly, the literate elite, whether sitting for exams in Zhejiang province, Shandong province, or Sichuan province, had all mastered the same canonical works and, it was hoped, had all come to embody Confucian virtues and ideals in the process. It was these virtues and ideals they were expected to uphold if they were fortunate enough to win official appointment. This is to say that the examination system served as a powerfully integrative force in Chinese history. It ensured that as far-flung as Chinese territory was, as large and diverse as the population might have been, there nonetheless would exist a widely shared culture, a system of values, beliefs, and customs that would create a semblance of unity among the people and make them more readily governable from an imperial center.

Interestingly, although the examinations promoted the values and interests of the Confucian school, beginning in the Tang dynasty the examination system was subject to a litany of critiques by Confucian literati themselves. Common objections to the system included:

- It rewarded rote memorization and adherence to rigid literary regulation, not originality or analytical thinking.
- It promoted bookish, antiquarian knowledge, not knowledge of practical use in governing the country.
- It was not an effective means of assessing the moral character of candidates; a system of recommendations would be more effective in finding men of good character and thus should replace or supplement the examination system.
- It distracted students from genuine learning, which is to say learning for the sake of moral cultivation; instead, learning had come to serve the pursuit of hollow fame and worldly success.
- It induced heated and vulgar competition, and a good Confucian is not supposed to compete, according to Confucius.

These objections were not dismissed out of hand and at times provoked serious debate. Indeed, over the centuries the examination system underwent frequent change and reform. Still, as a system it persevered intact for nearly fifteen hundred years and was a most powerful force in shaping and sustaining China's cultural and social norms. It was the very foundation of Chinese imperial order.

Confucianism and the common people

If the scholar-official elite could be called Confucian, what about the common people, those who had no access to education? How "Confucian" were they? They clearly shared many of the beliefs and ideals associated with Confucius and his tradition. Most, no doubt, recognized (even if they did not necessarily fulfill) their filial obligations to parents and grandparents; and most who could afford to celebrate their ancestral line through ritual offerings probably did so. Chinese society encouraged elite and non-elite, by means both formal and informal, to adopt the social practices and beliefs sanctioned by the state: Village schools instructed children, even those who would not go on to serious examination study, in basic Confucian teachings and principles;

local officials and village elders read aloud from proclamations and so-called community compacts that promoted proper social behavior; emperors circulated moral instructions, Confucian in tone and sentiment, throughout the empire; and families observed the family and ancestral rites codified by the Confucian school and passed on from generation to generation.

Whether the common people, socialized in the values and practices of the dominant culture, would have identified these values and practices as "Confucian" is doubtful. More likely they would have simply regarded them as the favored conventions of Chinese culture. Yet in being filial toward parents, respectful toward elders, and reverential toward ancestors, they were embracing practices and ideals that by the second century BCE had come to be closely associated with Confucian teachings. In characterizing China's non-elite, I propose that we err on the side of caution: most could not be called "Confucian" in that they did not give themselves to the study of Confucian teachings or identify in any substantive manner as followers of the Confucian school; and yet the lives they lived were in no small measure shaped by the teachings and practices of Confucianism.

Indeed, distinguishing between "Confucian" and "Chinese" can be historically challenging for students of China. Take filial piety. It was a centerpiece of the teachings of Confucius. No person in imperial China could reasonably claim to be a "Confucian" follower and at the same time expressly turn his back on the value of filial piety. Yet this value was in place long before Confucius celebrated it. When Confucius remarks to his disciples, "I transmit and create nothing of my own" (7.1), filial piety would have been just one of many of the tradition's teachings and practices he had in mind. So, is filial piety "Chinese" because its origins are deep within the Chinese cultural past and pre-date the emergence of Confucius and his school? Or is it "Confucian" because Confucius, in selecting from the past, gives new relevance and life to an ideal at risk and ensures its ongoing diffusion among the Chinese people through its integral association with the Confucian orthodoxy of the state? I would argue that it is both.

In any event, when I refer in this book to those ideals appropriated by Confucius from the earlier Chinese tradition as "Confucian," I trust the reader will recognize that I am not suggesting either that their origins lie with the Master or that their practice is limited to his true followers. The orthodox status attained by his teachings guaranteed them a wide, general diffusion in Chinese society.

Confucianism and the ruler

The tradition of one-man rule in China dates back to long before the institutionalization of Confucianism in the second century BCE, to no later than 1400 BCE, when inscriptions on oracle bones attest to the authority and power of Shang kings. But Confucian teachings' high praise for the virtues of one-man rule no doubt lent further legitimacy to China's traditional system of monocratic governance.

Confucius, of course, assumed that one-man rule would be effective because the ruler acted as *paterfamilias*, a benign and gentle authority guiding his subjects as a father would his children, with affection and concern for their well-being. His monocratic rule was justified by his perfect virtue and the moral charisma that naturally attracted the loyalty and obedience of his subject "children"—the common people who did not have the education or virtue to govern themselves. Through his goodness and exemplary ritual practice he would teach them proper behavior and a respect for hierarchical order, and thereby establish harmony throughout the realm. And just as a father was expected to make decisions on behalf of his family, so too was the ruler expected to make decisions on behalf of his people. The ideal government for Confucius was government *for* the people, but not *of* or *by* the people.

If the ruler were indeed benevolent, this system would work quite well. But, in fact, the sort of ruler idealized by Confucius would hardly have been typical. The question arises: How, according to the Confucian system, would the political order operate effectively in the absence of a truly good Confucian ruler? Confucius, to be sure, believed and hoped that Confucian-trained officials would be a check on the ruler's power—and provide the direction he needed. But the fact remained that the bureaucracy was staffed with "his" men. They had come to office through his beneficence, through success in the examinations that his government sponsored and an additional palace examination that he personally had overseen. The emperor was responsible for appointing and dismissing them; even exiling or killing them was entirely his prerogative. This is not to say that scholar-officials did not offer criticism of imperial decisions, but they did so at great personal risk. Challenges to the authority of the emperor were not made casually—or routinely, I imagine.

The fundamental problem in imperial Chinese history was this: when Confucian ideology proved ineffective in guiding and constraining the imperial will, there was little recourse. There were no constitutional or legal limits on the power or conduct of the emperor and no institutions or offices with legitimate authority to check imperial behavior when it veered far from Confucian ideals. As a consequence, rulers could—and at times did—abuse their power or neglect their responsibilities with impunity.

Take the case of the first emperor of the Ming, Taizu (r. 1368–98), a commoner who came to the throne as the leader of a rebel movement. Barely literate, he is said to have had a deep distrust—and envy—of the highly educated scholar-official class. In 1380, suspicious that his prime minister was plotting to overthrow him, Taizu abolished the secretariat—the central administrative organ of government—and took over personal and direct control of virtually all aspects of government. The opinion of Confucian scholar-officials carried no weight. Those officials who displeased him he had flogged and beaten with clubs (often to death) in full view of the court. Under Taizu, benevolent, paternalistic rule gave way to cruel, sometimes savage despotism.

The Tianqi emperor (r. 1620–27) was a ruler of the negligent variety, preferring to spend his days at carpentry, making fine furniture, rather than oversee the administration of the realm. His disregard—indeed distaste—for affairs of state gave the court eunuch Wei Zongxian the opportunity to seize control of government. Wei proceeded quickly to fill positions of power with opportunistic cronies, levy exploitative taxes on the people, and conduct a brutal purge of hundreds of scholar-officials who dared oppose him. In short, Tianqi's imperial disinterest resulted in a notorious regime of terror, from which the dynasty never recovered. Within two decades of Wei's rise to power, the Ming collapsed.

These cases are somewhat extreme but are offered to make the point that (because there existed no constitutional checks) bad things could happen when those at the highest levels of government did not embrace Confucian ideals. Most of the time, however, even if rulers and officials did not fully embody Confucian ideals, they were sufficiently able and competent to oversee the affairs of the state and defend the interests of their dynasty.

Confucianism and the family

As we saw in chapter 2, Confucius makes a case in the *Analects* for the foundational importance of the family in Chinese society, arguing that it is the locus of moral-ethical assimilation. It is here that the individual learns to be "Chinese," that he is introduced to the values, customs, and practices that distinguish Chinese people from the rest of the "barbarian" world. And it is here that he is introduced to the normative hierarchy of society: that senior generations are superior to junior ones; that older people are superior to younger ones; and that males are superior to females.

The family was patrilineal, meaning simply that the family line was traced through the male from a founding male ancestor. Children, although descended from both a mother and father, inherited their family membership from the father. The family's descent line thus would continue only if the family continued to produce male offspring. It is for this reason that the birth of a son was from the earliest times in Chinese history regarded as a "great happiness," while the birth of a daughter was considered but a "small happiness." A son could carry on the family line; a daughter would marry "out" into her husband's family, with the principal responsibility of ensuring the continuity of his family line for another generation. In a remark that would echo through the ages, Mencius said, "There are three ways to be unfilial, and the worst is to have no heir" (*Mencius* 4A.26).

What were the consequences of a family line coming to an end? Most grievous was that there would be no one to care for the ancestors. And the importance of ancestors in Chinese culture can hardly be overstated. These ancestors were entirely responsible for a person's existence. Without his father, and his father's father, and the generations of fathers before his father's father, a man simply would not be. His feeling of indebtedness to generations past was to be repaid with reverential treatment of their spirits through the performance of the so-called ancestral rites. These rites, passed down through texts like the canonical *Book of Rites* and the *Family Rituals* (compiled by the Neo-Confucian thinker Zhu Xi), kept alive the memory of the ancestors and sustained them in their existence in the spirit realm. When the rites came to an end, so too did the memory and spirits of the ancestors.

Of course, in the Judeo-Christian-Islamic West, forebears commanded devotion, affection, and respect as well. But there is a fundamental difference between these Western Abrahamic traditions and the Chinese Confucian tradition. In the West, the one God was thought responsible for the creation of all that was and all that is. It was God who created humankind in the form of

Adam and Eve; it was thus God who was ultimately responsible for the existence of all human beings. To be sure, people bound to these traditions honored their family line, but their highest show of reverence and respect went to God, who first created their family line. In a culture where an indigenous belief in a creator deity did not exist—and where a foreign belief in one did not become widespread—it was the biological line alone that accounted for one's existence and deserved the gratitude and praise of the individual.

Like all other normative relationships in China, that between ancestor and descendant is built on the principle of reciprocity. Just as parents and grandparents guide and protect the young, ancestors, too, continue to provide guidance and protection for the family. They do what they can to ensure good fortune, good

8. Family members paying respects to their ancestors at the family altar. (The family here appears to be posing for the photographer, as normally they would be facing the altar)

harvests, and good child-bearing, and in return, on their birthdays and other commemorative occasions, the family pays respects to the ancestral spirits, placing offerings of foodstuffs (e.g., oranges, pork, liquor, and sweets) and provisions (e.g., playing cards, scrolls, tobacco, a paper model of a fine carriage) that the ancestors were known to have enjoyed in life on the family altar in the home. If it is a family from a well-to-do lineage (in Chinese terms, a lineage is made up of all the family branches that trace their descent from a single male ancestor), the offerings are placed in the offering hall at the lineage temple. Failure to remember an ancestor, it was thought, could to lead to misfortune—family illness, diseased crops, or a failed business venture. Attending to the neglected ancestor, remembering him dutifully in accord with the rites, might bring some relief or improvement to the troubles the family was experiencing.

This raises another striking difference with mainstream Western tradition. In the West, the gulf between this world and the "other world" is vast. An unfamiliar, immaterial God resides over the "other world." God is omnipotent, not bound by obligations of reciprocity. And God is ultimately unknowable, meaning too that God's plans for humankind are not fully unknowable. Hence in praying to God and looking beyond this world for guidance and hope, people are told that they must have faith. In the Chinese tradition, it is Second Uncle Feng and Grandpa Feng who reside in the other world. There is little about Second Uncle and Grandpa that is unfamiliar—or immaterial—to the younger generations of Fengs. The younger Fengs received instruction and counsel from them beginning in childhood. They shared meals with them and knew their favorite dishes. They joined them in all of the important family occasions—cappings, weddings, funerals, and ancestral ceremonies. And they helped care for them in their old age. The younger Fengs, in turning to the world beyond theirs, could be confident that the spirits of Second Uncle and Grandpa remained invested in the well-being of the family and would do all they could to benefit its members and protect them from harm.

This is to say that in China the "other-world" was not very "otherly" or remote. It is perhaps best, then, to understand the Chinese spirit world not as an "other" world but rather as part of a continuum in the world of the family.

The ancestral rites, whether performed at a modest altar in the family home or in a large offering hall in a lineage temple, serve multiple functions. They give expression to the family's indebtedness for all that previous generations provided, including, most importantly, life itself; they preserve the memory of the ancestors and sustain their vitality in the spirit world; they lessen the fear of death, demonstrating to the living that when *they* part from this world they will continue to play a role in the life of the family; and they cement family bonds—and enhance the family's corporate identity—by bringing the members together to commemorate their shared ancestry.

The focus here on sacrifice and the expression of reverence to ancestors is not meant to suggest that Chinese did not believe in gods and spirits. There were gods and spirits of the natural world, presiding over rivers, mountains, winds, seasons, and the like. And there were gods and spirits who provided assistance and comfort to practitioners of Daoism, Buddhism, and popular religious sects. But the belief in ancestral spirits—and the ceremonial respect shown them—was dominant in Chinese society, widely shared by almost all people (including those who considered themselves Daoists and Buddhists), irrespective of social or economic status.

Confucianism and women

Confucius said, "Women and petty men (*xiaoren*) are especially hard to handle" (17.23). Although many interpreters over the centuries have tried to soften the thrust of this remark, there is no getting away from its general disparagement of women. Indeed, nowhere in the *Analects* or other canonical texts is there the suggestion that the Confucian program for self-cultivation and moral perfection was applicable to women. The teachings of Confucius—and those of most of his later followers—were seemingly intended for men.

The assumption that they did not have comparable moral potential as men meant that in the Confucian view, women had no place in public life—a prejudice that would persist until the twentieth century. Never were women permitted to serve as civil officials, nor were they ever allowed to enter the examination compound. Their responsibilities were to be limited to the "inner quarters," to matters within the household.

This is not to say that women did not wield political power. But the power they exercised derived not from their own legitimate, institutionalized authority but from their proximity to a powerful male. Chinese history is filled with women who as consorts, wives, and mothers to magistrates, ministers, and emperors possessed considerable political influence. One need only think here of Empress Dowager Cixi (1835–1908) who controlled the Qing court for the entire second half of the nineteenth century, first as mother to the Tongzhi emperor (r. 1862–74), then as aunt to the Guangxu emperor (1875–1908, whom she herself appointed), and finally, after 1898, as de facto ruler. In fact, there was one truly notable exception to the rule—Empress Wu [r. 690–705] of the Tang dynasty. In 690, having been Emperor Gaozong's [r. 649–83] empress, Empress Wu ascended the throne and proclaimed herself the "Son of Heaven." She would be the first—and the last—female Son of Heaven in China's long history.

Though they might never sit for an exam or become a scholar-official, girls growing up in an elite household would commonly learn to read the Confucian primers and texts such as the *Analects*, the *Mencius*, the *Book of Poetry*, the *Book of Filial Piety*, and *Lessons for Women* by Ban Zhao of the Han dynasty. It was supposed that exposure to these works and their teachings would help make them into model, virtuous Confucian women. It was supposed, too, that literacy among girls in the family would enhance the family's status, indicating that it had the resources and cultural investment in educating its daughters as well as its sons. But there was an additional motivating force for providing instruction to girls: it made them more marriageable, which is to say more attractive to families looking for brides, who, as mothers, could take on the role of teaching their young sons the basic Confucian texts. Few girls in non-elite families would receive an education; rather, they would learn to carry out the domestic chores that would be theirs to do for much of the rest of their lives: sewing, weaving, cooking, cleaning, and perhaps farming the fields.

For a girl, marriage was *the* life-changing event. On her wedding day, the bride, typically in her mid-to-late teens, would leave her family's household for the groom's household to live there with his parents, his still unmarried sisters, his brothers, their wives, and their children. Arriving at the gate of groom's house or estate, she would bow to the senior generations of the groom's family and to the memory of the family's ancestors. Henceforth, his family would be hers; and his ancestors would be hers. It was to them, not to her birth family's ancestors, that she would sacrifice and pay reverence. She herself now belonged to the groom's family line.

The loss of identity that came with this transition to the husband's family must have been traumatic for many. Consider: the wedding day may have been the first time a bride set eyes not simply on her husband's extended family but on her husband himself. She had not known him and had played no part in arranging the union with him. The union was an agreement reached by his parents and her parents, perhaps with the assistance of a matchmaker, based on what served the mutual interests of the two families. It was decidedly *not* a contract of love entered into freely by wife and husband.

So here we have a very junior female entering into an unfamiliar household, with a jumble of new relationships to negotiate. There were the parents-in-law, the brothers-in-law, the sisters-in-law, the nieces, and the nephews, not to mention the possible servants, maids, concubines, cooks, and the like. Living now under one roof with them, it was essential that she get along with them—if only because it would make her new life easier.

From her natal family and from the teachings of Ban Zhao in *Lessons for Women*, the young bride had learned what was most necessary to "succeed" in her new family: to serve her parents-in-law dutifully, to obey their every command. The mother-in-law and the father-in-law were now her parents. Her principal responsibility was to please them, especially the mother-in-law, by every means possible. In *Lessons for Women* she had read:

> Nothing is better than an obedience that sacrifices personal opinion. Whenever the mother-in-law says, "Do not do that," and if what she says is right, unquestionably the daughter-in-law obeys. Whenever the mother-in-law says, "Do that," even if what she says is wrong, still the daughter-in-law submits unfailingly to the command. Let a woman not act contrary to the wishes and opinions of parents-in-law about right and wrong; let her not dispute with them what is straight and what is crooked. Such (docility) may be called obedience that sacrifices personal opinion.

It was important that as the outsider entering into the family, the daughter-in-law subordinate her will to the family's. Only by doing so might she, with time, gain welcome acceptance into it.

Some in-law families might be kinder, gentler, and more welcoming to the new bride and some less so. But they all had precisely the same expectation of this outsider: that she bear the husband's children and continue the family line—now her family line. Of course, she had been raised by her birth parents to understand as well that this was her obligation when she married.

So on entering her new household she knew what the expectations of her were; and she knew that the sooner she met them, the sooner her lot as an outsider in the family would likely improve. And because nothing would improve it more than producing an heir, she hoped, just as the in-laws did, that the child would be a boy. Their "big happiness" would be her "big happiness."

Having children did not simply improve her lot in her new family. When she had "married out," she had left behind all the emotional richness of her natal family; entering into the husband's family, she was little more than a stranger on probation in a sense. Likely, her existence there had been largely devoid of emotional fulfillment and bonds of real affection. Now, with a child or children of her own, her life would be much enriched emotionally—and much less lonely. Within the larger patrilineal family of her in-laws she had created her own close-knit "uterine family"—as some anthropologists call it—in which she at last could expect to enjoy some degree of emotional intimacy. (She might also imagine a day when she would become a mother-in-law to her sons' wives and enjoy the authority, respect, and privileged treatment her own mother-in-law enjoyed.)

It was her place as mother to provide instruction for the young children. She was to be their first teacher. The *Analects for Women*, a ninth-century text outlining the "Confucian Way for women" (*fudao*, 婦道), asserts: "Most all families have sons and daughters.... The responsibility to instruct them rests solely with the mother." The mother's instruction was to take the form of modeling good behavior and recounting stories, historical events, and anecdotes from the tradition that taught Confucian morality. Additionally, mothers who were literate would recite aloud the *Lessons for Women*, the *Analects*, the *Mencius*, the *Book of Filial Piety*, and other staple works to their children. Such recitation served a dual purpose: it furthered the moral development of the children and introduced to them the canonical texts their families hoped they (especially the boys) would someday master.

9. A lithographic illustration from *Wu Youru huabao* (1908, rpt. 1983) of a mother teaching her son to write

In the domestic sphere, then, the woman played the roles of dutiful daughter-in law and moral instructress. But she played yet another role, important and yet only infrequently mentioned in the scholarly literature—that of household manager. The *Analects for Women* states:

> A woman who manages the household should be thrifty and diligent. If she is diligent, the household thrives; if lazy, it declines. If she is thrifty, the household become enriched; if extravagant, it becomes impoverished.

In an elite household, the responsibilities associated with managing the household could be especially daunting and might include tracking the family finances; maintaining order among the various sons and their wives; apportioning their monthly allowances; supervising the domestic help and paying each his or her monthly "stipend"; overseeing the kitchen, which meant seeing to the purchase of all food provisions and the feeding of all members of the household; and, if it was a landowning family, collecting rents from tenants. In such a household the husband, disdainful of dirtying his hands over money matters and mundane domestic chores, most likely retreated to his study, leaving all these tasks to his wife. He might also well be away from home serving as an official, conducting business, or simply enjoying a spell in the city.

A woman's marriage was expected to be a lifelong commitment, continuing beyond the death of her husband—whether death struck at old age or in his teens. Confucian teachings viewed remarriage as a disgrace, likening a twice-married woman to a disloyal minister who serves two lords. When she married, she had not simply entered into a relationship with the groom but into a relationship with his entire family. His death thus did not bring an end to her responsibilities to the family. Were her parents-in-law still alive, her duty to serve them persisted; and were her children, or her children's children, living in the household, her duty to nurture and instruct them persisted. The Confucian tradition—and associated texts like the *Analects for Women*—required the faithful wife to remain chaste until the end of her days. The state embraced and promoted this ideal, building stone commemorative arches (some of which still stand) to honor those widowed women whose deeds had won them particular renown for chastity.

If we were to read only the normative writings for women—works like Ban Zhao's *Lessons for Women* and the *Analects for Women*—it would be easy to assume that women were passive, submissive creatures, ruthlessly subordinated first to the demands of their fathers and mothers and then to the demands of their husbands and in-laws. Yet within the family they could be a commanding force. A passage from a nineteenth-century instruction manual for women by Zeng Jifen (1852–1942), a daughter of the illustrious Confucian statesman Zeng Guofan (1811–72), speaks eloquently, even if perhaps self-interestedly, to the central role played by the wife in the fate of the Chinese Confucian family:

> To whom, then, does the responsibility of ruling the family members belong? I say the wife.... The wife is the one who rules inside of the house. There is not even one matter of the entire family that is not closely related to the wife. These matters cannot be delegated to the husband. Why can't the husband rule the home? I say, he does not have the free time. Also, his ambitions lie everywhere but with the home. Regardless of whether he is a scholar or peasant, artisan or merchant, the husband wishes to devote all of his talents to making a living outside of the house. He exhausts his intelligence, accumulates wealth, relies on the wife for management, and keeps to it in order to establish the family. Thus the rise and fall of a family's destiny is completely tied to whether the wife is worthy or not.

Although polemical, to be sure, this remark cautions us against concluding that because the recorded regulations governing women's behavior in Chinese society emphasized their subordination, women were without power or authority in pre-modern China. Some women were able—much to the distress of Confucian commentators—to exert influence, and even to dominate, in the political realm. Still more to the point, within the family, the basic unit of Chinese society, women were granted legitimate access to authority, as mothers, teachers, and household managers.

Epilogue: Confucianism in the twentieth and twenty-first centuries

The pervasive influence that Confucian teachings had on premodern Chinese politics, society, and thought would meet with harsh condemnation in the early decades of the twentieth century by leaders of the nationalist May Fourth movement. Distressed by a century of assaults on Chinese sovereignty by Western imperialist powers and Japan—and by the ineffectuality of China's recently established republican government (1912–49)—students and workers in China staged mass protests beginning on May 4, 1919. These May Fourth reformers dedicated themselves to building a strong and, above all else, "modern" China capable of taking its place in the world. To build this modern China, they first sought the source of their nation's weakness. They found that source in Confucianism.

In the late 1910s and the 1920s, they launched a frontal attack on the Confucian tradition, insisting that "Mr. Confucius" and his antiquated customs and beliefs had to go if China truly wished to become a strong and healthy society. "Down with Confucius" and "smash the Old Curiosity Shop of Confucius," they chanted. An entirely new order was needed; and while liberals like Hu Shi (1891–1962) and Marxists like Chen Duxiu (1879–1942) could disagree over the particular form this new world order should take, they were of one mind that it was time to abandon Mr. Confucius in favor of Mr. Democracy and Mr. Science.

In 1918 Lu Xun (1881–1936), perhaps the greatest Chinese writer of the twentieth century, published the short story "Diary of a Madman" as a call to his fellow countrymen to throw off the shackles of Confucian culture. He tells of a madman who spent a whole night reading history, and in this history the words "true goodness, righteousness, and morality" appeared on every page. But as the night wore on, and his reading continued, the madman "began to see the words between the lines, the whole book being filled with the two words—'Eat People.'" "Diary of a Madman" was a savage condemnation of the Confucian tradition. Dressing itself up in the pieties of goodness and righteousness, Confucianism, in actuality, cannibalized and destroyed people; its hierarchical structure, which insisted that children be filial, that women be subordinate, and that inferiors be obedient to superiors, robbed people of their autonomy and vitality, and crushed the human spirit.

Events of the nineteenth century did much to shape the attitudes of intellectuals like Chen Duxiu and Lu Xun. Battered by imperialist powers beginning in 1839, China had been forced over the course of the century to open up so-called treaty ports to foreigners; to recognize the rights of these foreigners in China to be tried under their own laws (known as extraterritoriality); to pay huge indemnities to a host of imperialist powers; and to cede territory to the British and the Japanese. Chinese had come to feel strongly that their sovereign rights as a people and a nation had been grossly violated by foreign aggressors.

Statesmen and intellectuals of the late nineteenth and early twentieth centuries could agree in principle that reform was necessary if China were to meet the challenge of the Western powers and Japan. But finding a coherent program of reform they could all sign onto proved rather more difficult. Much of the disagreement occurred over the particular balance that should be struck between the adoption of Western techniques and learning and the preservation of traditional Confucian values. Undermined by such conflicts, court infighting, and heightened imperialist pressures, the efforts at reform failed. And in 1912, to a considerable extent as a result of the failure of these efforts, the Qing dynasty fell, bringing to an end a two-thousand-year history of imperial rule in China.

Leaders of the May Fourth movement showed no ambivalence about the course the country now needed to take. To establish a new strong order, China had to make a complete break with its Confucian heritage. For some in the movement, abandoning Confucianism meant looking elsewhere for intellectual traditions and political ideologies that would serve China in the twentieth century. Chen Duxiu and Li Dazhao (1888–1927), the May Fourth leaders, turned to the Russian Revolution of 1917 and the writings of Marx. As faculty at Beijing University, they organized informal Marxist study groups on campus, out of which developed a core of intellectuals increasingly knowledgeable about and dedicated to Marxist teachings. In 1921 Chen and Li would found the Chinese Communist Party (CCP) in Shanghai. The May Fourth exhortation to break with the native cultural tradition thus laid the necessary groundwork for the establishment of the Communist Party in China.

Of course, not all Chinese were eager to reject Confucianism so decisively. Some intellectuals continued to find meaning in the Confucian tradition. For instance, Liang Shuming (1893–1988), in *The Cultures of East and West and Their Philosophies* (1921), countered the May Fourthers, insisting that Chinese traditional culture, and Confucianism in particular, could—indeed must—assist in the rebuilding of China in the twentieth century. And in the hinterland areas distant from the urban centers of reform and revolution, many people still embraced and practiced Confucian values and rituals; many children there continued to read the Four Books as well as the "modern" textbooks of the new school curriculum.

The Nationalist Party, under the leadership of Chiang Kai-shek (Jiang Jieshi, 蔣介石, 1888–1975), also continued to find value in

Confucianism. In 1934 Chiang launched the New Life movement, calling for the moral regeneration of the country and its people. Echoing one of Confucius's fundamental premises, he insisted that only a morally strong people could make for a strong nation—militarily, economically, and ethically. The New Life movement promoted in particular four virtues closely associated with the Confucian tradition: ritual propriety, righteousness, integrity, and a sense of shame. In his 1934 speech inaugurating the movement, Chiang said:

> The four virtues are the essential principle for the promotion of morality. They form the major rules for dealing with men and human affairs, for cultivating oneself, and for adjustment to one's surroundings. Whoever violates these rules is bound to fail, and a nation that neglects them will not survive.

The New Life movement had a short life, however, as it failed to engage the interest or support of the primarily urban populations at which it was directed. Within a couple of years it was largely forgotten.

A two-decade civil war between the Nationalists led by Chiang Kai-shek and the CCP under the leadership of Mao Zedong (毛澤東) (1893–1976) came to an end in 1949. On October 1, Mao stood atop the Gate of Heavenly Peace (Tiananmen) and proclaimed the establishment of the People's Republic of China (PRC).

In 1978 Deng Xiaoping (1904–97) became China's paramount leader, setting China on a course of economic and political reform. Since 2000, the leadership in Beijing, eager to advance economic prosperity and promote social stability, has talked of the goal of achieving a "harmonious society," citing approvingly the passage from the *Analects*, "harmony is something to be cherished" (1.12).

The Confucius compound in Qufu has been renovated and is now the site of annual celebrations of Confucius's birthday in late September. In recent years, colleges and universities throughout the country—Beijing University, Qufu Normal University, Renmin University, Shaanxi Normal University, and Shandong University, to name a few—have established Confucian study and research centers. And, in the opening ceremonies of the 2008 Olympics, the Beijing Olympic Committee welcomed guests from around the world to Beijing with salutations from the *Analects*, "Is it not a joy to have friends come from afar?" and "Within the fours seas all men are brothers."

Many observers interpret this "endorsement" of Confucianism by the Chinese government to be to foster stability, order, and harmony. In the first decades of the twenty-first century, there seems to be genuine interest among the Chinese people, particularly middle-class urbanites, in embracing the teachings of the ancient sage. In 2006 a little-known professor of media studies from Beijing Normal University, Yu Dan, was invited to give a series of seven lectures on Confucianism for public television's program, "Lecture Room." Explaining the significance of the *Analects* to daily life today—in a manner accessible to non-academics—she became an overnight sensation. Her lectures struck a chord with the Chinese.

The success of Yu Dan is but one expression of the renewed interest in the native Confucian tradition. Observers explain this twenty-first-century "revival" of popular interest in the Confucian tradition as the result of a confluence of factors. Crucially, rising nationalist sentiments have fueled a desire to find meaning *within the native tradition*—and to offset the malignant effects of Western decadence and materialism.

Confucius has thus played a variety of roles in China's twentieth and twenty-first centuries. At times praised, at times vilified, he has been both good guy and bad guy. Yet whether good or bad, he has always been somewhere on the stage. These days Confucius appears to be gaining favor again among the people. But what the future holds for him and his teachings is difficult to predict. All we can say with any certainty is that Confucius will continue to matter.

References

Chapter 1: Confucius (551–479 BCE) and his legacy: An introduction

References to the *Analects* are to standard book and passage number (9.13 refers to Book 9, passage 13), as found in *A Concordance to the Analects of Confucius*, in the Harvard-Yenching Institute Sinological Index Series. Translations of the *Analects* throughout this volume are drawn from Daniel K. Gardner, *The Four Books* (Indianapolis: Hackett Publishing, 2007); D. C. Lau, *The Analects* (London: Penguin Books, 1979); James Legge, *Confucian Analects*, vol. 1, *The Chinese Classics*, rev. ed. (Hong Kong: Hong Kong University Press, 1960); Edward Slingerland, *Confucian Analects: With Selections from Traditional Commentaries* (Indianapolis: Hackett Publishing, 2003); Arthur Waley, *The Analects of Confucius* (New York: Vintage, 1989); and E. Bruce Brooks and Takeo Brooks, *The Original Analects* (New York: Columbia University Press, 1998), or are my own. For a discussion of the formation of the text of the *Analects*, see John Makeham, "On the Formation of *Lun yu* as a Book," *Monumenta Serica* 44 (1996): 1–25. The passage from Sima Qian, "Whenever a visitor wearing a Confucian hat comes" is from Burton Watson's translation, *Records of the Grand Historian of China*, 2 vols. (New York: Columbia University Press, 1961), 1:270. The exchange between Liu Bang and Lu Jia is found in Watson, *Records of the Grand Historian of China*, 1:278. On the "cosmological gulf," see Frederick Mote, *Intellectual Foundations of China*, 2nd. ed. (New York: Alfred A. Knopf, 1989), 12–25.

Chapter 2: The individual and self-cultivation in the teachings of Confucius

When speaking of self-cultivation, Confucius had in mind the self-cultivation of men, not of women. There was no expectation that women should, or could, morally perfect themselves. See chap. 6 for a discussion of women and the Confucian tradition. "There is a common saying among the people" passage is from *Mencius* 4A.5 (Book 1, Part A, passage 5), translated in Daniel K. Gardner, *The Four Books: The Basic Teachings of the Later Confucian Tradition* (Indianapolis: Hackett Publishing, 2007), 75. "From the Son of Heaven on down" passage from the *Great Learning* is translated in Gardner, *The Four Books*, 6. For a discussion of the "empirical data" Confucius finds in the early texts, see Benjamin Schwartz, *The World of Thought in Ancient China* (Cambridge, MA: Harvard University Press, 1985), 86ff. The "Now, ritual furnishes the means" passage is based on the translation in Legge, *Li Chi*, 1:63. "The parrot can speak" passage is based on the translation in Legge, *Li Chi*, 1:64–5. "Ruler and subject" passage is based on translation in Legge, *Li Chi*, 2:313. "Do not roll the rice into a ball" passage is based on the translation in Legge, *Li Chi*, 1:80–81. "The instructive and transforming power of rituals" passage is based on Legge, *Li Chi*, 2:259–60. "In music the sages found pleasure" passage is based on the translation in Legge, *Li Chi*, 2:107. "A filial son, in nourishing his aged" passage is based on the translation in Legge, *Li Chi*, 1:467–68. "Although his parents be dead" passage is based on the translation in Legge, *Li Chi*, 1:457.

Chapter 3: Government in Confucian teachings

For oracle bone inscriptions, see W. T. de Bary, *Sources of Chinese Tradition*, 2nd ed., 2 vols. (New York: Columbia University Press, 1999), 1: 3–23. "Now, Zhou, the great king of Shang," from the *Book of History*, is based on James Legge's translation in *The Shoo King or Book of Historical Documents*, vol. 3, *The Chinese Classics*, 284–85. "Wailing and calling to heaven" passage is based on the translation in Legge, *The Shoo King*, 426. "Heaven sees as the people sees" passage is based on the translation in Legge, *The Shoo King*, 292. "The Mandate is not easy to keep" passage from the *Book of Odes* is translated in de Bary, *Sources of Chinese Tradition*, 1:39 (with slight modification here). "The empire is not an individual's private property" is cited in Frederic Wakeman Jr. *The Fall of Imperial China* (New York: Free Press, 1975), 81.

Chapter 4: Variety within early Confucianism

References to the *Mencius* text are to standard book, part, and passage number (e.g., 6A.2 is Book 6, Part A, passage 2); references to the *Xunzi* text are to standard section number. Translations of the *Mencius* are from Gardner, *The Four Books* or D. C. Lau, *Mencius* (Hammondsworth: Penguin, 1970), with occasional slight revision. Translations of the *Xunzi* are from Burton Watson, *Xunzi* (New York: Columbia University Press, 2003), with occasional slight revision.

Chapter 5: The reorientation of the Confucian tradition after 1000 CE: The teachings of Neo-Confucianism

"Be they adults or children" is from the *Conversations of Master Chu* [Zhu Xi's *Zhuzi yulei*], translated in Daniel K. Gardner, *Learning to Be a Sage* (Berkeley: University of California Press, 1990), 12. "Qi moves and flows in all directions" is based on the translation in de Bary, *Sources of Chinese Tradition*, 1:687. "Heaven is my father" is found in de Bary, *Sources of Chinese Tradition*, 1:683. "The interaction of the two *qi*" is based on the translation in W. T. Chan, *Source Book in Chinese Philosophy* (Princeton: Princeton University Press, 1963), 463. Zhu Xi's explanations of principle are cited in Gardner, *Learning to Be a Sage*, 90, with slight modification here. The discussion of Zhu Xi's understanding of human nature and the self-cultivation process is based on Gardner, *The Four Books*, 133-38. "Human nature is simply this principle" and "human nature is principle" passages are cited in Gardner, *Learning to Be a Sage*, 98, with slight revision here. "Those of antiquity" is translated in Gardner, *The Four Books*, 5. "What is meant by the extension of knowledge" passage is translated in Gardner, *The Four Books*, 8. Zhu Xi's remarks about letting go of the mind and preserving the mind are cited in Gardner, *Learning to Be a Sage*, 51. The summary of the program of learning is drawn from Gardner, introduction to *The Four Books* and Gardner, *Learning to Be a Sage*, 35-6. "All things in the world have principle" is cited in Gardner, *Learning to Be a Sage*, 63. "Ease, immediacy, and brevity" is Zhu's description of the Four Books, cited in Gardner, *Learning to Be a Sage*, 39. "In reading, begin with passages" is from Gardner, *Learning to Be a Sage*, 43-4. A translation of Zhu Xi's hermeneutics can be found in Gardner, *Learning to Be a Sage*, 128-62. "In reading, you want both body and mind" is found in Gardner, *Learning to Be a Sage*, 146. "When the number's sufficient" is from Gardner, *Learning to Be a*

Sage, 136. "Practice the Way with all his strength" is cited in Gardner, *Learning to Be a Sage*, 38.

Chapter 6: Confucianism in practice

John Chaffee, *Thorny Gates of Learning in Sung China* (Cambridge: Cambridge University Press, 1985), 15, estimates that successful candidates in the examination accounted for 6–16 percent of the pre-Song civil service. On cheating in the examinations, see Benjamin Elman, *A Cultural History of Civil Examinations in Late Imperial China* (Berkeley: University of California Press, 2000), 174–205; and Chung-li Chang, *The Chinese Gentry* (Seattle: University of Washington Press, 1955), 188–97. On Confucian critiques of the examination system, see David S. Nivison, "Protest Against Conventions and Conventions of Protest," in Arthur Wright, ed., *The Confucian Persuasion* (Stanford, CA: Stanford University Press, 1960), 177–201. For instances of uxorilocal marriage, where the husband moves in with the wife's family, see Susan Mann, *The Talented Women of the Zhang Family* (Berkeley: University of California Press, 2007). "Nothing is better" passage is from Ban Zhao's *Lessons for Women* and is found in Nancy Lee Swann, *Pan Chao, Foremost Woman Scholar of China, First Century* A.D. (New York: Century Co., 1932), with slight modification. Passages from the *Analects for Women* are from de Bary, *Sources of Chinese Tradition*, 1:830–31. Zeng Jifen's remark, "To whom, then, does the responsibility" is cited by Joseph McDermott, "The Chinese Domestic Bursar," *Ajia bunka kenkyū*, November 1990, 18–19.

Epilogue: Confucianism in the twentieth and twenty-first centuries

"Began to see the words between the lines" is from Hsien-yi Yang and Gladys Yang's translation, "A Madman's Diary," in *Selected Stories of Lu Hsun* [Lu Xun] (Peking: Foreign Language Press, 1972), 10. Chiang Kai-shek's "New Life Movement" speech of 1934 is translated in de Bary, *Sources of Chinese Tradition*, 2:342.

Further reading

General studies of early Chinese intellectual history

Graham, A. C. *Disputers of the Tao: Philosophical Argumentation in Ancient China*. La Salle, IL: Open Court, 1989.
Schwartz, Benjamin I. *The World of Thought in Ancient China*. Cambridge, MA: Harvard University Press, 1985.
Van Norden, Bryan W. *Introduction to Classical Chinese Philosophy*. Indianapolis, IN: Hackett Publishing, 2011.

Translations of Confucian texts

A. The *Analects*
Brooks, E. Bruce, and Taeko Brooks. *The Original Analects: Sayings of Confucius and His Successors*. New York: Columbia University Press, 1998.
Lau, D. C. *The Analects/Confucius*. London: Penguin Books, 1979.
Slingerland, Edward. *Confucius Analects: With Selections from Traditional Commentaries*. Indianapolis, IN: Hackett Publishing, 2003.
Waley, Arthur. *The Analects of Confucius*. New York: Vintage, 1989.

B. The *Mencius*
Lau, D. C. *Mencius*. Hammondsworth: Penguin, 1970.
Van Norden, Bryan W. *Mengzi: With Selections from Traditional Commentaries*. Indianapolis, IN: Hackett Publishing, 2008.

C. The *Xunzi*
Knoblock, John. *Xunzi: A Translation and Study of the Complete Works*, 3 vols. Stanford, CA: Stanford University Press, 1988–94.

Watson, Burton. *Xunzi: Basic Writings*. New York: Columbia University Press, 2003.

D. The *Book of Rites*

Legge, James. *Li Chi: The Book of Rites*, 2 vols. New Hyde Park, NY: University Press, 1967.

E. The Four Books

Gardner, Daniel K. *The Four Books: The Basic Teachings of the Later Confucian Tradition*. Indianapolis, IN: Hackett Publishing, 2007.

Studies of early Confucian thought

Fingarette, Herbert. *Confucius: The Secular as Sacred*. New York: Harper & Row, 1972.

Goldin, Paul. *Rituals of the Way: The Philosophy of Xunzi*. Chicago: Open Court, 1999.

Ivanhoe, Philip J. *Confucian Moral Self-Cultivation*. Indianapolis, IN: Hackett Publishing, 2000.

Loewe, Michael. *Dong Zhongshu: A "Confucian" Heritage and the Chunqiu fanlu*. Leiden; Boston: Brill, 2011.

Makeham, John. *Transmitters and Creators: Chinese Commentators and Commentaries on the Analects*. Cambridge, MA: Harvard University Press, 2003.

Nylan, Michael. *The Five "Confucian" Classics*. New Haven, CT: Yale University Press, 2001.

Queen, Sarah. *From Chronicle to Canon: The Hermeneutics of the Spring and Autumn Annals, according to Tung Chung-shu*. Cambridge: Cambridge University Press, 1996.

Van Norden, Bryan W., ed. *Confucius and the Analects: New Essays*. Oxford: Oxford University Press, 2002.

Studies of later Confucian thought

de Bary, Wm. Theodore, ed. *Self and Society in Ming Thought*. New York: Columbia University Press, 1970.

de Bary, Wm. Theodore, ed. *The Unfolding of Neo-Confucianism*. New York: Columbia University Press, 1975.

Bol, Peter. *Neo-Confucianism in History*. Cambridge, MA: Harvard University Asia Center. Distributed by Harvard University Press, 2008.

Chow, Kai-wing. *The Rise of Confucian Ritualism in Late Imperial China: Ethics, Classics, and Lineage Discourse*. Stanford, CA: Stanford University Press, 1994.

Gardner, Daniel K. *Learning to Be a Sage: Selections from the Conversations of Master Chu, Arranged Topically*. Berkeley: University of California Press, 1990.

Graham, A. C. *Two Chinese Philosophers: Ch'eng Ming-tao and Ch'eng Yi-chuan*. London: Lund Humphries, 1958.

McMullen, David. *State and Scholars in T'ang China*. Cambridge: Cambridge University Press, 1988.

Tillman, Hoyt. *Confucian Discourse and Chu Hsi's Ascendancy*. Honolulu: University of Hawaii Press, 1992.

Tu, Wei-ming. *Neo-Confucian Thought in Action: Wang Yang-ming's Youth (1472-1509)*. Berkeley: University of California Press, 1976.

Wilson, Thomas. *Genealogy of the Way: The Construction and Uses of the Confucian Tradition in Late Imperial China*. Stanford, CA: Stanford University Press, 1995.

Wright, Arthur, ed. *The Confucian Persuasion*. Stanford, CA: Stanford University Press, 1960.

Education and the examination system

de Bary, Wm. Theodore, and John W. Chaffee, eds. *Neo-Confucian Education: The Formative Stage*. Berkeley: University of California Press, 1989.

Chafee, John W. *The Thorny Gates of Learning in Sung China: A Social History of Examinations*. Cambridge: Cambridge University Press, 1985.

Elman, Benjamin A. *A Cultural History of Civil Examinations in Late Imperial China*. Berkeley: University of California Press, 2000.

Elman, Benjamin A., and Alexander Woodside, eds. *Education and Society in Late Imperial China, 1600-1900*. Berkeley: University of California Press, 1994.

Miyazaki, Ichisada. *China's Examination Hell: The Civil Service Examinations of Imperial China*. New Haven, CT: Yale University Press, 1981.

Wu, Jingzi. *The Scholars*. Translated by Gladys Yang. Rockville, MD: Silk Pagoda, 2006.

Confucianism and the state

Chang, Chung-li. *The Chinese Gentry: Studies on Their Role in Nineteenth-Century Chinese Society*. Seattle: University of Washington Press, 1955.

Dardess, John. *Blood and History: The Donglin Faction and its Repression, 1620–27*. Honolulu: University of Hawaii Press, 2002.

Elliott, Mark C. *Emperor Qianlong: Son of Heaven, Man of the World*. New York: Longman, 2009.

Huang, Liu-hung. *A Complete Book Concerning Happiness and Benevolence: A Manual for Local Magistrates in Seventeenth Century China*. Tucson: University of Arizona Press, 1984.

Huang, Ray. *1587, A Year of No Significance: The Ming Dynasty in Decline*. New Haven, CT: Yale University Press, 1981.

Guy, R. Kent. *The Emperor's Four Treasuries: Scholars and State in the late Ch'ien-lung Era*. Cambridge, MA: Council on East Asian Studies, Harvard University. Distributed by Harvard University Press, 1987.

Confucianism and the family

Baker, Hugh. *Chinese Family and Kinship*. New York: Columbia University Press, 1979.

Cao, Xueqin. *The Story of the Stone: A Novel in Five Volumes*. Translated by David Hawkes. Hammondsworth: Penguin, 1973–86.

Ebrey, Patricia Buckley. *Chu Hsi's Family Rituals: A Twelfth-Century Manual for the Performance of Cappings, Weddings, Funerals, and Ancestral Rites*. Princeton, NJ: Princeton University Press, 1991.

Knapp, Ronald G., and Kai-yin Lo, eds. *House, Home, Family: Living and Being Chinese*. Honolulu: University of Hawaii Press, 2005.

Confucianism and women

Ebrey, Patricia Buckley. *The Inner Quarters: Marriage and the Lives of Women in the Sung Period*. Berkeley: University of California Press, 1993.

Ko, Dorothy. *Teachers of the Inner Chambers: Women and Culture in Seventeenth-Century China*. Stanford, CA: Stanford University Press, 1994.

Ko, Dorothy, Jahyun Kim Haboush, and Joan R. Piggot. *Women and Confucian Cultures in Premodern China, Korea, and Japan*. Berkeley: University of California Press, 2003.

Mann, Susan. *Precious Records: Women in China's Late Eighteenth Century*. Stanford, CA: Stanford University Press 1997.

Mann, Susan. *The Talented Women of the Zhang Family*. Berkeley: University of California Press, 2007.

Pruitt, Ida. *A Daughter of Han: The Autobiography of a Chinese Working Woman*. Stanford, CA: Stanford University Press, 1945.

Wang, Robin, ed. *Images of Women in Chinese Thought and Culture: Writings from the Pre-Qin Period through the Song Dynasty*. Indianapolis, IN: Hackett Publishing, 2003.

Confucianism since the twentieth century

Alitto, Guy. *The Last Confucian: Liang Shu-ming and the Chinese Dilemma of Democracy*, 2nd ed. Berkeley: University of California Press, 1986.

Chow, Tse-tsung. *The May Fourth Movement: Intellectual Revolution in Modern China*. Cambridge, MA: Harvard University Press, 1960.

Harrison, Henrietta. *The Man Awakened from Dreams: One Man's Life in a North China Village, 1875–1942*. Stanford, CA: Stanford University Press, 2005.

Levenson, Joseph R. *Confucian China and Its Modern Fate: A Trilogy*. Berkeley: University of California Press, 1968.

Lin, Yü-sheng. *The Crisis of Chinese Consciousness: Radical Antitraditionalism in the May Fourth Era*. Madison: University of Wisconsin Press, 1979.

Louie, Kam. *Critiques of Confucius in Contemporary China*. Hong Kong: The Chinese University Press, 1980.

Yu, Dan. *Confucius from the Heart: Ancient Wisdom for Today's World*. New York: Atria Books, 2009.

"牛津通识读本"已出书目

古典哲学的趣味	福柯	地球
人生的意义	缤纷的语言学	记忆
文学理论入门	达达和超现实主义	法律
大众经济学	佛学概论	中国文学
历史之源	维特根斯坦与哲学	托克维尔
设计，无处不在	科学哲学	休谟
生活中的心理学	印度哲学祛魅	分子
政治的历史与边界	克尔凯郭尔	法国大革命
哲学的思与惑	科学革命	民族主义
资本主义	广告	科幻作品
美国总统制	数学	罗素
海德格尔	叔本华	美国政党与选举
我们时代的伦理学	笛卡尔	美国最高法院
卡夫卡是谁	基督教神学	纪录片
考古学的过去与未来	犹太人与犹太教	大萧条与罗斯福新政
天文学简史	现代日本	领导力
社会学的意识	罗兰·巴特	无神论
康德	马基雅维里	罗马共和国
尼采	全球经济史	美国国会
亚里士多德的世界	进化	民主
西方艺术新论	性存在	英格兰文学
全球化面面观	量子理论	现代主义
简明逻辑学	牛顿新传	网络
法哲学：价值与事实	国际移民	自闭症
政治哲学与幸福根基	哈贝马斯	德里达
选择理论	医学伦理	浪漫主义
后殖民主义与世界格局	黑格尔	批判理论

德国文学	儿童心理学	电影
戏剧	时装	俄罗斯文学
腐败	现代拉丁美洲文学	古典文学
医事法	卢梭	大数据
癌症	隐私	洛克
植物	电影音乐	幸福
法语文学	抑郁症	免疫系统
微观经济学	传染病	银行学
湖泊	希腊化时代	景观设计学
拜占庭	知识	神圣罗马帝国
司法心理学	环境伦理学	大流行病
发展	美国革命	亚历山大大帝
农业	元素周期表	气候
特洛伊战争	人口学	第二次世界大战
巴比伦尼亚	社会心理学	中世纪
河流	动物	工业革命
战争与技术	项目管理	传记
品牌学	美学	公共管理
数学简史	管理学	社会语言学
物理学	卫星	物质
行为经济学	国际法	学习
计算机科学	计算机	化学
儒家思想		